I0021430

THE BEST OF THE INDEPENDENT
RHETORIC AND COMPOSITION JOURNALS

The Best of the Independent Rhetoric and Composition Journals
Series Editor: Steve Parks

Each year, a team of editors selects the best work published in the independent journals in the field of Rhetoric and Composition, following a competitive review process involving journal editors and publishers. For additional information about the series, see http://www.parlorpress.com/bestofrhetcomp.

THE BEST OF THE INDEPENDENT RHETORIC AND COMPOSITION JOURNALS

2014

Edited by Steve Parks, Brian Bailie, James Seitz, Jessica Pauszek, Tamara Bassam Issak, and Heather Christiansen

Parlor Press
Anderson, South Carolina
www.parlorpress.com

Parlor Press LLC, Anderson, South Carolina, USA

© 2016 by Parlor Press. Individual essays in this book have been reprinted with permission of the respective copyright owners.
All rights reserved.
Printed in the United States of America

SAN: 254-8879

ISSN 2327-4778 (print)
ISSN 2327-4786 (online)

978-1-60235-823-2 (paperback)
978-1-60235-824-9 (Adobe eBook)
978-1-60235-825-6 (ePub)
978-1-60235-826-3 (iBook)
978-1-60235-827-0 (Kindle)

1 2 3 4 5

Cover design by Heather Christiansen and David Blakesley.
Printed on acid-free paper.

Parlor Press, LLC is an independent publisher of scholarly and trade titles in print and multimedia formats. This book is available in paper and digital formats from Parlor Press on the World Wide Web at http://www.parlorpress. com or through online and brick-and-mortar bookstores. For submission information or to find out about Parlor Press publications, write to Parlor Press, 3015 Brackenberry Drive, Anderson, South Carolina, 29621, or email editor@parlorpress.com.

Contents

Introduction

James Seitz and Jessica Pauszek

As one might expect from a collection of articles from ten independent journals, the essays gathered here represent a wide range of concerns, interests, and questions in the field of rhetoric and composition. Indeed, the diversity of issues and methodologies found among these articles poses a challenge for those hoping to discern a general pattern that might reveal something about the present trajectory of the field. Rather than a unified movement, what we find are the signs of a broad-minded scholarly discipline that enables multiple, even conflicting, research agendas at once—as is the case in other disciplines throughout the academy. While the question of whether rhetoric and composition should imitate or reject the models offered by other disciplines is important, it seems useful to indicate what those of us who serve as editors of this collection recognize as an accomplishment: the salutary breadth of issues that our discipline now includes in its purview. From the practices of a multilingual writing center and a youth activism summer camp to theories of visual rhetoric and computer interface; from defending the value of basic writing programs to exploring the ideologies informing educational pragmatism; from cognitive psychology and queer theory to archival research and the history of literacy—the articles assembled here display a field eager to spread its wings.

Such a broad array of scholarly activity reflects the freedom of inquiry sponsored by independent journals in our field. Yet certain affinities among these articles enable us to group them according to three distinct but overlapping concerns: 1) pedagogical and institutional change, 2) literacies and technologies, and 3) writing and social justice. In this introduction, we describe how the articles in this collection contribute to these scholarly conversations, and we consider the ways in which such conversations not only identify salient questions for further study but also point to the significance of such questions for all of us in rhetoric and composition, regardless of our areas of specialization.

PEDAGOGICAL AND INSTITUTIONAL CHANGE

While the pedagogical preoccupation displayed by much of the scholarship in rhetoric and composition has generated a good deal of critique in recent years, some of the most important work in the field continues to devote itself to pedagogical and institutional change, as three articles in this collection attest. In "Practice, Patience, And Process In the Age of Accountability: What Cognitive Psychology Suggests about the Teaching and Assessment of Writing," Kathleen Cassity draws on studies in cognitive psychology in order to discuss how a "training approach," similar to that received by a musician or athlete, can help students learn to write more effectively. Cassity notes that cognitive psychology supports much of what writing teachers already know about the value of offering students frequent practice in and response to their writing, but she suggests we need to do more to systematize the goal of "helping novice writers to automate key aspects of the writing process during the developmental years." Ultimately, Cassity suggests that institutions should not only increase their commitment to WAC and WID programs but also design assessments within a framework that accounts for what cognitive psychology reveals about the ebb and flow of learning a complex activity like writing, wherein students sometimes appear to take steps backward at precisely the moments when they are making progress. Through her close attention to the learning process, Cassity asks us to rethink how we understand ourselves as instructors and how we assess our students' work.

Turning to the writing center as a particular site for writing pedagogy, Noreen Lape, in "Going Global, Becoming Translingual: The Development of a Multilingual Writing Center," reflects on the transformation of an English writing center into a Multilingual Writing Center at Dickinson College. Through research on multilingual and translingual learning, Lape explores the various cultural roles of academic writing in languages other than English, acknowledges the institutional cooperation required among various language programs, and addresses the fluid sense of purposes—accommodation, resistance, and so on—that tutors and students might bring to their work in a Multilingual Writing Center. In particular, Lape explores the role that peer tutors play in a writing center that engages in multiple languages, whether the peers are international students studying at the college or American students studying abroad. Arguing that a Multilingual Writing Center can position writing in a global context and help "construct pluralistic definitions of 'good' academic writing that acknowledge culturally-specific rhetorics and conventions.", Lape offers a strong model of pedagogical and institutional change.

Institutional change concerns Victor Villanueva as well, though the changes proposed by various administrators Villanueva has encountered across three decades of teaching underserved students have not always been welcome. In "Subversive Complicity and Basic Writing Across the Curriculum," Villanueva recounts his successful attempts to rescue basic writing programs from budget cuts by making use of "a rhetoric that cobbles together multiculturalism or equal opportunity and assimilation." At various times in his career, Villanueva found himself explaining to provosts that basic writing courses are not remediation but enculturation: these courses aim to place students on the margins of American culture into conversation with the mainstream. Admitting that such rhetoric is in part duplicitous, Villanueva goes on to clarify his vision of a basic writing program in which those who tutor students who are first generation or of color or from poverty learn the grammars of the dominant dialects spoken by such students, study "contrastive rhetorics," and practice forms of conscious listening discussed by Krista Radcliffe. Likewise, the students who are tutored "learn precisely the same things: rhetorical listening and rhetorics (as plural), and of course, matters of correctness, since infelicities obtain in every dialect and language." What Villanueva ultimately seeks is an approach to basic writing in which students "become the agents of their own basic writing across the curriculum" (59).

LITERACIES AND TECHNOLOGIES

One of the most vital strands of contemporary scholarship in rhetoric and composition investigates how changes in technology have altered what constitutes literate habits and practices. David Reider, for example, in "From GUI to NUI: Microsoft's Kinect and the Politics of the (Body as) Interface," addresses the possibilities and challenges of the replacement of the Graphical User Interface [GUI] by the Natural

User Interface [NUI]. Such a shift in computer interface might be represented by the user who once clicked on graphics (e.g., desktop file icons) but who now speaks to or gestures at the computer, tapping or drawing on the screen with a stylus or using a remote control in what might be considered more "natural" and "embodied" actions. Reider suggests that this change in the way we interact with computers—which may soon become far more prevalent—encourages us "to focus on the production of novel interfaces that embody our critical values and concerns, rather than limiting ourselves to the analysis and critique of someone else's technologies." In other words, NUI offers the possibility of creating "new relations between bodies and code."

Reider's recognition of the complexity of contemporary literacy is further explored and historicized by Annette Vee in "Understanding Computer Programming as Literacy." Vee offers readers not only a way of thinking of computer programming as a kind of literacy but also ways of approaching the history of writing and reading as material practices in relation to the development of societal infrastructures. Vee's use of historical accounts of the emergence of literacy (touching, for example, on eleventh century census-taking in the form of the Domesday Book, the use of written contracts, and the rise of document culture) and her parallel account of the emergence of computer programming show that "[p]rogramming is not replacing writing, but is rather interlacing with it, augmenting it. . . . Looking at the writing of code through a concept of computational literacy allows us to focus on the writing practices that undergird our complex, contemporary composition environments." By understanding computer programming as a form of literacy, we can work toward a more comprehensive approach to the teaching of writing.

While Reider and Vee concern themselves with computer literacy, Fred Johnson, in "Perspicuous Objects: Reading Comics and Writing Instruction," considers the visual rhetoric of comic books and their potential in writing courses. Looking closely at comics, Johnson discusses their rhetorical power and complexity, and he investigates how writing instructors might help their students engage with comics in the composition classroom. Comics, Johnson argues, push teachers and students to look at how each object—through its form, visual representations, and text—"contributes to the voice of the comic and is part of the comic's content." Through his close readings of comics and comic theory, he pushes teachers and students to be more rigorous with their analysis and discusses the tools that visual artists use. Johnson provides a vocabulary and discussion grounded in visual rhetoric analysis that serves as a model for readers to make connections between the form and content of visual examples.

WRITING AND SOCIAL JUSTICE

Although the field of rhetoric and composition has long acknowledged the "social" and "public" nature of writing, connections between writing and social justice seem particularly salient today. Indeed, in recent moments of increased social and political tension, many scholars in the field are attempting to think through their role as teachers, compositionists, rhetoricians, and activists. The articles in this section illustrate various forms of writing and social justice work that enable us to re-think which communities, identities, and histories we highlight in the field. As these authors show, social justice work can connect to our research methodologies and pedagogies, as well as to the rhetorics we use to describe ourselves and the political events that occur around us.

Sometimes social justice work relies on a reconception of which histories and texts we acknowledge and understand as rhetorical. In her article, "Chicanas Making Change: Institutional Rhetoric and the Comisión Femenil Mexicana Nacional," Kendall Leon explores the programmatic writing (committee reports, flow charts, questionnaires, marginalia, etc.) of the Comisión Femenil Mexicana Nacional (CFMN), one of the first Chicana feminist organizations. Closely reading the archive of these materials, where she locates nuanced strategies for effecting political change, Leon argues "that it is valuable to examine community-based groups and to listen to histories like the CFMN and Chicana rhetoric broadly, as a way to learn about the rhetorical abilities we need to operate as both part of and outside of publics and institutions." Leon offers a detailed examination of how the CFMN sought to influence employment training programs so that the need for employment among Latinas would be recognized, and she demonstrates how the CFMN "developed a rhetoric that was at once responsive and effectual; public and internal; activist and institutional." By attending to documents that rhetorical scholarship might otherwise overlook, Leon enriches our narratives for how community organizations create change and establish possibilities for connecting to and learning from the past.

While Leon highlight behind-the-scenes writing practices of a community organization, Adela C. Licona and J. Sarah Gonzales consider how a community organization can make use of a pedagogy that connects writing and social justice initiatives. In "Education/Connection/Action: Community Literacies and Shared Knowledge as Creative Productions for Social Justice," Licona and Gonzales describe their collaboration through the Nuestra Voz Racial Justice Summer Camp (where Gonzales served as Director of the Racial Justice Program at the summer camp and Licona worked as Co-Director of the Crossroads Collaborative at the University of Arizona). Gonzales and Licona explain the Education/Connection/Action approach, which "begins with a commitment to engaging local histories with an understanding of youth as knowledgeable and as interested in learning." The camp's goal is to challenge deficit-minded stories by providing a space where youth engage in cultural issues relevant to them (which together they identified in this particular camp as the Ethnic Studies Ban in Arizona; The School-to-Prison Pipeline; and Youth, Sexuality, Health and Rights). Through their analysis, Gonzales and Licona provide a model for how youth engage in creative learning and social action through multimodal productions (PSAs, literacy remixes, poetry), and they reveal projects that allow youth to take an active role in creating social change.

In "Let Me Queer My Throat: Queer Rhetorics of Negotiation: Marriage Equality and Homonormativity," Hillery Glasby explores how an alternative, queer rhetoric can help negotiate the sometimes troubling nexus of the personal and the political. Glasby begins by acknowledging her ambivalence regarding queer marriage in the face of marriage equality laws and radical queer questioning of same-sex marriage—but rather than writing to resolve this ambivalence, she seeks a rhetoric that will help "to navigate the vast wastelands of [her] multiple subjectivities." While recognizing the value of queer critiques of heteronormativity, Glasby questions whether queer marriage will have the effect of domesticating and normalizing queer partners in the ways that these critiques propose. To the contrary, Glasby suggests that queer marriages might instead make queer lives more visible and thereby disrupt normative conceptions of marriage as a result. Admitting her uncertainty as someone engaged to marry her queer partner, Glasby asks readers to explore possibilities with her rather than insisting on a single perspective, thereby upending more familiar rhetorics of persuasion.

In the final piece in this section, Kurt Spellmeyer articulates what it might mean for compositionists to become more explicitly political rather than quietist and professional. In "Fighting Words," Spellmeyer laments the ways that a combination of rightwing celebration of the free market and liberal pragmatism has led to a public sphere in which true politics—which always involves conflict over what citizens view as the good life—has been eviscerated in the name of finding a "middle ground." For Spellmeyer, President Obama is a prime exemplar of this pragmatic approach, which constantly identifies two supposedly equal extremes on the left and right and then offers a conciliatory middle as the best answer. Spellmeyer sees this maneuver as a kind of anti-politics. In his view, composition needs to fight for the Humanities instead of leave them for some safer place in the university, however tempting it might be to escape the Humanities at a time when they're struggling. Spellmeyer doesn't specify what this might involve by way of pedagogical or curricular practice, but he concludes that "[e]ducation in a democracy must teach citizens not only that power is inescapable but also that nothing will improve unless they exercise it."

Taken together, the articles in this collection serve as a reminder of the important work being done by independent journals in rhetoric and composition. To a great extent, we see these journals as incubators for the emergent ideas, theories, and practices that may become dominant paradigms in our field—and for that reason, we believe independent journals to serve as a vital element in the development of our discipline. It is important to end this brief introduction, then, by highlighting that much of the important work accomplished by these journals is undertaken by editors and editorial staff who often receive no institutional support for their efforts. While the proceeds of this collection will go towards efforts to raise the profile of independent journals at academic conferences, we believe it is equally important that faculty at institutions housing such journals become advocates for supporting the work of these editors; that all faculty work to ensure their libraries subscribe to these journals; and that, as a field, we continue to find venues to recognize the significant work achieved by these journals.

A Note on the Selection Process

The ten articles selected for this volume represent discerning, innovative, eloquent scholarship from independent journals in rhetoric and composition. Each journal submitted a set of articles for review, and we called upon faculty and graduate students from a range of institutions to read the articles and rank them according to the following criteria:

- Demonstrates a broad understanding of the discipline, including the ability to explain how its specific focus in a sub-disciplinary area addresses broader concerns of the field.
- Makes an original contribution to the sub-disciplinary area, expanding or rearticulating central premises.
- Articulates its concerns in a style that addresses, in addition to members of the sub-disciplinary area, a wider audience.

Based on the recommendations of the reviewers, the editors of this collection selected the final list of essays.

We are very grateful, then, to all of the associate editors who have organized and participated in reading groups that helped choose the selected essays. Their generosity, insight, and collaboration made this volume possible, and we are happy to list them here:

Jen Arena, Rutgers-Newark
Steve Bailey, Central Michigan University
Liz Bauer, Central Michigan University
Britany Becker, California State University – San Bernadino
Marne Benson, Rutgers-Newark
Mark Blaauw-Hara, North Central Michigan College
Mirabeth Braude, Michigan State University
Liz Brockman, Central Michigan University
Beth Brunk-Chavez, University of Texas—El Paso
Michael Van Calbergh, Rutgers-Newark
Esmeralda Castaneda, California State University – San Bernadino
Pisarn Bee Chamcharatsri ,University of New Mexico
Brent Chappelow, Arizona State University
Katie Chavez, California State University – San Bernadino
Sana Clason, University of Cincinnati- Blue Ash
Anthony Cirilo, Rutgers-Newark
Jonathan Covos, California State University – San Bernadino
Nicole Crouch, California State University – San Bernadino

Christine Peters Cucciare, University of Delaware
Ben Delloiacano, Rutgers-Newark
Tom Hong Do,University of Arizona
Candace Epps-Robertson, Michigan State University
Kristina Fennelly, Kutztown University
Cassandra Fetters – University of Cincinnati-Blue Ash
Brandon Fralix, Bloomfield College
Debra Freeland, California State University – San Bernadino
Moe Folk, Kutztown University
Bree Gannon, Michigan State University
Angelia Giannone, University of Arizona
Brenda Glascott, California State University – San Bernadino
Mathew Gomes, Michigan State University
Laura Gonzales, Michigan State University
McKinley Green, Michigan State University
Denice Gsoell, California State University – San Bernadino
Max Gray, Rutgers-Newark
Laura Feibush, University of Pittsburgh
Al Harahap, University of Arizona
Brian Hendrickson, University of New Mexico
Chris Kapp, Rutgers-Newark
Devon Kehler, University of Arizona
Matt Kelly, University of Pittsburgh
Latonya Kuzak, California State University – San Bernadino
Daniel Lawson, Central Michigan University
Tabitha Lehouillier, California State University – San Bernadino
Barbara L'Eplattenier, University of Arkansas—Little Rock
Jerry Won Lee, University of California—Irvine
Daniel Libertz, University of Pittsburgh
Karen Lunsford, University of California—Santa Barbara
Amy Lynch Biniek, Kutztown University
Alex Malanych, University of Pittsburgh
James Maya, California State University – San Bernadino
Neely McLaughlin, University of Cincinnati-Blue Ash
Dan Melzer, University of California—Davis Rochelle Rodrigo, University of Arizona
Christopher Minnix, University of Alabama—Birmingham
Amanda Morris, Kutztown University
Paula Neves, Rutgers-Newark

Maria Novotny, Michigan State University
Kevin Oberlin, University of Cincinnati-Blue Ash
Trisha O'Neal, California State University – San Bernadino
Laurie Pinkert, University of Central Florida
Emily Pioszak, Central Michigan University
Patricia Pytleski, Kutztown University
Erika Quinonez, California State University – San Bernadino
Yvette Quintana, California State University – San Bernadino
Heather Reyes, California State University – San Bernadino
Lori Rogers, Central Michigan University
Viola Rowe, California State University – San Bernadino
Kathleen J. Ryan, Montana State University
Dustin Shepherd, California State University – San Bernadino
Virginia Schwarz, University of Wisconsin—Madison
Matthew Sheehan, Rutgers-Newark
Jake Slovis, Rutgers-Newark
Laura Spence-Ash, Rutgers-Newark
Allegra W. Smith, Michigan State University
Courtney Stanton, Rutgers-Newark
Melissa Adamo, Rutgers-Newark
Fabian Torres, California State University – San Bernadino
Stephanie Vie,University of Central Florida
Brian Walker, Rutgers-Newark
Rangel Zarate, California State University – San Bernadino
Ariel Zepeda, California State University – San Bernadino

THE BEST OF THE INDEPENDENT RHETORIC AND COMPOSITION JOURNALS

COMMUNITY LITERACY JOURNAL

Community Literacy Journal is on the Web at http://www.community-literacy.org

The Community Literacy Journal publishes both scholarly work that contributes to the field's emerging methodologies and research agendas and work by literacy workers, practitioners, and community literacy program staff. We are especially committed to presenting work done in collaboration between academics and community members. We understand "community literacy" as the domain for literacy work that exists outside of mainstream educational and work institutions. It can be found in programs devoted to adult education, early childhood education, reading initiatives, lifelong learning, workplace literacy, or work with marginalized populations, but it can also be found in more informal, ad hoc projects. For us, literacy is defined as the realm where attention is paid not just to content or to knowledge but to the symbolic means by which it is represented and used. Thus, literacy makes reference not just to letters and to text but to other multimodal and technological representations as well.

Education/Connection/Action: Community Literacies and Shared Knowledges as Creative Productions for Social Justice

"Education/Connection/Action" represents the kind of work that we aspire to publish. It is a model of a university and community partnership—written by a faculty member and a community-program administrator—that focuses on "lived and learned literacies to inform participatory media projects that critically and creatively address restrictions on access to local knowledges and information with particular relevance to youth sexuality, health, and rights."

The article's research draws on compelling frameworks for community action and interaction, and the art, activism, and youth-led productions provide a meaningful and memorable context for awareness of connections between overlapping systems of injustice, exclusion, and oppression.

1 Education/Connection/Action: Community Literacies and Shared Knowledges as Creative Productions for Social Justice

Adela C. Licona and J. Sarah Gonzalez

Abstract: This article highlights Education/Connection/Action (ECA), a locally developed community pedagogy deployed at a youth activism summer camp that served as a site for a community/academic teaching and research collaboration. Youth considered connections between a set of issues, including a local ban on Ethnic Studies, the School-to-Prison Pipeline, and Youth Sexuality, Health, and Rights. They drew from lived and learned literacies to inform participatory media projects that critically and creatively addressed restrictions on access to local knowledges and information with particular relevance to youth sexuality, health, and rights (broadly defined). In highlighting youth voices, desires, and needs across distinct youth communities, their collaborative productions demonstrated coalitional potential and a collective call for change.

> We, the youth, believe abstinence-only is not acceptable.
> Comprehensive sex education is not promoting sex, but knowledge.
> It's better to be aware, informed, and prepared instead of ignorant
>   and fearful of change.
> We are a new generation.
> We are change, tolerance, and understanding.
> No longer streets gathered of polychromatic lowriders and the compe-
>   tition of Macho Men stuck through cities and cries of "no homo."
> We need purified love, acceptance, forgiveness, understanding, and
>   bravery for change.

We, the youth, want love, no more ignorant love.

—Alexia Vazquez & Enrique Garcia,

TYPS Poets & Nuestra Voz Racial Justice Summer Camp Participants, 2011

The poem above, titled "No More Ignorant Love," instantiates the powerful, and powerfully creative, work written and performed at the 3rd Annual Nuestra Voz: Youth, Art and Activism Summer Camp. It reflects the arts-based approach engaged throughout the camp, while also elucidating the potential of using art to discuss and act on civic and social justice issues. Alexia, a high school senior, and Enrique, a high school junior, co-wrote this poem at the end of a series of round-tables that introduced participants to youth-identified themes of interest including the Ethnic Studies Ban (Arizona state laws ARS §§ 15-111 and ARS §§ 15-112), the School-to-Prison Pipeline, and Youth, Sexuality, Health, and Rights. In these roundtables, youth used their own lived experiences, interests, and desires to inform the discussions, and collaborated on action projects. The poem is an expression of an emergent consciousness about the interlocking relationship between sex, gender, race, and class and, thus, it served a pedagogical purpose in the camp by positioning poets as a peer educators.

In this report we intend to explore both the pedagogical strategies that enable young people, such as Alexia and Enrique, to emerge as poets and peer educators, and the collaborative approaches that support such strategies. We introduce a framework developed by community literacy practitioner J. Sarah Gonzales, the *Education / Connection / Action* (ECA) approach, and describe the ways that our collaboration around arts-based inquiry informed a number of youth-led productions. Youth were supported in their desire to speak back to the authoritative discourses pathologizing activist youth and to speak up regarding constraints on their pursuits of knowledge, interests, needs, and dreams. First, however, we will provide some background about the development of our particular collaboration, along with the contexts that framed the summer camp.

CREATIVE SPACE FOR YOUTH UNDER FIRE: BACKGROUND AND CONTEXT

We (J. Sarah Gonzales and Adela C. Licona) came together initially around our shared interest in racial justice.[1] Gonzales served as

Director of the Racial Justice Program, including the Nuestra Voz Latin@ Youth Initiative summer camp, at the YWCA Tucson. Licona is Co-Director of the Crossroads Collaborative at the University of Arizona, a project funded by the Ford Foundation to foster action-oriented research collaborations that seek to understand the constraints and possibilities around what youth know, what they want and need to know, and how they learn about sexuality, health, and rights. We both believe in the need for critical community education, and we each work on issues of social justice from our distinct locations in a community-serving organization and at a public university. We were interested in collaborating on issues of racial justice, sexual and gender justice, as well as immigrant/immigration, economic, and reproductive justice. We each positioned ourselves as adult allies to local youth, and to the youth movements that were emerging in Tucson as a response to regressive legislation in the state of Arizona.

We started our collaboration in the midst of a political climate that fueled, and was fueled by, social panic expressed in particularly regressive legislation with dramatic implications for youth participants (see Herdt, 2009, on moral and sexual panics). It was a time marked by the passage of such legislation as SB 1070, officially named the "Support Our Law Enforcement and Safe Neighborhoods Act" but popularly referred to as the anti-immigrant, anti-immigration, "papers please" legislation. This act was considered among the most restrictive anti-immigrant legislation in the U.S. when it initially passed through the Arizona state legislature in 2010. Many youth participants felt threatened by this legislation because of its sanctioning of racial profiling, and because either they or their family members held differing immigration statuses.

Arizona House Bill (HB) 2281 (which later became state laws ARS §§ 15-111 and ARS §§ 15-112), popularly known as the ban on Ethnic Studies, was also a part of the suite of panic-inflected legislation. This bill prohibits public and charter schools in Arizona from promoting either the "overthrow of the U.S. government" or "resentment toward a particular race or class of people" and from advocating ethnic solidarity or curriculum designed for a "particular ethnic group." It was passed to ban the teaching of Mexican American Studies in the Tucson Unified School District, the largest district in the city; the law threatened other Ethnic Studies programs in the state as well. Youth experienced the ban as a restriction on their right to learn from and access culturally relevant material in their classroom contexts. The legislation fueled a youth movement that itself also fed into the panic that defined the Arizona legislature at this time. Several camp participants were active in protesting the Ethnic Studies ban at the local and state levels (see Basu; Planas).

Finally, a bill that received far less media attention, but was nonetheless a part of the panic-inflected legislation, was Senate Bill (SB) 1309, known as the Parent's Bill of Rights. This bill, like HB 2281, functioned to restrict students' access to knowledge and rights regarding their own health and sexual education by granting parents the right to opt students out of classes with any sexual content. The fervor in the local community was heightened by the intensity of national and global media in the city, and by the regularly occurring youth-organized protests.

In response to this local context, we planned a social justice summer camp focused on art as activist expression, using youth-creative multimodal productions to move their voices into public spaces where decisions were being made. Licona joined the weekly planning meetings in anticipation of the camp, and participated as a volunteer and teacher-researcher at the weeklong summer camp directed by Gonzales. As community workers, activists, and researchers, we came to know, and opened ourselves to learn from, one another. Our roles in our collaborations became that of action-oriented teacher-researcher with one another as well as with the youth (see Licona and Russell, in preparation), as we sought to develop guiding principles and strategies for facilitating community education, connection, reflection, and action explicitly with and for youth participants (see Mitchell on action research and new social movement mobilization).

THE *EDUCATION* / *CONNECTION* / *ACTION* (ECA) APPROACH: APPLIED PRINCIPLES OF COMMUNITY LITERACY AND ACTION-ORIENTED COLLABORATIONS

It was in the context of YWCA Tucson's Racial Justice Program that Gonzales actively developed and began to implement the Education/Connection/Action (ECA) approach, which aims to build pedagogical practices that honor spaces and practices of community education. ECA begins with a commitment to engaging local histories with an understanding of youth as knowledgeable and as interested in learning.[2] Each element of ECA identified and informed youth-centered practices to prepare participants for an arts-based approach to learning, teaching, and performing. ECA was specifically designed as a critical community pedagogy to work in community contexts and was, in fact, developed by a community activist and literacy practitioner outside of formal educational institutions (see Anzaldúa; Boggs; Freire; hooks). In the Nuestra Voz camp, ECA worked to foster youth voice and promote collaborative learning and action.

While the elements of ECA praxis elaborated upon in what follows are discussed as distinct, the framework is not linear. In other words, the categories that comprise this approach are related and not always neatly distinguishable.

Education

The first element of ECA, "Education," refers to the discussion of locally meaningful and culturally relevant topics and goals, determined in collaboration with youth and adult allies. This approach assumes youth have both something to say and to learn from each other and from their adult allies. Such an approach allows youth to participate in shaping the agenda for conversation, share distinct and even contradictory perspectives, and critically examine relevant topics.

Our camp planning committee comprised youth from the Nuestra Voz Youth Advisory Committee, members of the Crossroads Collaborative at the University of Arizona, and adult-ally directors from local youth-serving programs. Members of the committee brought ideas and research from their areas of interest and expertise to develop activities that facilitated participant engagement in the goals of the Nuestra Voz Camp. Together, we decided on three camp themes: the Ethnic Studies Ban; the School-to-Prison Pipeline; and Youth, Sexuality, Health and Rights.

The second key element of the ECA's "Education" principle is creating space for youth to be recognized as holders and producers of knowledge about these topics through their personal experiences and various ways of knowing. Because we intentionally recruited youth from several different activist organizations, the youth were able to share from their broad and distinct experiences, social locations, and perspectives. The youth participants from Kore Press's Grrls Literary Activism workshops, for instance, arrived at camp already trained to use their individual and collective voices to speak up in the public realm about injustices including gender oppressions. The youth participants from the Eon Youth Program at Wingspan, Southern Arizona's LGBT Community Center, arrived at camp well-versed in sexual health and sexual justice.

Finally, returning Nuestra Voz program participants arrived to the summer camp with a keen understanding of race, racism, racial trauma, and racial healing due to their participation throughout the year in the racial justice programs of YWCA Tucson. In other words, each of the youth groups arrived with lived and learned knowledges and forms of expertise that helped inform and enhance a cross-perspectival approach to the work emerging from the summer camp. We encouraged participants to share through a roundtable format that promoted group discussion.

We also collaborated with Crossroads Collaborative scholar Londie Martin and various teacher-researchers to develop a multimodal literacy activity called "I'm on the Map," which highlights the place-based, lived knowledges of youth and their spatialized practices. On this digital interactive map, youth located themselves, identified the places meaningful to them in their everyday lives, and highlighting the places where they were involved in change-oriented projects. It offered an opportunity for the development of relational literacies, or those practices that can make youth visible, and knowable, and understandable to one another, and allowed participants to realize that youth from across multiple community contexts were involved in related change-oriented activities. Through the "I'm on the Map" activity participants co-developed a critical awareness of other places and practices across the Tucson community.

Connection

"Connection," the second element of ECA, refers to the opportunities youth participants are given to explore how the youth-identified and developed camp topics are connected to one another across distinctions in race, class, gender, sexuality, education, and immigrant status. Participants worked through activities designed to challenge them to creatively identify connections between the topics, themselves, and their communities. It is through the "Connection" component that participants began to see themselves and their individual and community histories as meaningful and relevant. They began to identify not only as agents of local histories, but of social change as well.[3]

For example, to encourage youths' analytical connections between personal stories and broader histories of the topics, we created an "historic timeline" for youth to help populate, a practice we learned at the Gay-Straight Alliance Advocacy and Youth Leadership Academy held in Sacramento, CA. We used butcher paper along a wall to map out the international, national, local, and personal timeline of a topic, inviting consideration of the multiple relationships between events along these temporal and geographic axes. This timeline included major events in the world, in the United States, in the state of Arizona, and in the lives of youth participants that we discussed as a whole group. Youth were encouraged to identify and reflect on how their experiences correlated with broader historic events. This exercise not only helped youth to connect their individual lives to world events, it made them legible as social and historic actors in a local context.

To foster awareness of connections between overlapping systems of injustice, exclusion, and oppression, we additionally provided a tool to youth participants that was informed by the work of Critical Race theorist, Mari Matsuda and moved them to consider "asking the other question." Participants used the "other question" approach throughout the camp to first identify racism in a given context and then to see if, through critical inquiry (asking different questions about the same contexts), participants could also identify sexism, classism, and/or heterosexism. In this way, participants were encouraged to consider multiple perspectives and actively relate across differences to collaborate in projects for social justice. They also learned the importance of carefully constructing questions from multiple perspectives within the practice of critical inquiry.

Action

ECA's final component, "Action," refers to understanding the unique power of young people to address social justice issues in their communities. "Action" provides a space for youth to interpret their work as activism, to brainstorm and create art that uses their talents to support change, and to develop a perspective about "Action" that conveys both short- and long-term goals. Numerous examples of youth- and adult-ally created art activism served to inspire, encourage and model "Action." At the camp, participants developed groups around a focus topic and worked intensively on creating a project that was presented to a community audience of other youth, adults, family members, invited city officials, and supporters of the YWCA.

Participants chose to center our "Action" efforts on media literacy and civic and arts activism in the context of social marketing (see Duncan-Andrade). Youth were presented with definitions and examples of social and corporate marketing to consider the various ways marketing techniques are used to persuade, educate, and encourage change.[4] In small groups, youth viewed specific social marketing campaigns and discussed questions such as: What behavior is the ad targeting? What change are they asking the viewer to make? Who is their target audience? Who created the ad? Print media, DIY videos, and guerilla media styles were examined to show a wide range of possibilities, and to address the ways in which community-based social marketing can be utilized – particularly when access to technology is limited.

The social marketing approach was intended to teach youth about the rhetorical framing of media messages: Participants learned about the context within which a message is created, the role of the author/s, and the idea of "audience." Three groups formed around the camp themes of Ethnic Studies, the School-to-Prison Pipeline, and Youth, Sexuality, Health, and Rights. In whole-group discussions, youth explored how these topic areas were similar and dissimilar. We recognized that one commonality across the three topics was the restriction youth experienced in terms of access to knowledge and resources, and action projects addressed this restriction. Youth produced media from their own perspectives and social locations (see Henry Jenkins, 2007, on participatory culture and media education), through art forms including writing, spoken word, video production, and photography.

GROUP ONE: A FOCUS ON ETHNIC STUDIES

The group focusing on Ethnic Studies decided to address the violent and often racist language used in online comments (see Baym)[5] in response to local newspaper stories referencing Ethnic Studies debates in Tucson. They discussed the different ways in which they and their peers had experienced the efforts to ban Ethnic Studies, and noted their frustration at receiving negative messages and threats, in addition to being dismissed or ignored by adults in decision-making roles and other seats of power. Youth found that anonymous commenters expressed more discursive violence online, particularly when discussing issues of immigration and race.

Building on what they had learned about community-based social marketing, the group launched a mini-campaign around the slogan, "Online Comments Don't Stay Online." With this video, the group hoped to inform the community about the negative effects of violent language used to frame the debate and its possible correlation to verbal and physical threats made against youth in their efforts to save Ethnic Studies. Their video short highlighted the hostile online media climate that was created around the Ethnic Studies debates, and how it permeated their lives as students and as family and community members.

GROUP TWO: A FOCUS ON THE SCHOOL-TO-PRISON PIPELINE

The second group addressed the school-to-prison pipeline and zero-tolerance sentencing policies, using the media of stop motion photography and animation to create a short video. They worked to intervene in the predominant rhetorical framing of youth as disinterested in their education, unmotivated, criminal, and as predestined failures. Together with adult allies, youth researched statistics about bullying and the various forms of discrimination youth from diverse backgrounds experience in school. They also considered the consequences of being educated in schools with a police presence and harsh consequences for minor infractions. They found creative ways to educate one another on the statistics and labels that negatively affect young people. The video calls for youth, adults, and the greater community to reimagine youth as interested, motivated, and capable. Ultimately, their creative work calls on community members to take action to make schools safer, more productive, and a meaningful learning environment for all young people.

GROUP THREE: A FOCUS ON SEX ED

The third group focused on the *de facto* practice of abstinence-only education in Arizona schools. They discussed the consequences of abridged access to information on sexual health and healthy sexualities. They learned about recent legislation, termed the Parents' Bill of Rights that required parental permission for students' participation in sexual education courses, and simultaneously established the right for parents to opt their students out of any class with sexual content. They expressed the need, as did youth in the Ethnic Studies group, for curriculum to be relevant to their lives, and for a broad youth population to be represented in their curricula.

These youth expressed the desire to learn more about how to have healthy interpersonal relationships. They confronted the harsh realities of not having access to the knowledge that they knew they needed to be sexually and relationally healthy. Informed by the principles of community-based social marketing, this group decided to create a public service announcement for viewing by other camp participants and a public audience at the end of the camp, and for use by the Crossroads Collaborative. They interviewed one another about their experiences in sex education classes: some students had not had sex education; some had had abstinence-only health classes. Others had received comprehensive sexuality education at the Eon Youth Lounge.

Their conversations strategically employed the toolbox the planning committee had prepared, which included information about safe sex, as well as local and national statistics concerning youth sexual health. Youth drew damaging statistics on their bodies and added storytelling pieces from the interviews they conducted with one another to illustrate diverse perspectives and damaging consequences of youth experience with abstinence-only education. This creative approach served as a strategy to disrupt deficit-driven (limited and limiting) understandings of youth and their needs (see Solórzano & Yosso); to focus on the ill effects of abstinence-only education; and to intervene into practices that rendered all LGBTQ students, and any sexually active students, invisible in abstinence-only educational contexts. Additionally, and as an act we've come to understand as a literacy remix, they re-distributed speaking parts that situated them outside their own identities throughout the video (see Jenkins et al. on participatory culture and remixed media). For example, one student might speak on behalf of a transgender participant but not necessarily identify as transgender. This accomplished a kind of coalitional approach to the making of their PSA. By remixing stories, youth effectively disconnected bodies from their particular narratives to challenge dominant cultural logics (and their regulating powers) in order to produce images of youth as subjects who desire knowledge/s and claim the right to access them, produce them, and teach them (see Butler).[6]

The critical and creative work that youth generated at camp functioned rhetorically to intervene into deficit-driven stories and statistics that produce misunderstandings of youth and their lived contexts. Camp participants chose to produce slam poetry and video performances to address the intersections of their identities, experiences, and social locations. Through these productions, youth expressed an understanding that they were being kept from pursuing particular knowledges and resources. They believed that many adults in the community had low estimations of their abilities and potentials. They collectively questioned how it is possible to move through a system of formal education and still lack the knowledge needed to make informed and healthy choices about their lives.

Evidence of the successful integration of the "action" component of ECA included youths' self-presentation as holders and producers of knowledge; their coalition-efforts with each other; their expanded understanding of connections across types of oppression; and their ultimate actions to change something in the world. Youth creatively and confidently integrated their lived knowledges and experiences with new knowledges, and spoke with confidence and conviction about their needs. Spoken word and slam poetry, has become a site and practice for youth from diverse locations in Tucson to continue to express and to take action on their shared needs, dreams, and desires.

ECA FOR COMMUNITY / ACADEMIC COLLABORATIONS: POSSIBILITIES, LIMITATIONS, AND IMPLICATIONS

In creating a space in which youth experienced themselves and their communities as important and informative, and in facilitating youth voice and advocating for the rights of youth to engage in social issues that impact them and their communities, the Nuestra Voz summer camp succeeded in meeting its objectives. Youth participated in a practice of relational and remixed literacies when they made themselves legible to one another by sharing life stories and deeply held interests. In learning from one another, and allowing that learning to inform broader inquiry, all participants – youth and adult allies alike – engaged in a generative reciprocity of teaching and of research. Adults learned, or were reminded, that youth care about themselves, one another, their schools, homes, and communities.

Pre-surveys and post-surveys, designed and developed by youth and adult participants and members of the Crossroads Collaborative, also suggest the effectiveness of the ECA approach we engaged at the camp. Pre-surveys revealed that youth arrived feeling "sad," "frustrated," and "angry," as well as with a clear desire to better understand both passed and pending legislation in Arizona. They also wanted to learn about how to respond to issues they considered relevant to their lives in a way that was meaningful, effective, and that would be heard and seriously considered especially by those in positions to facilitate change. Post-surveys indicated that participants learned that the broad issues the camp addressed were connected and mutually relevant; that they had a right to use their voices and visions to express needs, interests, dreams, and desires; and that art can serve as a tool for education and activism. They reported feeling "passionate" about change and "determined" to participate in their schools and communities – particularly around the right to comprehensive knowledge and information.

While these camp successes were significant, there were also challenges to implementing, and collaborating within the ECA framework – particularly in the camp's one-week timeframe. One challenge that we had not anticipated was the arrival of already-formed groups of young people. It was a challenge to encourage participants out of the groups they were first affiliated with – even though the work that was ultimately produced expressed strong coalitional potential. With more time, and perhaps better-developed strategies, we can imagine a more robust mixing of youth participants across creative productions and performances.

While we understand that there are elements of the camp that cannot be replicated across distinct contexts, we do believe there is much here that can inform related efforts. Literacy practitioners in many situations may be able to draw from ECA principles to create effective learning and action communities. ECA's first principle of "Education" calls for the participation of learners in the selection of content, and the honoring of learners as holders and producers of knowledge, concepts that can be implemented through practices such as advisory councils. The concept of "Connection" draws attention to the need for coalitional work. Collaborations can be designed to explicitly encourage participants to connect across social spaces and identifications, learning how to organize themselves toward critical inquiry and creative collaborations. ECA's final principle, "Action" allows participants the space to empower each other to co-present their projects and knowledges about social justice to one another and to the greater community.

When Alexia Vazquez' and Enrique Garcia's poem, "No More Ignorant Love," was performed at the community event concluding the camp, youth voice was made audible. The performance served as a reminder that there is much to learn from youth whose own lives are expressions of lived knowledges and lived desires. The production and performance of the poem became a form of youth community action. When youth are supported to bring their lived and learned knowledges together, they learn to use their voices to tell about their lives (and so their histories), to teach, and to call for needed change as an expression of informed action.

Camp youth emerged as critical and creative peer educators and collaborators fully capable of participating in the civic realm and of making themselves legible and recognizable to one another as allies in broad-based social justice work. Youth called on their formal and experiential literacies – including academic, community, and family literacies – to craft creative participatory media productions addressing injustices and inequities in Tucson and beyond.

ACKNOWLEDGMENTS

The authors wish to thank Tucson youth for their work and collaborations to plan, facilitate, and create the productions and performances we consider here. We thank Stephen T. Russell and Brenda O. Daly for their helpful reviews and comments on early drafts of our manuscript and Leah Stauber for her editorial assistance. We offer special thanks to Rachael Wendler for her support, wisdom, and insightful suggestions. Finally, we would like to thank the Ford Foundation for their generous support.

NOTES

1. Prior to the collaboration, Gonzales worked with local middle and high school students in Tucson for a three year focus on race, racism, racial trauma, and racial healing through performance. Licona had just finished work on her book on zines, or self-published magazines: Zines in Third Space: Radical Cooperation and Borderlands Rhetorics. In the book Lico-

na explores the counter-cultural productions and coalitional potentials and practices of queer and queer-of-color zinesters or zine authors.

2. Licona's work as a critical feminist pedagogue is further informed by a Funds of Knowledge approach to learning contexts, the principles of place-based pedagogy, and the concept of critical localism (see Stephen Goldzwig, 1998; Gonzáles, Norma, Luis Moll, and Cathy Amanti, 2005). In terms of community literacies, these concepts are connected to Goldblatt's belief that we should be actively aware of the real problems faced by everyday members of the communities in which we live (see Eli Goldblatt, 2007).

3. Principles of radical and feminist pedagogies together with LatCrit and Critical Race Theory (CRT), as well as literatures in youth action research, inform our understanding of participants as agents of local histories and social change. On radical pedagogy, see Elizabeth Ellsworth; Henry Giroux and Peter McLaren; and Carmen Luke. On youth action research, especially relevant to our local context, see Julio Cammarota and Michelle Fine.

4. Gonzales draws from the work of Doug McKenzie-Mohr and William Smith in *Fostering Sustainable Behavior: An Introduction to Community-based Social Marketing* (2011) to inform her approach to social marketing as a practice that puts broad notions of societal benefit over profit.

5. The process and practice of "extremely argumentative communication," understood as "messages that include swearing, insults, name calling, negative affect, and typographic energy," is also called flaming, and is highlighted in the work of Nancy Baym, who focuses her attentions on social networking sites, SNS, and other social media (Personal Connections in the Digital Age, 2010, 57).

6. Licona is at work developing and connecting concepts of remixed and relational knowledges and literacies to community practice, participatory media production, and subcultural contexts. She is interested in the potential of such remixes to disrupt notions of the exceptional or "deserving" youth and sees such a strategy as potentially coalitional (see Karma Chávez' forthcoming work on coalitional possibilities). Relational literacies, related to Licona's work on community literacies and relational knowledges, is a concept named and taken up explicitly in Londie Martin's 2013 dissertation titled "The Spatiality of Queer Youth Activism: Sexuality and the Performance of Relational Literacies through Multimodal Play."

WORKS CITED

Anzaldúa, Gloria. Ed. *Making Face, Making Soul/Haciendo Caras: Creative and Critical Perspectives by Feminists of Color.* San Francisco: Aunt Lute, 1990. Print.

Basu, Kaustuv. "The Next Target?" Inside Higher Ed, April 17, 2012. Web. 1 July 2013.

Boggs, Grace Lee. *The Next American Revolution: Sustainable Activism for the 21st Century*. Berkeley: University of California Press, 2012. Print.

Butler, Judith. *Gender Trouble*. New York: Routledge Classics, 2006. Print

Cammarota, Julio. "A Social Justice Approach to Achievement: Guiding Latina/o Students toward Educational Attainment with a Challenging, Socially Relevant Curriculum." *Equity & Excellence in Education* 40 (2007): 87–96. Print.

Cammarota, Julio, and Michelle Fine. *Revolutionizing Education: Youth Participatory Action Research*. New York: Routledge, 2008. Print.

Chávez, Karma R., "Counter-Public Enclaves and Understanding the Function of Rhetoric in Social Movement Coalition-Building." *Communication Quarterly* 59.1 (2011):1-18. Print.

—. *Queer Migration Politics: Activist Rhetoric and Coalitional Possibilities*. Urbana: University of Illinois Press, (in press).

Delgado Bernal, Dolores. "Critical Race Theory, Latino Critical Theory, and Critical Raced-Gendered Epistemologies: Recognizing Students of Color as Holders and Creators of knowledge. *Qualitative Inquiry* 8 (2002):105-26. Print.

Duncan-Andrade, Jeff. "Urban Youth, Media Literacy, and Increased Critical Civic Participation." *Beyond Resistance! Youth Activism and Community Change: New Democratic Possibilities for Practice and Policy for America's Youth*. Ed. Shawn Ginwright. Pedro Noguera, and Julio Cammarota. New York, Routledge, 2006. 149-170. Print.

Ellsworth, Elizabeth. "Why Doesn't This Feel Empowering? Working Through Repressive Myths of Critical Pedagogy." *Feminisms and Critical Pedagogy*. Ed. Carmen Luke and Jennifer Gore. New York: Routledge, 1992. 90-119. Print.

Finley, Susan. "Critical Arts-Based Inquiry: The Pedagogy and Performance of a Radical Ethical Aesthetic. *The Sage Handbook of Qualitiative Research*. Ed. Norman K. Denzin and Yvonna S. Lincoln. Los Angeles: Sage, 2011. 435-450. Print.

Freire, Paulo. *Pedagogy of the Oppressed*. Trans. Myra Bergman Ramos. New York: Continuum Books, 1993. Print.

—. *Pedagogy of Hope: Reliving Pedagogy of the Oppressed*. New York: Bloomsbury Academic, 2004. Print.

Giroux, Henry and McLaren Peter. "Radical Pedagogy as Cultural Politics: Beyond the Discourse of Critique and Anti-Utopianism." *Theory/Pedagogy/Politics: Texts for Change*. Ed. Donald Morton and Mas'ud Zavarzadeh. Urbana: University of Illinois Press, 1991. 152-186. Print.

Goldblatt, Eli. *Because We Live Here: Sponsoring Literacy Beyond the College Curruciculum*. Cresskill: Hampton Press, 2007. Print.

Gonzáles, Norma, Luis Moll, and Cathy Amanti. *Funds of Knowledge: Theorizing Practices in Households, Communities, and Classrooms.* New Jersey: Lawrence Erlbaum, 2005. Print.

Herdt, Gilbert. *Moral Panics, Sex Panics: Fear and the Fight over Sexual Rights.* New York: New York University Press, 2009. Print.

hooks, bell. *Teaching to Transgress.* New York: Routledge, 1994. Print.

Jenkins, Henr, Ravi Purushotma, Margaret Weigel, Katie Clinton and Alice J. Robison. "Confronting the Challenges of Participatory Culture-Media Education for the 21st Century (Part Two)." *Digital Kompetanse: Nordic Journal of Digital Literacy* 2 (2007): 97-113. Web. 1 July 2013.

Licona, Adela C. *Zines in Third Space: Radical Cooperation and Borderlands Rhetoric.* Albany: State University of New York Press, 2012. Print.

Licona, Adela C., Stephen T. Russell, and the Crossroads Collaboration. "Teachers-Researchers in Engaged Transdisciplinary Public Scholarship: The Mixed and Messy Practices of Critical and Creative Inquiry." Manuscript in preparation. 2013.

Luke, Carmen. "Feminist Politics in Radical Pedagogy." *Feminisms and Critical Pedagogy.* Ed. Carmen Luke and Jennifer Gore. New York: Routledge, 1992. 25-53. Print.

Martin, Londie. The Spatiality of Queer Youth Activism: Sexuality and the Performance of Relational Literacies through Multimodal Play. Unpublished dissertation. University of Arizona, 2013. Print.

Matsuda, Mari J. "Beside My Sister, Facing the Enemy: Legal Theory Out of Coalition." *Stanford Law Review* 43.6 (1991): 1183-92. Print.

McKenzie-Mohr, Doug, and William Smith. *Fostering Sustainable Behavior: An Introduction to Community-based Social Marketing.* New Society Publishers, 2011. Print.

Mitchell, Gordon R. "Public Argument Action Research and the Learning Curve of New Social Movements." *Argumentation and Advocacy* 40 (2004): 209-225. Print.

Planas, Roque. "Arizona Official Considers Targeting Mexican American Studies in University." Fox News Latino, March 28, 2012. Web. 1 July 2013.

Solórzano, Daniel G., and Tara J. Yosso. "From Racial Stereotyping and Deficit Discourse Toward a Critical Race Theory in Teacher Education." *Multicultural Education* 9 (2001): 2-8. Print.

HARLOT

Harlot is on the web at http://harlotofthearts.org

Harlot: A Revealing Look at the Arts of Persuasion is a peer-reviewed digital journal dedicated to exploring rhetoric in everyday life. The journal's title gestures toward historical references to rhetoric as "the harlot of the arts," a pejorative perspective that Harlot seeks to challenge. The mission of the journal is to bridge rhetorical scholarship and popular discourse by creating a space for critical—but inclusive and informal—conversations about rhetoric amongst diverse publics. To that end, its peer review process includes reviewers from within and outside academic contexts who prioritize collaboration and revision; accepted submissions are typically succinct, savvy, and richly mediated.

"Let Me Queer My Throat" Queer Rhetorics of Negotiation: Marriage Equality and Homonormativity" by Hillery Glasby

http://harlotofthearts.org/index.php/harlot/article/view/210/145

"Let Me Queer My Throat" is personal-political-critical-creative contribution to the discourses surrounding same-sex marriage. The author's own upcoming wedding, along with some heavy theory reading, served as the exigence for this exploration of identity, ambivalence, and performativity. The author considers and critiques homonormative positions against marriage, arguing instead that "queer participation in marriage also has the power to undo the category of married rather than round it out, thereby disrupting its historically discriminatory ideologies, regulatory functions, and exclusivity." Whether the audience agrees with that conclusion is far less important than that they accepted the author's invitation to participate in the conversation. Resisting academic pressure "to argue rather than explore, to speak rather than listen, to tidy up and close rather than unravel and invite," this webtext invites audience engagement. Its combination of visual, video, audio, and alphabetic elements deepen the reading experience with layers of everyday life and theory. The article enacts the queer praxis Glasby advocates.

2 Let Me Queer My Throat: Queer Rhetorics of Negotiation: Marriage Equality and Homonormativity

Hillery Glasby

Creator's Statement: This project grew from the personal tension I faced when, late last summer, two life-altering events took place in the same week: 1. I started reading a lot about homonormativity and queer resistance to marriage equality, and 2. My girlfriend asked me to marry her in a very sweet and traditional sort of way, which quickly gave way to wedding planning. Blending photography, personal writing, alternative rhetorics, and more traditional academic discourse, I investigate what's at stake with my upcoming same-sex wedding, while remaining conscious of my queer politics. This project argues that critical queer participation in marriage has the power to disrupt and undo the institution rather than round it out and make it whole(some).

PAGE 1: HOME

Embedded Video

"They Told Me" by Sallie Ford and the Sound Outside. Chorus: *"Never have I had a rational mind. Never have I been rational inside. My gut, my heart, and my head, that's the way they've always been. Never gonna change who I am just because you'll never understand. Never gonna apologize for being. How the hell would that make any sense?"*

PAGE 2: PURPOSE

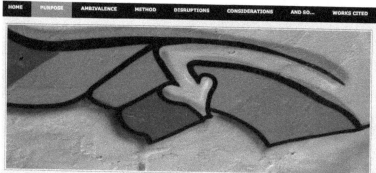

"Bubble Gum." Toronto Street Art. 2013.

> PURPOSE

I AM COMPELLED TO WRITE

The exigence of this essay lies at the heart of the intersection between my personal and political lives – between my *being* and *doing* queer [1]. My recent queer studies work centers on my personal negotiation of the marriage equality movement, homonormativity, and understanding my own upcoming, same-sex wedding as a political act. I see getting married to a woman as *being* queer; I consider refusing to get married because it is a heteronormative institution as *doing* queer – both are personal and political. I find myself sitting defiantly on the side of marriage equality, yet I feel ambivalent about marriage itself. It seems to make sense that queers should, at the very least, have the option to refuse participation in marriage rights/rites. **This project is a way for me to negotiate the "queer feelings" I am experiencing, and to better verse and insert myself in the ongoing conversation on gay marriage from a critically queer perspective.**

My approach draws on alternative, specifically queer, rhetorics as a way of negotiating these competing discourses and the tension between publics and the private. More than not, academic writing asks writers to argue rather than explore, to speak rather than listen, to tidy up and close rather than unravel and invite. Using Jonathan Alexander and Jacqueline Rhodes' theories of queer rhetoric alongside David Wallace's explorations of what compels us, as scholars and whole human beings, to write, I employ alternative rhetorical strategies as a vehicle to navigate the vast wastelands of my multiple subjectivities. Rather than confidently moving forward with a clear, linear argument in mind, I am instead inspired by Eve Kosofsky Sedgwick's question: "what if instead there were a practice of valuing the ways in which meanings and institutions can be at loose ends with each other? What if the richest junctures weren't the only ones where everything means the same thing" (Sedgwick 6-7). This project is my investigation of those loose ends.

I Am Compelled To Write

The exigence of this essay lies at the heart of the intersection between my personal and political lives – between my *being and doing* queer [1]. My recent queer studies work centers on my personal negotiation of the marriage equality movement, homonormativity, and understanding my own upcoming, same-sex wedding as a political act. I see getting married to a woman as *being* queer; I consider refusing to get married because it is a heteronormative institution as *doing* queer – both are personal and political. I find myself sitting defiantly on the side of marriage equality, yet I feel ambivalent about marriage itself. It seems to make sense that queers should, at the very least, have the option to refuse participation in marriage rights/rites. **This project is a way for me to negotiate the "queer feelings" I am experiencing, and to better verse and insert myself in the ongoing conversation on gay marriage from a critically queer perspective.**

My approach draws on alternative, specifically queer, rhetorics as a way of negotiating these competing discourses and the tension between publics and the private. More than not, academic writing asks writers to argue rather than explore, to speak rather than listen, to tidy up and close rather than unravel and invite. Using Jonathan Alexander and Jacqueline Rhodes' theories of queer rhetoric alongside David Wallace's explorations of what compels us, as scholars and whole human beings, to write, I employ alternative rhetorical strategies as a vehicle to navigate the vast wastelands of my multiple subjectivities. Rather than confidently moving forward with a clear, linear argument in mind, I am instead inspired by Eve Kosofsky Sedgwick's question: "what if instead there were a practice of valuing the ways in which meanings and institutions can be at loose ends with each other? What if the richest junctures weren't the only ones where everything means the same thing" (Sedgwick 6-7). This project is my investigation of those loose ends.

PAGE 2A: PURPOSE >> AUDIENCE

Audience Awareness

Those of us who enjoy rhetoric know for a fact that our audiences shape the texts we produce; but how often do we expect a text's audience to (re)shape our thinking? Sometimes a clearly defined audience can be more problematic for readers than an ambigous one.

When I started reading *gay marriage* by Jonathan Rauch, I was immediately struck at his clearly defined hetero audience, which he appeals to using a hypothetical anecdote laced with pathos: "imagine a community, a whole culture, without marriage. In your community, no one is married, no one has ever been married" (2). A few things strike me about the move Rauch makes here. First, he deploys a simple, yet provoking anecdote making a complex and moving comparison. It is peculiar to be a part of a community that doesn't have many people married, inside of a culture where almost everyone you know is married, plans on being married, or talks about someday getting married. Second, not everyone in queer community, at the time of this book's publication (2004), was void of some form or interpretation of marriage. Many GLBTQ folks have either been married in prior heterosexual couplings or they have been married – or in some sense, committed – to another GLBTQ person. Both scenarios provide very different perspectives on the idealism of marriage.

Difference in audience is the most pervasive component of the aforementioned rhetorical situation. I have come to the realization that I am no longer engaged in the public discourse that comes from the GLBTQ community and their allies explaining to heteronormative structures and individuals why we seek marriage equality, why we deserve marriage equality, and why marriage inequality is nonsensical and hypocritical – all a sort of asking. I've realized that the intended audience of the materials I read regarding marriage equality has undergone a major shift. **After reading countless texts by queer writers and scholars discussing homonormativity, I'm shocked by the tone of a text aimed at a heteronormative audience – an audience I no longer belong to – in which every sentence is haunted by invisible discrimination and assumptions.**

So now I find myself enmeshed in the "insider's" – queer community conversation about how marriage equality is problematic, specifically why it's something that shouldn't serve as a distraction from larger systemic issues. And it feels completely liberating to engage in critical debate with the person sitting to my immediate right rather than someone across the room. This shift in audience has completely changed my perspective on every conversation I've had about marriage equality. I suppose advocacy has given way to critique.

Dear reader, I invite you to locate and position yourself within my audience.

PAGE 3: AMBIVALENCE

Ambivalence: A State of Mixed and Contradictory Feelings

[EMBEDDED AUDIO.

> *MORNING MASSAGE: When I see my massage therapist, Sara, she tells me how happy she is to hear that Ginny and I are engaged, and she recalls how she teared up when she first heard the news because she feels so strongly for marriage equality. Her boyfriend has two siblings who are gay, pushing her progressive politics even further. "It used to be a social issue for me, but now it's personal," she explains. I felt myself having two conversations at once – one with Sara about marriage equality and another with myself as I critiqued the typical marriage equality sentiments. I used to never do this, but ever since I've become more critical of marriage equality and the queer political resistance, it's*

something I find myself doing more often. I'm not sure how I feel about it. For one, I feel bad because here's this person articulating her support in the best way she knows how; she sees herself being critical and resistant in her support of marriage equality. She, like most hetero supporters, wouldn't understand why gays wouldn't want to get married because that's not really the message they hear. Equality is a positive umbrella in their eyes, no worries for them about the normalizing implications. And then I hate myself for interrogating their support because it feels so genuine and important. So I let myself go and allow myself to feel loved and supported, even if it means being considered normal, the same.

AFTERNOON LUNCH: An hour and a half later I find myself sitting down for breakfast with our favorite waitress, Julie. We haven't seen her in awhile; we tell her the news and she's excited. Another waitress comes over to chat: she is also getting married. We share ideas, caterers, and wedding site plans. We find out, after four years of knowing her, that she has two children and has been dating the same man for ten years. She explains how she's getting married, finally, because they can afford it, because their children are old enough to be involved and remember it, and because it's a way for her family and friends to come together and celebrate. Then she says something that surprises us: they aren't actually going to sign the marriage certificate because she doesn't want "Emmett County and the state of Michigan regulating [her] family." She also doesn't want to lose $3,000 in tax credits. I would have never expected her to be so resistant, and it felt really good to hear a hetero critique of the state. As we are getting up to leave, a woman at the table next to us says, "I didn't mean to eavesdrop, but I heard the good news. Congratulations! That's so exciting. And you're doing it all on your own, which you'll never regret." Although I wasn't too sure what the doing it on our own bit was about (most likely because we are having the ceremony and dinner at a private home and not in a hall or at a church), I could see that this was the woman's way of saying, "I don't carry any prejudice against the gay community and I am happy to see you are getting married whether it's legal or not." She was saying that she supported us, and, again, that meant *something to me. How much power do we grant the institution of marriage when we avoid it because of its tradition and systemic longitude? How disempowered and disenfranchised do we allow our(queer)selves to become when we allow an institution, albeit in a backward sort of manner, to determine the decisions that affect our lives? And how do we rewrite the connections people forge by reading their support as normalizing when that is not their intention?]*

Ambivalence is the best word to describe my current state. Reading radical queer critiques of same-sex marriage and getting engaged in the same week has me confused. As I look forward toward my relationship's future, I can't help but look behind to historicize the (nation-)state's endorsement and promotion of compulsory heteronormativity, homophobic institutions, and systemic violence against queers. The nation-state both grants and refuses. It is a mechanism of legitimacy and illegitimacy, and it (and its regulating powers) factors into the decisions GLBTQ folks make every day. In *Who Sings the Nation State?*, Judith Butler and Gayatri Spivak ask, "what kind of state are we in when we start to think about the state?" (3). **I would answer: an ambivalent, queer, genealogical, critical state of (non/)being and doing.**

J. Jack Halberstam further complicates this 'state' for me as I read *Gaga Feminism*, where ze [2] provides a scathing critique of the marriage equality movement. Ze admits ze is "grumpy" about gay marriage, and argues, "while gay, lesbian, and trans people may think that, by tying the knot and going legal, they are changing a very old and conventional institution, be warned: before you change it, it changes you" (97). The more I read, the more enraged I became. Ironically, Halberstam writes about how ze and hir [3] lesbian partner co-parent as lesbian/femme-mom and butch-stepdad *at the same time* ze critiques such models of domesticity vis-à-vis an attack on marriage. This hypocritical move doesn't change the fact that Halberstam makes some excellent points about why I shouldn't want to participate in marriage, as a queer.

Almost immediately after reading this section of Halberstam's book, I saw FCKH8's post of Ellen and Portia de Rossi; it's like a punch in the heart. I love it. If I have an emotional reaction to this, am I a bad queer? I react just as strongly to FCKH8's image as I do to Halberstam's arguments about marriage...How many other queers are with me on this? How many of us are actually discussing the ambivalence this is causing, and how many of us wonder how we can refocus that political energy on something more pressing? What if my "getting married" and ideas of marriage are totally different than the traditional sense? If my idea of getting married means being with a woman on a daily basis, isn't that already different? Should it even matter how different or same it is? Am I going to lose my queer-card if I marry my girlfriend?

PAGE 3A: AMBIVALENCE >> WHICH SELF?

[VISUAL SLIDESHOW]

A month after we got engaged, my mother, my two godmothers, and my cousin came to visit, and we talked about the wedding – guest lists, dress ideas, dates, venue options, colors, flowers, shower ideas, and everything else emphasized by the Wedding Industrial Complex (WIC). To brainstorm ideas, Ginny and I went to a bookstore to browse through bridal magazines and purchase a Wedding Planner/ Organizer. Heteronormativity was rampant. Capitalism was rampant. Access and decadence were rampant. We were both excited and frustrated.

We are both coming to understand our politics and ourselves as we begin to see our pre-wedding selves in terms of "knowledge of identity as performed among competing social discourses" (Gonçlaves 14). As a queer scholar and lesbian bride-to-be, I see how I have been constructed, and constructed myself, as a radical queer who resists-just-to-resist and as a person who is engaging in the WIC for reasons that are important to me: to enjoy a celebration with family and friends in an up-north lakeside ceremony, to partake in a(n albeit) limited right (courts are currently debating Michigan's ban on same-sex marriage) that many others who have come before us have worked so hard for – and against. *Which self do I honor?*

PAGE 4: METHOD

Method: Queer and Alternative Rhetor(ic)s

> *We needed for there to be sites where the meanings didn't line up tidily with each other, and we learned to invest those sites with fascination and love.* —Eve Kosofsky Sedgwick

> *What does it mean for you to negotiate this tension through writing?* —Rachael Ryerson, colleague and dear friend

What does it mean to be a queer rhetor? What happens to ethos when the rhetor is queer and writes to "sort out her identity"? What kind of knowledge can be (re/de)generated when that queer rhetor authorizes him/her/themself to compose queerly? David Wallace lays a foundation for such rhetorics (and, subsequently, rhetors) in assuming that "rhetoric becomes alternative when it engages the individual's subjectivity rather than attempting to erase it and accounts for the positioning of that subjectivity within the discourse of power that enfranchise some and marginalize others" (5). Wallace is not the first queer composition scholar to "call to expand the linguistic and rhetorical canon [...and articulate a] need we need alterative rhetorics that work in practice" (11, 19). He explains:

> For alternative rhetoric as I define it, embodiment must be more than autobiographical self-revelation or other rhetorical and stylistic innovations; it must bring the operation of culture into relief in a way that accounts for the interlocutors' positions not only within culture at large but also in relation to each other in the immediate context. (Wallace 12)

I want to write in a queer rhetorical space – a third space that Sedgwick might describe as an "open mesh of possibilities, gaps, overlaps, dissonances and resonances, lapses and excesses of meaning" (8). Rather than writing from either the center or the margins, I see myself existing in the narrow space between the columns on the page. **Rhetorical modes that exist outside the conventions of dominant academic discourse are vital to demythologizing and dismantling the canon and expanding the representations of lived experience.**

Queer Ethos

Too often, regulated discourses contain the kind of meaning that can be made and the kinds of subjectivities that can be represented and articulated. Academic writing often elides the personal connections, stories, trauma, and experiences that guide and shape the knowledge (especially transnational and queer) scholars-as-human-beings can produce. Rather than adhering to a strict set of codes and conventions the academic elite employ as gate-keeping standards, alternative and queer composing and rhetorics allow for the new forms of resistance, agency, and countermobilization queer scholars and activists call for.

In their wiki *queer-rhetoric*, Jacqueline Rhodes and Ellen Gil-Gómez agree and call attention to what's at stake for marginalized academics who write within and outside the lines: "To be authorized in the system means to accept one's 'authoring' by the system. In our scholarly work, this 'authoring' takes on a particular weight, since we live or die professionally by our ability to immerse ourselves in language, to think critically about discourse. We are not, however, often called upon to reflect on the bodies through which such discourse is mediated, controlled, foiled, and itself further provoked" ("home"). Clean, controlled, disembodied, and tightly focused discourse is the expectation, but to what extent does that limit, refuse, and even erase who we are as authors? **Rather than asking for the authority to speak and write, we must grant ourselves the ethos to speak, without fear of being censored or censured.**

In the "Ethos" section of their video *Queered*, Jonathan Alexander and Jacqueline Rhodes ask the following questions: "what kind of ethos is the queer allowed?"; "who has the right to speak, and on what and with what credibility?"; is it possible to "write" a coherent queer life? Rather than coherence, we need complex, chaotic, and excessive modes of composing in order to more adequately capture and (con)figure the multiple and messy subject positions we queers write from. Queer and alternative rhetorics allow for a "dialectic between academia and activism" to unfold in ways that are critical for increased queer agency and ethos (Malinowitz 10). In their webtext *The Pleasures of the Archive*, Alexander and Rhodes necessitate a place for "rhetorical practices arising out of the specificity of queer experience and queer possibility" and add, "a focus on queer rhetorical practice, then, seeks to catch those moments in which a self-conscious intervention is made in discourses of normalized, and normalizing, sexuality" ("Introduction").

My Queer Ethos

In the spirit of Wallace, Butler, Alexander, Rhodes, and Mary from Harriet Malinowitz's case study in *Textual Orientations*, I want to play "with social [political, cultural, and textual] signifiers and choreograph provocative rhetorical moments" through "queer positionality and everyday speech acts" (245, 240). Queers need the space to generate new meaning vis-à-vis new rhetorics since, as Malinowitz explains, "being condemned to always write about what [one] already knows, rather than being permitted the intellectual excitement of writing [oneself] into some new epistemological place," can feel inadequate and impersonal (178).

I claim the right to write from a contested queer subjectivity. This is my rhetoric, a first-person negotiation – a conglomeration and twisting of others' rhetoric – both disempowering and empowering; my rhetoric can only hope to mirror a shade of my social and political identity.

PAGE 4: DISRUPTIONS

Disrupt(ure/ion)s within the Marriage Equality Movement
--Homonormativity
--Legalize Gay
--Sanitize Queer

PAGE 4A: DISRUPTIONS >> HOMONORMATIVITY

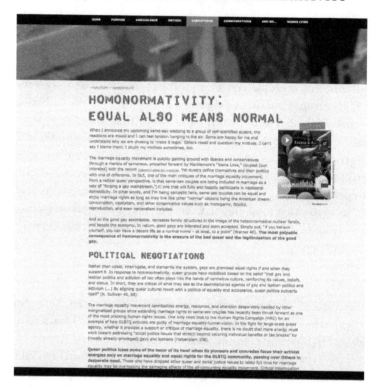

Homonormativity: Equal Also Means Normal

[EMBEDDED AUDIO

Transcript: *Nothing succeeds like excess – Oscar Wilde The excess body. The excess of money spent on the average wedding – over $23,000, average. The excess baggage of walking down 50 stone, moss-lined steps toward the beach and the rocks and Lake Michigan to Ginny. The excess scrutiny I face, from the anti-gay marriage camp and from my own queer comrades. The excess scrutiny I put upon myself. I recently attended a drag* *show, which got me thinking about drag performance – the wardrobe, the make-up, the implants….the next day, I'm in a dressing room at Macy's, squeezing myself into a DDD bra for my wedding dress: my main concern is that my physical body won't fit appropriately (adequately or by my own stupid standards) into that dress. I feel like my conceptual self will "fit" but my body won't….where drag seems to embrace, flaunt, and aim for this "spillage," I brainstorm how to conceal it, hide it, erase it. Standing at the check-out buying the bra, I knew the employee assumed I am marrying a man. Even though Ginny was standing right next to me, re-written as friend, shopping girl-friend. Not girlfriend. Sometimes I feel compelled to clarify, sometimes I just don't have the energy.]*

When I announce my upcoming same-sex wedding to a group of self-identified queers, the reactions are mixed and I can feel tension hanging in the air. Some are happy for me and understand why we are chosing to 'make it legal.' Others resist and question my motives. I can't say I blame them; I doubt my motives sometimes, too.

The marriage equality movement is quickly gaining ground with liberals and conservatives through a mantra of sameness, propelled forward by Macklemore's "Same Love," coupled (pun intended) with the recent *Grammy's same sex weddings*. Yet queers define themselves and their politics with one of difference. In fact, one of the main critiques of the marriage equality movement, from a radical queer perspective, is that same-sex couples are being included in marriage as a way of "forging a gay mainstream,"[4] one that will fully and happily participate in neoliberal domesticity. In other words, and I'm being sarcastic here, same-sex couples can be equal and enjoy marriage rights as long as they live like other "normal" citizens living the American dream: consumption, capitalism, and other conservative values such as monogamy, fidelity, reproduction, and even nationalism included.

And so the good gay assimilates, recreates family structures in the image of the heteronormative nuclear family, and boosts the economy. In return, good gays are tolerated and even accepted. Simply put, "if you behave yourself, you can have a decent life as a normal homo – at least, to a point" (Warner 40). **The most palpable consequence of homonormativity is the erasure of the bad queer and the legitimization of the good gay.**

Political Negotiations

Rather than upset, interrogate, and dismantle the system, gays are promised equal rights if and when they support it. In response to homonormativity, queer groups have mobilized based on the belief "that gay and lesbian politics and activism all too often plays into the hands of normative culture, reinforcing its values, beliefs, and status. In short, they are critical of what they see as the assimilationist agenda of gay and lesbian politics and activism [...] By aligning queer cultural revolt with a politics of equality and acceptance, queer politics subverts itself" (N. Sullivan 46, 89).

The marriage equality movement cannibalizes energy, resources, and attention desperately needed by other marginalized groups since extending marriage rights to same-sex couples has recently been thrust forward as one of the most pressing human rights issues. One only need look to the Human Rights Campaign (HRC) for an example of how GLBTQ activists are guilty of marriage-equality-tunnel-vision. In the fight for large-scale queer agency, whether it provides a support or critique of marriage equality, there is no doubt that more energy must work toward addressing "social justice issues that stretch beyond securing individual benefits or tax breaks" for (mostly already-privileged) gays and lesbians (Halberstam 108).

Queer politics loses some of the tenor of its howl when its pioneers and comrades focus their activist energies only on marriage equality and equal rights for the GLBTQ community, passing over Others in desperate need. Those who have dropped other queer and social justice issues to lobby full time for marriage equality may be overlooking the damaging effects of the all-consuming equality movement. Critical interrogation of exclusionary systemic power is a constant lens for queers – it guides everything we do and are. But I'm learning that sometimes we must resist and subvert queer(ness) vis-à-vis queer(ness). We must always ask ourselves: how much are we willing to sacrifice in our own lives to conform to the nonstandard?

PAGE 4B: DISRUPTIONS >> LEGALIZE GAY

HOME   PURPOSE   AMBIVALENCE   METHOD   DISRUPTIONS   CONSIDERATIONS   AND SO...   WORKS CITED

LEGALIZING(THE)GAY

> Marriage is coercive, but in the best possible way, which is to say, the softest. The reward for marrying successfully is approval and respect.
> – Jonathan Rauch

The marriage equality movement is guilty of arguing that without the right to enjoy legalized – and legitimized – loving, monogamous relationships, life isn't quite complete. Jonathan Rauch, member of IGF and advocate of GLBTQ mainstreaming in his book gay marriage, claims that without access to marriage, "their world remains incomplete, unfinished [...] they live in a world turned upside down" (3). In endorsing an idealistic vision of normative - even upright - marriage rather than a critique of the institution itself, Rauch aligns himself with other conservatives who oppose and deny the radical social change queer opponents of marriage promote.

It is frightening to witness the candor of some gay marriage equality activists from the IGF camp; Rauch argues that same-sex marriage "makes marriage not just a norm (the one for heterosexuals) but the norm (for everybody)" (6). Clearly this line of thinking is problematic since it moves to totalize the experience of all relationships under the institution of marriage, one that will only gain power in granting status to same-sex couples. Furthermore, it only supports couple-hood in a move toward compulsory monogamy that elides various alternative family structures throughout (and beyond) the GLBTQ community. What about the couple or family that doesn't care much for meeting social expectations (Rauch 33)? For the political queer, inclusion means absorption, assimilation, and a new level of invisibility and the erasure of difference. **Although "norms are important" for Rauch, they are of little concern for queers, like myself, who are politically inclined.** In fact, his claim that "norms are what respectable people regard as respectable behavior" is proof enough for most queers to stay as far away from gay marriage as possible (149).

Historically, marriage and its heteronormative, heterosexist underpinnings are just one example of "how sexuality is used to enable participation in the democratic project for some, while constraining it for others (2004, 287-8)" (Banks qtd in Alexander 15-16). With political moves such as the now-ruled-unconstitutional Defense of Marriage Act (DOMA), marriage - as an extension of the state's authority - has been positioned as a regulatory mechanism used to curtail "dissident sexual citizenship." Alexander reminds us, "the proper citizen is the one whose life and intimacies are most closely allied with those of the reigning (hetero)normative constructions of sex, gender, and sexuality" (54 my emphasis). Warner concurs, "if the campaign for marriage requires such a massive repudiation of queer culture's best insights on intimate relations, sex, and politics of stigma, then the campaign is doing more harm than marriage could ever be worth" (Warner 91). Alexander sees queer participation in marriage as an endorsement of 'proper' citizenship; Warner takes it a step further and points out how being 'proper' erases and elides much of the foundation upon which queer culture has been built – queer sex.

There is no doubt that marriage plays a normalizing role in the lives of many individuals, even for heterosexuals. Why else would we collectively refer to it as 'setting down'?

Legalizing(the)gay

> *Marriage is coercive, but in the best possible way, which is to say, the softest. The reward for marrying successfully is approval and respect.* —Jonathan Rauch

The marriage equality movement is guilty of arguing that without the right to enjoy legalized – and legitimized – loving, monogamous relationships, life isn't quite complete. Jonathan Rauch, member of IGF and advocate of GLBTQ mainstreaming in his book *gay marriage*, claims that without access to marriage, "their world remains incomplete, unfinished [...] they live in a world turned upside down" (3). In endorsing an idealisitic vision of normative–even *upright*–marriage rather than a critique of the institution itself, Rauch aligns himself with other conservatives who oppose and deny the radical social change queer opponents of marriage promote.

It is frightening to witness the candor of some gay marriage equal-ity activists from the IGF camp; Rauch argues that same-sex marriage "makes marriage not just a norm (the one for heterosexuals) but *the* norm (for everybody)" (6). Clearly this line of thinking is problematic since it moves to totalize the experience of all relationships under the institution of marriage, one that will only gain power in granting sta-tus to same-sex couples. Furthermore, it only supports couple-hood in a move toward compulsory monogamy that elides various alternative family structures throughout (and beyond) the GLBTQ community. What about the couple or family that doesn't care much for meet-ing social expectations (Rauch 33)? For the political queer, inclusion means absorption, assimilation, and a new level of invisibility and the erasure of difference. **Although "norms are important" for Rauch, they are of little concern for queers, like myself, who are political-ly inclined.** In fact, his claim that "norms are what respectable people regard as respectable behavior" is proof enough for most queers to stay as far away from gay marriage as possible (149).

Historically, marriage and its heteronormative, heterosexist under-pinnings are just one example of "how sexuality is used to enable par-ticipation in the democratic project for some, while constraining it for others (2004, 287-8)" (Banks qtd in Alexander 15-16). With political moves such as the now-ruled-unconstitutional Defense of Marriage Act (DOMA), marriage—as an extension of the state's authority—has been positioned as a regulatory mechanism used to curtail "dissident sexual citizenship." Alexander reminds us, "the *proper* citizen is the one whose life and intimacies are most closely allied with those of the reigning (hetero)normative constructions of sex, gender, and sexual-ity" (54 my emphasis). Warner concurs, "if the campaign for marriage requires such a massive repudiation of queer culture's best insights on intimate relations, sex, and politics of stigma, then the campaign is doing more harm than marriage could ever be worth" (Warner 91). Alexander sees queer participation in marriage as an endorsement of 'proper' citizenship; Warner takes it a step further and points out how being 'proper' erases and elides much of the foundation upon which queer culture has been built–queer sex.

There is no doubt that marriage plays a normalizing role in the lives of many individuals, even for heterosexuals. Why else would we collectively refer to it as 'settling down'?

PAGE 4C: DISRUPTIONS >> SANITIZE QUEER

Sanitizing(the)queer

The normalizing and cleansing strategies utlitized by dominant culture do not wait until marriage to begin; GLBTQ individuals are regulated and disciplined from a very young age, directly and indirectly by blatant and insidious messages of heteronormativity and heterosexism (truth be told, the same is true for straight-identified youth, too). As an example, in her investigation of the rhetorical ethos of students involved in the Speakers Bureau, intended to address heteronormativity and homophobia from a student speaker's perspective, Zan Gonçalves quotes the Bureau training workshops, which suggest that student rhetors, "choose vignettes that set a particular tone, and consider how to invite humor, if possible, *as a way to bring ease to a traditionally loaded topic*" (36 my emphasis). In a move that sanitizes queer discontent (and subsequently, agency), the students are strongly encouraged to filter any rage or discomfort out of the rhetorical situation for the audience's sake. Young GLBTQ folks are also being sent mixed messages: come out and share your story, but keep it normal – don't come across as one of *those* people. Rauch uses the same logic, for GLBTQ adults: it's okay to be different, but don't be so different that it makes other people uncomfortable.

While Rauch's intentions could be argued as being sincere by those who do desperately want to just fit in, his arguments are essentially damaging for those who remain critical of the oppression caused by colonization: "Marriage is the great civilizing institution. No other institution has the power to turn narcissism into partnership, lust into devotion, strangers into kin" (7). **Arguing for marriage equality as a sure-fire way to "civilize" gays and lesbians, therefore benefiting all of society, is dangerous and offensive.** It is evident that Rauch has succumbed to her-focused discourse that sees the individualistic, promiscuous, random sexual appetite of gays as needing to be tamed, controlled, and suppressed. In addition to arguing that marriage "confers status," Rauch also claims that "marriage creates a safe harbor for sex" (20), but who's to say that gays want to dock their boats into just one slip?

Keepin' It Dirty

Warner has complained, more than any other queer scholar, about the use of marriage to squelch non-normative queer sexualities, promiscuity, public sex, and sexual freedom. Rather than welcome queers as they are (perhaps even the really bad ones!), "marriage, in short, would make for good gays – the kind who would not challenge the norms of straight culture, who would not flaunt sexuality, and who would not insist on living differently from ordinary folk" (Warner 113). He continues, "a marriage license is the opposite of a sexual license. Sexual license is everything the state does not license, and therefore everything the state allows itself to punish or regulate," and he is spot on when he declares, "the state merely certifies a love that is beyond law; but by doing so, it justifies its existence as keeper of the law" (Warner 97, 103). What sexual, rhetorical, social, and political agency can queers gain when they refuse license by the state?

Queers are a multifaceted threat to mainstream America and its capitalist machine. Marriage can corral those restless, roaming queers, tag 'em, and round 'em up safely in a pen. Rest assured; (of course, I'm being facetious here) marriage will magically turn all those weird gays into an ordinary, stabilized and settled community – no social disruptions, "sexual underworlds," "disease," or "moral cost" here. Perhaps for those who view their sexuality as a problem in need of a remedy, marriage is a path toward normalization and acceptance. **This is extremely problematic, though: queers have pride and political resolve–they would rather see the system radically reconstructed than change what they understand to be distinctive characteristics of their own identity/ies.**

Most radical queers—and disability studies scholars—will join me in being seriously disturbed to hear Rauch bluntly state, "As it happens, I experience my own homosexuality as a (mild) disability. If I could have designed myself in the womb, I would have chosen to be heterosexual" (100). This is what the hetero-logic of marriage equality can do to GLBTQ individuals who are susceptible to the dominant discourse's messages about queerness-as-badness. When marriage is positioned as "the normal thing for adults to do," stigma attaches itself to those who can't or refuse to participate, even if they have good reason to turn their backs and run in the opposite direction.

PAGE 5: CONSIDERATIONS

Considerations: Why Marriage is a Good Start
—Queer articulations
—Linguistic Performativity
—Occupy Marriage

PAGE 5A: CONSIDERATIONS >> QUEER ARTICULATIONS

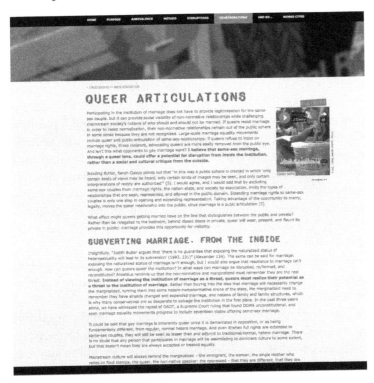

[EMBEDDED AUDIO

Transcript: *Already anticipating the coming out process at the dress shops. Wondering if I should have my mom call ahead and let them know so there is no awkwardness for me, maybe just for them. I know they'll say, "so, tell me about your fiancé," and I'll respond, "well, she's great...." If I'm lucky they'll call her Ginny and not Jenny.*]

Participating in the institution of marriage does not have to provide legitimization for the same-sex couple, but it can provide social visibility of non-normative relationships while challenging mainstream society's notions of who should and should not be married. If queers resist marriage in order to resist normalization, their non-normative relationships remain out of the public sphere in some sense because they are not recognized. Large-scale marriage equality movements include queer and public articulation of same-sex relationships; if queers refuse to insist on marriage rights, those insistent, advocating queers are more easily removed from the public eye. And isn't this what opponents to gay marriage want? **I believe that same-sex marriage, through a queer lens, could offer a potential for disruption from inside the institution, rather than a social and cultural critique from the outside.**

Reading Butler, Sarah Claeys points out that "in this way a public sphere is created in which 'only certain kinds of views may be heard, only certain kinds of images may be seen, and only certain interpretations of reality are authorized'" (5). I would agree, and I would add that by excluding same-sex couples from marriage rights, the nation-state, and society by association, limits the types of relationships that are seen, represented, and allowed in the public domain. Extending marriage rights to same-sex couples is only one step in opening and expanding representation. Taking advantage of the opportunity to marry, legally, moves the queer relationship into the public, since marriage is a pubic articulation [5].

Call it a Freudian slip, but I refuse to sanitize this amusing error in the spirit of Alexander's discussions of excess and Warner's points on queer resistance to the zoning out of sex.

What effect might queers getting married have on the line that distinguishes between the public and private? Rather than be relegated to the bedroom, behind closed doors in private, queer will wear, present, and flaunt its private in public: marriage provides this opportunity for visibility.

Subverting Marriage. From the Inside

Insightfully, "Judith Butler argues that 'there is no guarantee that exposing the naturalized status of heterosexuality will lead to its subversion' (1993, 231)" (Alexander 124). The same can be said for marriage: exposing the naturalized status of marriage isn't enough, but I would also argue that resistance to marriage isn't enough. How can queers queer the institution? In what ways can marriage be disrupted, re/formed, and reconstituted? Anzaldua reminds us that the non-normative and marginalized must remember they are the real threat. **Instead of viewing the institution of marriage as a threat, queers must realize their potential as a threat to the institution of marriage.** Rather than buying into the idea that marriage will necessarily change the marginalized, turning them into some hetero-homonormative drone of the state, the marginalized need to remember they have already changed and expanded marriage, and notions of family and family structures, which is why many conservatives are so desperate to salvage the institution in the first place. In the past three years alone, we have witnessed the repeal of DADT, a Supreme Court ruling that found DOMA unconstitutional, and seen marriage equality movements progress to include seventeen states offering same-sex marriage.

It could be said that gay marriage is inherently queer since it is demarcated in opposition, or as being fundamentally different, from regular, normal hetero marriage. And even if/when full rights are extended to same-sex couples, they will still be seen as lesser than and adjunct to traditional/normal, hetero marriage. There is no doubt that any person that participates in marriage will be assimilating to dominant culture to some extent, but that doesn't mean they are always accepted or treated equally.

Mainstream culture will always remind the marginalized – the immigrant, the woman, the single mother who relies on food stamps, the queer, the non-native speaker: the oppressed – that they are different, that they are deficient, and that they will never really fit, no matter how hard they try. The most pressing issue, of course, is the systemic, cultural logic that tells itself that once slavery is abolished, once women are granted the right to vote, and once same-sex marriage is legalized, discrimination disappears and equality abounds. Because we all know this couldn't be further from the truth.

PAGE 5B: CONSIDERATIONS >>
LINGUISTIC PERFORMATIVITY

[EMBEDDED AUDIO.

Transcript: *During a recent trip to Seattle, we stopped in an antique jewelry store to look at Old European diamonds. But the girl behind the counter was much more interested in looking at my diamond than showing me the store's …She called the owner, who was perched in an oversized chair with a little dog on her lap, over to see it. Same narrative: she told me how lucky I was. And before she made any heteronormative assumptions – as I've gotten pretty good at sensing them, I made it a point to gesture towards Ginny, to let the owner know she was the one who got the ring for me. It's moments like these when I realize I'm caught between tradition and a queer place.*]

More recent Butlerian notions of linguistic performativity stem from J. L. Austin and John Searle's discussions of speech acts, which can be broken down into three components: the speaker's intention with the speech act, which is classified as illocution; the effect the speech act has on the listener, which is classified as perlocution; and the linguistic elements of the speech act, which are classified as locution. The aspects I am most interested in for the purposes of this project are illocution and perlocution – the generative space where a speech act becomes performative and is able to queer, disrupt, and provide agency to the non-normative speaker. For example, if I am speaking about my girlfriend, the listener can, whether consciously or unconsciously, alter the meaning of my intended message. Very quickly my girlfriend will be become a friend who happens to be female. Or, I may decide to refer to her as my partner, which can also be misunderstood or misconstrued.

During a recent trip to Los Angeles, I met an acquaintance's acting partner—they were rehearsing a scene together, and when he was introduced to me as my girlfriend's partner, he first assumed we were also acting partners. After a few moments, "partner" reregistered, to which he responded, "Oh. Ohhhh. Partner." Both girlfriend and partner can easily be misread, reconstituted, and recycled in a way that erases a large part of our relationship, since we are, of course, both friends and partners. Here is where marriage can offer explicit rhetoric for those who need/want it. If my intention/illocution is intended to make the relationship between us explicitly clear, all I have to do is refer to her as my wife. **The perlocution of this particular speech act—my wife—leaves no space for misunderstanding.** I gain more control of how my relationship is read, which grants rhetorical agency while disrupting the space in which the conversation is taking place.

Saying. Doing. Being.

The linguistic performativity of a woman referring to her wife is powerful, yet rarely are people exposed to such a speech act. Even in states and countries that extend marriage rights to same-sex couples, the impact is undeniable, for these are "speech acts that actually do something rather than merely represent something" (Felluga "Modules on Butler"). Inserting queerness into (perceived traditional) marriage is potential through performativity. Claeys addresses the power of performative utterances, "using a performative sentence, therefore, is not just saying something, it is doing something as well [...] saying something is always doing something" (6-7, 8). The performativity of a woman intentionally referring to her wife is resignification of what a wife can be and to whom she can be a wife; since wife is defined as what it is not—a husband—interference occurs, and the speech act can be said to constitute what Butler calls a "subversive redeployment," especially when wife is used in response to a heteronormative, heterosexist, or homophobic speech act.

Malinowitz also supports the conflation of linguistic and social change: "political change means linguistic change and the concomitant production of new knowledge; empowerment entails creating a new discourse within which to fashion and position yourself" (245). There is hope for queers who want to remain resistant and radical in the context of such a problematic context as marriage. Judith Butler "insists on the importance of critical writing and the use of language for political mobilization," and more specifically, she "is thus interested in the speech which makes people 'uncomfortable' and makes people think" (Claeys 5). **In this way, queers can occupy marriage literally and linguistically.**

PAGE 5C: CONSIDERATIONS >> OCCUPY MARRIAGE

[EMBEDDED AUDIO.

Transcript: *On the way out of the post office, immediately after mailing our Save the Date cards, we notice a bumper sticker on the car parked next to mine: my Jeep dons a large rainbow strip and a Michigan LOVE sticker; the other car has a yellow and red marriage encounter® sticker that reads, "I believe in marriage". I guess we do, too. (I have a sneaking suspicion that these folks don't necessarily support same-sex marriage.) It feels like, since we started planning our wedding, these moments of tension are everywhere. With each plan comes another reminder that we aren't subscribing to a "normal" mode of marriage. Some would argue that by getting married, we are becoming normalized; I would argue that getting married has done nothing but prove how different we really are.*]

Butler effectively argues for "making use of language to invoke, incite, and solicit a different future" (Butler *Who Sings the Nation State?* 51). Using the platform and solidarity of the recent Occupy movements, I suggest a performative politics that moves queers into the realm of marriage, civil unions, or fill-in-the-blank, if and when they wish to do so. Increasing visibility and rearticulating queer desires can destabilize what dominant discourse tells us about ourselves. But where do we start? While arguing for a new state of feminism, gaga feminism, Halberstam argues that "these feminists are not 'becoming women' in the sense of coming to consciousness, they are unbecoming women in every sense – they undo the category rather than rounding [sic] it out" (xiv). **Similarly, I would argue that queer participation in marriage also has the power to undo the category of married rather than round it out, thereby disrupting its historically discriminatory ideologies, regulatory functions, and exclusivity (Halberstam xiv).** As ze explains,

> they dress it up and down, take it apart like a car engine and then rebuild it so that it is louder and faster. This feminism is about improvisation, customization, and innovation. The gaga feminist [and, I would add, queer], in other words, cannot settle into the house that the culture has built for her[/them]. S/he has [/they have] to tear it down, reimagine the very meaning of the house in form and function and only then can s/he [/they] rebuild. (xiv)

In the same way Halberstam sees feminists working to "occupy gender" (xiv), I see a generative space for queers to "occupy marriage" in order to dismantle its systemic power from the inside. Malinowitz takes a more realistic and moderate approach (not that such an approach is ideal – what is ideal anymore, especially in the context of queerness?), and points out that "though people usually want to leave the margins, they do want to be able to bring with them the sharp vision that comes from living with friction and contradiction" (Malinowitz 251-52). Here is where the task begins: occupy marriage, but bring the meta-knowledge along.

(Or, just say fuck it and don't get married.)

PAGE 6: AND SO...

This project has been a keyhole into my opacity, into the spaces where I am caught between an older, het set of norms and a newer queer set of values. As I attentively plan my upcoming wedding, I can't help but wonder, how might refusing to get married, just to remain radically queer, be understood as *queernormativity* – the dominant, queer non-status-quo? Yes, my same-sex marriage can be read as normative, but I believe it will result in more queer visibility. If I refer to my wife, who is present and also refers to me as her wife, in that moment, we upset the norm; we undo the binary of traditional marriage that says opposite wife is husband. In this way, as Sedgwick points out, "language really can be said to produce effects" (10). Ultimately, I see my participation in same-sex marriage as a moment of "queer assertiveness" and as an "openly queer articulation" (Sedgwick 14), one that will not and cannot be easily ignored. I can't live outside of heteronormativity, nor can I escape capitalism and domesticity because, as Wallace points out, "we are all reliant on social norms beyond our control" (6).

Even though I can't move outside the system, or live life outside of its margins, I can use the meta-knowledge I have gained from the margins, beyond those margins, in order to remain critically 'engaged'. [EMBEDDED VIDEO.

Transcript: *When people learn that Ginny and I are getting married, they always ass, "Iiiis that legal in Michigan?" To which we answer, "no, not yet." We explain the initial delay, the exciting March 21st Supreme Court ruling that found the marriage ban unconstitutional, and the disheartening stay that was promptly filed the following day. Although we plan on filing for a marriage license in our home state to be married legally, we will hold our ceremony in Harbor Springs, Michigan whether it is legal or not. For us, it's land over law. Place is incredibly important to us: Lake Michigan, this yellow house, the bright canopy of green leaves and sunshine hold memories only our hearts know. This wedding is our way of inviting others in to experience a piece of ourselves. I knew from the start that this project would be personal – what queer writing isn't? When I shared my conceptual vision for the project, Ginny remarked, "part of me is written into this." The obvious metaphor here reminds me that my personal life and partner would normally be written out of an academic essay, but queer rhetoric welcomes it, welcomes me, whole—a messy, emotional, conflicted, multiple queer subject.*]

WORKS CITED

Ahmed, Sara. "Queer Feelings." *The Routledge Queer Studies Reader*. Eds. Donald E. Hall and Annamarie Jagose with Andrea Bebell and Susan Potter. New York: Routledge, 2013: 3-17. Print.

Alexander, Jonathan. *Literacy, Sexuality, Pedagogy*. Logan: Utah State University Press, 2008. Print.

Alexander, Jonathon and Jacqueline Rhodes. *Queered*. Technoculture 2 (2012). Web. 9 Mar. 2012. http://tcjournal.org/drupal/vol2/queered

— "Queer Rhetoric and the Pleasures of the Archive." *Enculturation* 16 Jan. 2012. Web. 9 Mar. 2012. http://enculturation.net/files/QueerRhetoric/queerarchive/intro.html

Butler, Judith. "Performative Acts and Gender Constitution: An Essay in Phenomenology and Feminist Theory." *Theatre Journal* 40.4 (1988): 519-531. Print.

Butler, Judith and Gayatri Spivak. *Who Sings the Nation State?* London: Seagull Books, 2010. Print.

Claeys, Sarah. "How to do Things with Butler: An Inquiry on the Origin, Citation, and Application of Judith Butler's Theory of Performativity" Diss. Universiteit Gent, 2006. Print.

Felluga, Dino. "Modules on Butler: on performativity." Purdue University. *Introductory Guide to Critical Theory* 31 Jan. 2011. Web. 6 Dec. 2013. http://www.cla.purdue.edu/english/theory/genderandsex/modules/butlerperformativity.html

Gonçalves, Zan Meyer. *Sexuality and the Politics of Ethos in the Writing Classroom.* Carbondale: Southern Illinois University Press, 2005. Print.

Halberstam, J. Jack. *Gaga Feminism.* Boston: Beacon, 2012. Print.

Malinowitz, Harriet. *Textual Orientations.* Portsmouth: Boyton/Cook Publishers, 1995. Print.

Mercer, Johnny and Hoagy Carmichael. "Skylark." Perf. Maxine Sullivan. 1947. mp4.

Partisan Records. "Sallie Ford & The Sound Outside-They Told Me (Official Video)." *YouTube.* YouTube, 11 Jul. 2013. Web. 4 April 2014.

Rauch, Jonathan. *gay marriage.* New York: Holt, 2004. Print.

Rhodes, Jacqueline and Ellen Gómez. *queer-rhetoric.* 2013. Web. 2 Dec. 2013. http://queer-rhetoric.wikispaces.com/

Sedgwick, Eve Kosofsky. "Queer and Now." *The Routledge Queer Studies Reader.* Eds. Donald E. Hall and Annamarie Jagose with Andrea Bebell and Susan Potter. New York: Routledge, 2013: 3-17. Print.

Sullivan, Andrew. *Virtually Normal.* New York: Vintage Books, 1995. Print.

Sullivan, Nikki. "Queer: *A Question of Being or Doing?" A Critical Introduction to Queer Theory.* New York: New York University Press, 2003. Print.

Wallace, David. *Compelled to Write.* Logan: Utah State University Press, 2011. Print.

Warner, Michael. *The Trouble with Normal.* Cambridge: Harvard University Press, 1999. Print.

Interface

Background image-Mo, Atle. *White Wall.* nd. Digital image. Subtle Patterns. Web.

Navigation bar Bogdan Bogdan. *Menu Matic.* 2011. Dynamic drop down menu. *Adobe Widget Browser.*

Slideshow widget-mssdvm. *FlexSlider.* 2011. Slideshow or image rotator. *Adobe Widget Browser.*

Typeface-Tension Type. *Impact Label* and *Impact Label Reversed.* 2009. *Font Squirrel.*

JOURNAL OF BASIC WRITING

The Journal of Basic Writing is on the Web at http://wac.colostate.edu/jbw/index.cfm

Journal of Basic Writing is a refereed journal founded in 1975 by Mina Shaughnessy and is published twice a year with support from the Office of Academic Affairs of the City University of New York. Basic writing, a contested term, refers to the field concerned with teaching writing to students not yet deemed ready for first-year composition. Originally, these students were part of the wave of open admissions students who poured into universities as a result of the social unrest of the 1960s and the resulting reforms. Though social and political realities have changed dramatically since then, the presence of "basic writers" in colleges and universities, and the debates over how best to serve them, persist. *JBW* publishes articles related to basic and second-language writing as well as freshman writing transitions. Articles exploring the social, political, and pedagogical questions related to educational access are at the core of *JBW*'s history and mission.

Subversive Complicity and Basic Writing Across the Curriculum

In this article, noted writing and rhetoric scholar Victor Villanueva draws from his Keynote at the Conference on Basic Writing workshop at the 2013 4C's to mobilize the BW community toward another radical affiliation. His assertion, he says, is "simple": "time for basic writing to get out from under," time "to inculcate a Basic Writing Across the Curriculum. . . a time yet again to move away from the concept that basic writers are in need of remedies." BW instructors understand rhetorical efficacy by way of recognizing their students' capacities for interesting and competent language. When shared, this understanding can impel our colleagues across the disciplines to see our students' rhetorics as constructively as we do. The impact would be a wider, more inclusive community for students deemed "basic," and opportunities of educational access stand to be renewed.

3 Subversive Complicity and Basic Writing Across the Curriculum

Victor Villanueva

Abstract: What follows is a simple assertion: time for basic writing to get out from under, a call for us to inculcate a Basic Writing Across the Curriculum. It is time yet again to move away from the concept that basic writers are in need of remedies, in part because all composition courses are in some sense remedial, and to a greater degree because the "illness" that we seek to remedy is in being at least discursively other-cultural. Within this essay there are reflections, speculations, considerations of how to go about what is demanded of us—enculturation and assimilation—while doing what it is we believe we ought to do—promote critical consciousness, something that many of us in many disciplines seek to do, even if those in other disciplines are unaware of the term.

A MEMORY, 1984

We finally have health insurance, so Carol can deliver the child who will be AnaSofía in a birthing room in a hospital, Virginia Mason, Seattle, Washington. The dilation has been sudden, precipitous. Unprepared for a long stay at the hospital, I call my friend Virginia for some help: my medicines, toothbrush, those kinds of things.

Virginia shows up in the midst of Carol's contractions. She tells me that the basic writing program that I have been in charge of is going to be cut, so she has made an appointment for me with the provost for the next day. I don't know what a provost is, but I get the idea: someone with power.

The baby is born. Some complications. The umbilical cord had become a noose. Two nurses and I unwrap the cord, cut it, rub the feet, and then the squall of life, the baby born. Mom and baby are fine. I've got a provost to meet.

Still shaken by the miracle, I show up at the provost's office. I don't understand where a provost stands in the hierarchy, but I do understand an office larger than the apartment that houses Carol, me, and three kids with a fourth about to move in. Offices in academics are hegemonically legitimating monuments, primary symbols of power (or the lack: TAs and instructors in the sub-basement).

The provost explains that the university is about higher education, not remediation, especially given the times (one of many budget crises in my career; they come often; financial crises are a normal part of capitalism, according to Marx and to Keynes, though each providing different ways of dealing with crisis). The university cannot afford the luxury of remediation.

Well, if that's the case, I say, then why do we offer algebra or even regular 101 comp courses? Seems like remediation to me. The only difference I see is who is being served. It was something like that, that I had said.

The provost appears to get defensive. I'm scared that I've crossed a line. She then explains, patiently, that those algebra and comp courses are the norm, that basic writing falls below the norm, is more a basic literacy, pre-university.

I understand, I say. But I go on to say that, based on personal experience, community colleges have their hands full, that culturally they are somewhat different from the university, and that the job of basic writing as I see it isn't teaching grammar or other discrete skills but moving from one way of doing language to another, moving to the ways of language of the university. Sometime not long after this particular conversation, compositionists began to write of "academic discourse communities."

My intention is not to denigrate the community college. I am finding the available means of persuasion—exploiting the discourse of elitism and the discourse of assimilation to this person in a football-field sized office. I argue that we don't remediate; we enculturate. And so, Basic Writing survives at that University (and remains to this day, nearly three decades later).

About ten years after that first meeting with a provost, the other state university in the same state: Same conversation, same threat, same result, given the promise of assimilation, a kind of enculturation.

I

First-year comp has always been remedial, but it gained special notice when it became designed for the poor and the folks of color, not Harvard's comp course but open admissions at City College of New York, in Harlem. In Harlem. And suddenly, these were the New Students (see McAlexander), "the true outsiders" (Shaughnessy, *Errors* 2). "New" reminds me of the somewhat recent national election's sudden realization that there are Latinos in the U.S., failing to remember that the Latinos, the Spanish, were the supposed discoverers of this continent, the first non-indigenous long-term inhabitants. Been here all along, and tied to the original inhabitants, insofar as rules against miscegeny applied mainly to the Spanish elite (Acuña). In much the same way, the New Students weren't all that new. They were the victims of a particular political economy.

So the university decided that those Harvard boys or those Yale boys, products of the best college prep schools of the second half of the nineteenth century, were not quite literate, certainly not for Harvard or Yale, Kelly Ritter reminds us. At Harvard the boys were assigned to English A, and some to English B, and even some to English D, the letters correlating to potential grades in writing in English A, to degrees of heads' boniness, "bonehead" the term used at the University of Utah for its remedial students in the 1940s (Ritter 68), with Shaughnessy saying that the new students weren't even up to par with the boneheads (*Errors* 2). Or there was Yale's "Awkward Squad," white, middle-class Ivy Leaguers of the 1920s through the 1960s who nevertheless required what we would now call basic writing (Ritter 43-4). And when the likes of Sharon Crowley shouted for an end to the universal requirement for first-year comp, she was hooted down. But when economic crises loom, the racialized, non-middle-class version of "remedial" writing is immediately slated for removal. And the way to save it is to invoke a rhetoric that cobbles together multiculturalism or equal opportunity and assimilation.

Monday, 11 March 2013, The Chronicle of Higher Education, *front page: A long column titled "The Second-Chance Club: Inside a Semester of Remedial English." It's a very nice piece, showing how the students have to pass a timed writing—clear thesis sentence, four paragraphs (well, at least it isn't five), answering three questions on the assigned writing. The* Chronicle's *column contains pictures of the students, Black students, and the white professor (though there is one white student in the pictures, as well; you just have to look closely to find him). The caption under a head-shot of the prof declares that "Professors in remedial courses often must be social workers, too." This exposure is good for the survival of basic writing. And the message is clear—a second chance at upward mobility, a dedication to assimilation, a multicultural imperative for an improved economy.*

But for all the inherent sympathy, multiculturalism tends to fail because by-and-large it tends not to be anti-racist. The problem with multiculturalism is that it relies on a conception of cultural pluralism, an ideal (a Platonic "Good," even), but given the political economy of the day (no matter which school of "political economy," the political liberal's Keynesian or the economic neoliberal's Friedmanian), the idea of all cultures living together in mutual understanding is not yet here. So we do an injustice in acting as if a mutuality already exists, that with a little effort on thesis sentences andcoherent paragraphs as defined by Cicero, Aristotle, or Bain, we can level the playing field (and put this way, resorting to a cliché, makes the absurdity apparent). But absurd or not, the rhetoric of the new racism, with its preference for *difference* over *racism*, allows for arguments based on assimilation and enculturation to become how best to sell basic writing, whether to central admin or to *The Chronicle of Higher Education*. Far be it for us to point to absurdity or even the violence inherent in our nation's dominant metaphor, the melting pot. Sometimes rhetoric actually is about duplicity, Plato notwithstanding.

Assimilation, enculturation, remains the general norm, even as we in writing try to write our ways out of that norm. Melting into the pot is seen as the way to maintain a nation, the rhetoric goes; identity politics risk the loss of a national identity. It's a strange notion, when we think in terms of all the cultures (as opposed to "races") contained beneath the umbrella term *America*. We're really quite capable, apparently, of clinging to ancestry and realizing our national identity. We do better to look to the relations among discourse, the cultural, the political (not only as ideology but as political power more broadly conceived), and the economic.

Gyatri Spivak begins to approach this recognition of the forces at play as she writes not only of epistemologies that give credence to the power of discourse as ideological, but also as she writes of the episte-mology of other political economic forces, what she calls (à la Foucault) an epistemology of violence. She is referring to the degree to which "subalterns" (like the disenfranchised, the poor, women, often) are never quite able to speak or write from their own ways of knowing. That is, when Spivak asks "Can the Subaltern Speak?" she argues that since our identities are formed in relation to others, power relations are such that there is no truly autonomous Other, no truly autonomous subaltern whose voice is separate from and stands alongside the voices of those in power. She concludes that the answer to whether the subaltern can speak is no. And this is surely no less true for so many of those, women and men, who find themselves in (or choose to enter into) basic writing classrooms, forced into a particular way of marshaling arguments: Edited American English and Aristotelian logic. Yet what choice do we have as teachers, we ask. Code meshing? It's a great concept: using the rhetorical power available in some dialects that are not available in the Standard, an intentional blending of dialectics. And it is more than simply a great concept; it is right; it is some assertion of the subaltern speaking. But before code meshing could work in sociology or in history or any place in the college or university outside of the English classroom, we would have to educate an awful lot of educators. We've been trying for over forty years now, but some notion of "proper English" continues to hold sway.

But maybe, rather than throw up our hands and say that the *reality* is that we must give in to the power and the economy, to students' own wishes for a chance at the middle class, say in resignation that we teach academic discourse lest the folks in sociology or history or whatever hurt the students, maybe we can gain a force in numbers, forge alliances, insinuate basic writing into WAC. We have our expertise—literacy and its pedagogy—but they have theirs. And as often, they too recognize the politics, just not necessarily the politics in believing writing is simply writing, in believing that the codes are agreed upon, a given. On the one hand, we would do well to insinuate our knowledge into theirs. Some of the most interesting writing and research about racism obtains in sociology (like Bonilla-Silva or Winant); some of the most interesting research and writing about language is happening in psychology (like Martín-Baró in Aron and Corn or Mishler); some of the most interesting uses of written narrative is happening in the medical professions (also Mishler); there's even an entire field of study called Narrative-Based Medicine (see, for example, Greenhalgh and Hurwitz). What we know that they might not is that as language carries meaning, meaning carries cultures and their ideologies, ideologies and their economies.

I have made this argument before, though in another context ("Politics"), that we cannot presume to be the purveyors of critical consciousness. In terms of racism, we stand to learn from those other disciplines while we inform them of the ways of writing and rhetoric. We can learn from folks in business who have economists among them, from historians, from political scientists, from sociologists, as well as from the literary figures and critical theorists from whom we have grown accustomed to learning. We give something to the disciplines—matters of literacy and rhetoric grounded in the sociopolitical; and they give us something—their considerations of the political and the economic. And we introduce them to basic writers, not as needing remedies or in need for proper development (Rose), but as rhetorical power players (Villanueva, *Bootstraps*). It's time. And it's bound to succeed, since we'd be in the business of justice and maybe even real equality somewhere down the line, not composition teachers who "must be social workers," not missionaries converting the natives to the religion of "proper" discourse.

The missionary. Some of us read Shaughnessy's "Diving In" as a spoof on developmental schemes. So much of the work in education was being tied to developmental models at the time of Shaughnessy: William Perry, Maslow, Bloom, and especially Piaget. Shaughnessy was clearly poking fun at the missionary mentality of teachers like her: trained in literature, suddenly faced with the New Student. But it turns out not to be so funny a scheme, since somehow it seems that we can't quite get past "converting the natives" because of the exigencies of power and economics. We remain stuck in the idea that there is only one way for students to succeed: learn the discourse of power, doing almost nothing outside of our closed conversations in Writing Studies to alter that discourse. That *Chronicle of Higher Ed* article mentioned above clearly honors the successful conversion of the natives. If basic writing is to be no longer missionary in its method, though, no longer social work, then we should be engaging with the other minds across the disciplines who also face the students we face, having those faculty work with us rather than point accusatory fingers at us. We should enter into a dialogue across the disciplines so as better to understand the social processes that could relegate such a large number to the trouble-heap. All of us can use the tools at our disposal to circumvent reproducing a school system that has traditionally failed to educate the woman, the poor, or the person of color at the same rate of efficiency as others. And while we learn from them, we pass on contact zones and critical pedagogies and world Englishes and meshed codes, passing on our particular ways of understanding what many other disciplines also understand, that language is not just the conveyor of knowledge but is the way knowledge becomes known.

II

But the problem remains: how to teach the written rhetoric of power without negating students' power, the power inherent in their own ways with words. One answer might be to teach a conscious mimicry. This is not a new idea, of course (see, for instance, bell, Bhabha, Fuss). As I mentioned some years ago ("Rhetoric"), Puerto Ricans, as the longest continuous colonial subjects of the modern world, have long used a strategy called *jaibería*, a *jaiba* rhetoric. Puerto Rico's situation is one in which political power makes colonialism no longer tenable, yet there remains an economic situation in which nationalism is not feasible. The trick then is maintaining a cultural identity while complying with dominance. That's achieved through a *jaibería*, a "subversive complicity" (Grosfoguel), kind of like shining someone on, a conscious mimicry. Sociologists Grosfoguel, Negrón-Muntaner, and Goeras call on Diana Fuss's reading of Fanon in *Black Skin, White Masks* to describe a *jaiba* politics as a mimicry rather than a masquerade: According to Diana Fuss in her essay on Frantz Fanon, there is a tendency within postcolonial and psychoanalytic discourse to distinguish between the practices of mimicry and masquerade. While in psychoanalysis, masquerade is understood as the unconscious assumption of a role, mimicry, according to Homi K. Bhabha, is understood as a colonial strategy of subjugation. Fuss, however, stresses that there can be a mimicry of subversion where the deliberate performance of a role does not entail identification. The performance's contexts thus become crucial in determining its subversive potential . . . [In] both Fanon's and Fuss's texts, the most powerful example of subversive mimicry is that of the Algerian Nationalist woman militant who "passes" as a Europeanized subject in order to advance the cause of National liberation. (26-28)

In comp terms, this is where "inventing the university" is a mutually conscious decision, not just foisted on basic writers but encouraged as a jointly agreed upon strategy, not with the idea that students become like teachers but rather that students learn how to gain the trust of teachers so that a communal learning can take place, what Fanon calls "a world of reciprocal recognitions" (218). This is the strategy of a particular program with which I am currently involved, CLASP, which I'll describe a little further below.

Gail Okawa outlines a pedagogy wherein students are asked to look at how people of color are represented in ways that hide their political identities, asking students to remove these masks. By the same token, folks of color can quite intentionally choose to conceal by the wearing of masks, consciously enacting Fanon's white masks, though Okawa refers to Mitsuye Yamada's use of the mask metaphor. In a similar vein, Malea Powell tells tales of the trickster's ways, a rhetoric which "exposes the lies we tell ourselves and, at the same time, exposes the necessity of those lies to our daily material existence" (9). And there is *imitatio*, a forming of the self through a learning process of mimicry. *Jaibería* is not a new idea. I talk to a provost, imitating the discourse of assimilation disguised as multiculturalism, so as to be able to provide critical opportunities critically.

Acknowledge that Basic Writing Programs are always subject to the political economy because of a structural racism; recognize the institutional belief that higher education cannot be responsible for what it sees as the shortfalls of lower education (blame always flowing downstream), and we are perforce pulled into a rhetoric of survival, a complicit rhetoric with somewhat subversive motives. In other words, I'm calling for *imitatio* with an anti-racist critical pedagogy, *imitatio* taking on a particular mental state—a *jaibería*, masking in a discursive trickery—while students work *with* us on discourse, work critically and consciously on conventions, and while we—both the students and the teachers of writing—work on introducing those in other disciplines to the basic writer and swap discoveries and conceptions of economics and political power and language.

In the pages of this journal some years back, I told of how I introduce basic writing students (and others) to the idea of writing as epistemological, that language comes from the self in dialogue with one's culture ("Theory"). It's a fun exercise. I invite you to try it. What that article doesn't mention, however (since that wasn't its intent), is what happens after the opening gambit. Once we establish something about language as epistemological and a social construction, we discuss conventions. This is pretty straightforward at first, matters of registers and codes that all students understand immediately—speaking to an elder versus speaking to a peer, say. Then to the "logic" behind academic discourse, the idea that whereas the writing with which they are most familiar within a school context (the fiction and poetry) is designed for surprise, expository and argumentative academic writing tends to work from an older Roman oral legal tradition, in which the jurors or judges must know an argument's general premises or assertions first, so as to prepare listeners for the arguments to follow (and thereby judge). I even show them a short passage from Cicero's *de Inventione*. Then we go into the matter of vocabulary. This is, of course, an issue for graduate students no less than basic writers, graduate students given to preferring "that's problematic" to "that's a possible problem," just as undergraduates learn "to be cognizant of" rather than simply "get it." Inspired decades ago by a rhetoric by Patrick Hartwell, I provide a number of clichés in "academic" speech, and we work these together: "Refrain from being lachrymose over precipitately decanted lacteal fluid" or "Male cadavers are incapable of yielding any testimony." Soon they see the problem in using a vocabulary which has not yet become their own. As a class, we work through these examples. The students tend to respond. So students are encouraged to let go of the fear, to the extent that's possible, asked to write "naturally," in their own ways. Then we work through papers together. Unlike the standard stage model of *the* writing process, we begin with editing, mainly marking sentence breaks (since fused sentences and run-on sentences tend to be the greatest problems). Then we translate. Using a student-volunteer's paper, we work together to translate the student's discourse onto something akin to academic discourse, especially as pertains to audience. In the process, students become conscious translators of their own ways with words to those of the academic discourse community. The process thereby calls on a conscious understanding of Aristotle's logic, and a conscious understanding of contrastive rhetorics.

I have used this process successfully for many years with students from other cultures, including those students who might look white and middle class but who are at least at one remove from the supposed traditional student. As with any pedagogy (including the one discussed below), I can't claim classes full of critically conscious literacy epiphanies, but most get most of it in the mere fifteen weeks, the forty contact hours, that we have.

III

Gaining more than forty hours in the acquisition of academic discourse means having to involve our colleagues across the curriculum. At my institution right now, we are involved in a program called CLASP (Critical Literacies Achievement and Success Program). Although the students are those who are first generation, of color, and from poverty, there is no assumption that students are operating from a lack. We take their presence in college at face value, meaning that we simply accept what they themselves believe: that they are capable of college work, a belief substantiated by their very presence at an institution with no open admissions policy, an institution, in fact, subject to a state mandate against racial preferences on admissions (a ban now upheld by the Supreme Court's April 2014 decision in Schuette v. Coalition to Defend Affirmative Action). CLASP is not a remedial program. Rather, it operates from Fanon's "reciprocal recognitions," that whatever the students don't know about how professors operate, the professors are equally ignorant of how these "New Students" operate. At the heart of the program is discussing how to talk with professors, discussing with the students the kinds of questions they might have of the instructor, having the students jot down their questions, and mandating a series of visits during the professors' office hours. The best learning is one-with-one; novice students' great fear is the one-with-one with professors. Through this program, the professors get to discover the students as more than victims; the students get to discover the professors as less than geniuses.

Within CLASP, we include the Writing Commons, an offshoot of the Writing Center, wherein tutors are trained in the grammars of the dominant dialects of the students who participate in CLASP: Chicano English (see Fought) or African American Language (see Smitherman and Villanueva). They're also shown the workings of contrastive rhetoric. And they are taught how to listen—rhetorically—that kind of conscious listening (and even eavesdropping) that Krista Ratcliffe describes. And the students learn precisely the same things: rhetorical listening and rhetorics (as plural), and of course, matters of correctness, since infelicities obtain in every dialect and language. The

CLASP Writing Commons provides an introduction to the ways of a writing center but within a community with which they are familiar, even though the students contain all the variations on ideology one would expect of "traditional" students. They get to hear each other on racism, class, assimilation, sexuality—the hot-button subjects that are typical of humanities and social science courses. They get to hear each other; they learn to discuss; and again, the tutors get to discover how not-at-all-different the students are. What's more, the students gather more and more awareness of themselves as rhetorical beings, gain greater metalinguistic awareness, develop a vocabulary with which to speak with their professors during those office hours that the program mandates. They become the agents of their own basic writing across the curriculum.

And those of us who work at training faculty who are interested in CLASP from across the curriculum (and the interest is in fact across the curriculum) reinforce what students discover about the organizational patterns and other discourse markers (matters other than simple mechanics) that are manifest in students' early draft writing. The faculty learn from us and from the students that often the students' writing does not reflect a lack of organizational abilities but different organizational patterns. The Arab student or the Latina student who seems to go on long tangents can discuss with faculty, thanks to contrastive rhetoric, how the tangent might not be (and discover the discursive footnote). And the student, in discussion with the faculty who is conscious of contrastive rhetoric, might also discover when a tangent really is a tangent—and would be a tangent in Spanish or in Arabic academic discourse. So while professors learn (or recall, since many are not monolingual in English) the conventions of other languages and deliver the conventions of particular disciplines, the students—and the professors—become conscious of the conventions-as-conventions. In remaining conscious of students' patterns of predispositions by way of early drafts that give vent to culturally specific discursive ways, the conversation is opened up; the professors and the students work together in assuring students gain access to the places they wish to go by way of the academy without erasing where they've been. Their mimicry, their conscious invention of the university, has the potential of changing the university, broadening the university's conceptions of discourses in action, of the rhetorics that are always at play, more members of the university discovering that, at bottom, we are all creatures of the word.

FROM PABLO NERUDA:

Nació
la palabra en la sangre,
creció en el cuerpo oscuro, palpitando y voló con los labios y la boca.

Más lejos y más cerca aún, aún venía
de padres muertos y de errantes razas, de territorios que se hicieron piedra que se cansaron de sus pobres tribus, porque cuando el dolor salió al camino los pueblos anduvieron y llegaron
y nueva tierra y agua reunieron para sembrar de nuevo su palabra.
Y así la herencia es ésta:
éste es el aire que nos comunica
con el hombre enterrado y con la aurora de nuevos sere que aún no amanecieron

The word
was born in the blood,
grew in the dark body, beating,
and took flight through the lips and the mouth.

Farther away and nearer still, still it came
from dead fathers and from wandering races, from lands which had turned to stone,
lands weary of their poor tribes, for when grief took to the roads the people set out and arrived and married new land and water to grow their words again.
And so this is the inheritance:
this is the wavelength which connects us with dead men and the dawning
of new beings not yet come to light

WORKS CITED

Acuña, Rodolfo F. *Occupied America: A History of Chicanos* (7th ed.). Boston: Longman, 2010. 36. Print.

Aron, Adrianne and Shawn Corne, eds. *Writings for a Liberation Psychology: Ignacio Martín-Baró.* Cambridge, MA: Harvard University Press, 1996. Print.

Bartholomae, David. "Inventing the University." *Journal of Basic Writing* 5.1 (1986): 4-23. Print.

Berlin, James A. *Writing Instruction in Nineteenth-Century American Colleges.* Carbondale, IL: Southern Illinois University Press, 1984. Print.

Bhabha, Homi. "Of Mimicry and Man: The Ambivalence of Colonial Discourse." *October* 28 (1984): 125-33. Print.

Bizzell, Patricia. "William Perry and Liberal Education." *College English* 46.5 (1984): 447-54. Print.

Bonilla-Silva, Eduardo. *Racism without Racists: Color-Blind Racism and the Persistence of Racial Inequality in the United States.* Lanham, MD: Rowman and Littlefield, 2006. Print.

Crowley, Sharon. "Composition's Ethic of Service, the Universal Requirement, and the Discourse of Student Need." *JAC* 15.2 (1995): 227-39. Print.

Fanon, Frantz. *Black Skin, White Masks.* Trans. Richard Philcox. New York: Grove Press, 2008. Print.

Fought, Carmen. *Chicano English in Context.* New York: Palgrave Macmillan, 2003. Print.

Fuss, Diana. "Interior Colonies: Frantz Fanon and the Politics of Identification." *Diacritics* 24.2/3 (1994): 19-42. Print.

Greenhalgh, Trisha and Brian Hurwitz, eds. *Narrative Based Medicine.* London: BMJ Books, 1998. Print.

Grosfoguel, Ramón. "Feminizando la Politica." *El Nuevo Día.* 24 July 1990: 51. Web.

Grosfoguel, Ramón, Frances Negrón-Muntaner, and Chloé S. Goeras. "Beyond Nationalist and Colonialist Discourses: The Jaiba Politics of the Puerto Rican Ethno-Nation." *Puerto Rican Jam: Rethinking Colonialism and Nationalism.* Eds. Frances Negrón-Muntaner and Ramón Grosfoguel. Minneapolis: University of Minnesota Press, 1997. 1-36. Print.

Hartwell, Patrick and Robert H Bentley. *Open to Language: A New College Rhetoric.* New York: Oxford University Press, 1982. Print.

hooks, bell. "Representing Whiteness in the Black Imagination." *Displacing Whiteness: Essays in Social and Cultural Criticism.* Ed. Ruth Frankenberg. Durham: Duke University Press, 1997. 338-46. Print.

Hoover, Eric and Sara Lipka. "The Second-Chance Club: Inside a Semester of Remedial English." *The Chronicle of Higher Education*, 11 March 2013. Web.

McAlexander, Patricia J. "Mina Shaughnessy and K. Patricia Cross: The Forgotten Debate over Postsecondary Remediation." *Rhetoric Review* 19.1/2 (2000): 28-41. Print.

Mishler, Elliot. *The Discourse of Medicine: Dialectics of Medical Interviews.* New York: Ablex, 1984. Print.

—. *Storylines: Craftartists' Narrative of Identity.* Cambridge, MA: Harvard University Press, 1999. Print.

Neruda, Pablo. "La Palabra," *Plenos Poderes.* Buenos Aires: Editorial Losada, 1962. 4. Print.

—. "The Word." Trans. Alastair Reid. *The Poetry of Pablo Neruda.* Ed. Ilan Stavans. New York: Farrar, Straus and Giroux, 2003. 621. Print.

Okawa, Gail Y. "Removing Masks: Confronting Graceful Evasion and Bad Habits in a Graduate English Class." *Race, Rhetoric, and Composition.* Ed. Keith Gilyard. Portsmouth, NH: Heinemann Boynton/Cook, 1999. 124-43. Print.

Powell, Malea. "Blood and Scholarship: One Mixed-Blood's Story." *Race, Rhetoric and Composition.* Ed. Keith Gilyard. New Hampshire: Boynton/Cook Publishers, 1999. 1-16. Print.

Ratcliffe, Krista. *Rhetorical Listening: Identification, Gender, Whiteness.* Carbondale, IL: Southern Illinois University Press, 2005. Print.

Ritter, Kelly. *Before Shaughnessy: Basic Writing at Yale and Harvard, 1920-1960.* Carbondale, IL: Southern Illinois University Press, 2004. Print.

Rose, Mike. "Narrowing the Mind and Page: Remedial Writers and Cognitive Reductionism." *College Composition and Communication* 39.3 (1988): 267-98. Print.

Shaughnessy, Mina P. "Diving In: An Introduction to Basic Writing." *College Composition and Communication* 27.3 (1976): 234-39. Print.

—. *Errors and Expectations: A Guide for the Teacher of Basic Writing.* New York: Oxford University Press, 1977. Print.

Smitherman, Geneva and Victor Villanueva, eds. *Language Diversity in the Classroom: From Theory to Practice.* Carbondale, IL: Southern Illinois University Press, 2003. Print.

Spivak, Gayatri Chakravorty. "Can the Subaltern Speak?" *Marxism and the Interpretation of Culture.* Eds. b. Cary Nelson and Lawrence Grossberg. Urbana, IL: University of Illinois Press, 1988. 271-316. Print.

Villanueva, Victor. *Bootstraps: From an American Academic of Color.* Urbana: National Council of Teachers of English, 1993. Print.

—. "The Politics of Literacy Across the Curriculum." *WAC for the New Millennium: Strategies for Continuing Writing-Across-the-Curriculum Programs.* Ed. Susan McLeod, Eric Miraglia, Margot Soven, and Christopher Thaiss. Urbana: National Council of Teachers of English, 2001. 165-78. Print.

—. "On the Rhetoric and Precedents of Racism. *College Composition and Communication* 50.4 (1999): 645-61. Print.

—. "Theory in the Basic Writing Classroom? A Practice," *Journal of Basic Writing* 16.1 (1997): 79-90. Print.

Winant, Howard. *The World Is a Ghetto: Race and Democracy Since World War II*. New York: Basic Books, 2001. Print.

JOURNAL OF TEACHING WRITING

JOURNAL OF
TEACHING
WRITING
VOL. 28, NO. 2

ITW
Published by the
Indiana Teachers of Writing
Sponsored by
Indiana University-Purdue University Indianapolis

The *Journal of Teaching Writing* is on
the Web at http://journals.iupui.edu/
index.php/teachingwriting/

The *Journal of Teaching Writing*, now in
its thirty-fourth year of publication, is the
only national journal devoted to the teaching of writing at all academic levels, from
preschool through university, and in all
subject areas of the curriculum. It publishes refereed articles, book reviews, and
professional announcements. Contributors
of manuscripts receive signed and substantive reviews from members of our Editorial
Board, which is composed of distinguished
teachers and writers from all educational
levels and geographic regions of the U.S.; approximately 20% of manuscript
submissions are published annually. With its editors and Editorial Board,
the Journal has led the field in demystifying the editorial review process and
modeling the teaching of writing as a process of reflection and revision.

Practice, Patience, and Process in the Age of Accountability: What Cognitive Psychology Suggests about the Teaching and Assessment of Writing

This article offers writing teachers a cognitive perspective on learning to
compose, with implications and recommendations for writing instruction
and assessment. Exploring the concept of "deliberate practice" from Ronald
T. Kellogg and Alison P. Whiteford's research in cognitive psychology,
Cassity affirms and lends further support to what we already know and value
in the teaching of writing (e.g., frequent writing, formative feedback, revision, WAC/WID). This essay hits on important topics in the teaching of
writing on multiple levels and will help teachers fine-tune their teaching and
assessment approaches.

4 Practice, Patience, and Process in the Age of Accountability: What Cognitive Psychology Suggests about the Teaching and Assessment of Writing

Kathleen J. Cassity

It's a scenario experienced by many writing instructors: When chatting with colleagues from other disciplines at your institution, someone says, "You teach writing? So: How come our students can't write?" Or you meet someone who works outside academia who finds out where you teach and soon that person claims, "No one we've hired from that school can write."

To respond meaningfully yet concisely to such remarks is challenging. Most of us who teach writing are well aware of the complexity of the task we face, and regardless of where we place ourselves philosophically as composition instructors—whether we identify with "process," "post-process," "social-epistemic," "rhetorical," or other labels—we most likely agree that growth in writing requires extensive practice over a lengthy period of time, situated within a specific context. The recent work of cognitive psychologists Ronald Kellogg and Alison Whiteford not only confirms that this is so, but points toward some reasons *why* this is the case. Understanding how composition skills develop from the perspective of cognitive psychology can help us design and implement more effective writing instruction as well as more meaningful assessments. Such an understanding may also help us to articulate more effectively the need for extensive practice, time, and discipline-specific knowledge to the various constituencies we serve—

something especially crucial when dealing with those who mistakenly believe that helping students learn to write better should be the sole province of composition teachers, and/or that a good first-year writing course should be able to "take care of" any problems. Given the current high level of cultural anxiety regarding student writing abilities along with the intensified emphasis on programmatic and institutional accountability, the time is ripe for considering how we might ground our writing instruction and assessment in a scientific understanding of what actually happens in our brains as we write;[1] such a consideration is what I will attempt here.

I begin by elucidating some of Kellogg and Whiteford's most salient findings with regard to memory, deliberate practice, "knowledge-telling" versus knowledge transformation, and domain familiarity. I then explore the implications of these concepts for both teaching and assessment. Given the current emphasis on "measurable" and quantifiable data, I assert that cognitive psychology provides a scientific and evidence-based rationale for much of what composition has already come to value, as well as a means of both articulating that rationale to our constituencies and designing more meaningful assessment tools. Finally, I conclude by calling for a recommitment to revitalized writing instruction at all levels; enhanced Writing Across the Curriculum (WAC) and Writing in the Disciplines (WID) programs; and writing pedagogies and assessments that are grounded in awareness of cognitive processes rather than in any particular ideology of composition studies.

KELLOGG AND WHITEFORD: KEY PRINCIPLES

The concept of "deliberate practice" is arguably the most crucial aspect of composition instruction that Kellogg and Whiteford emphasize; in order to grasp why this is so crucial, it is helpful first to explore key aspects of memory and executive attention, and the high demands that composing places on both. *Working memory* (sometimes called "short-term memory") can be seen as analogous to the RAM in a computer in that the contents of our working memories never enter long-term storage. *Executive attention*—what we might refer to in lay terms as our "focus"—is the mindful and conscious attention that we bring to a task at any given moment, and is necessarily finite. (Our limited ability to focus executive attention on more than one thing at a time explains, for instance, why certain kinds of multi-tasking, such as driving a car while texting, is inadvisable.) Finally, *long-term memory* speaks for itself. It is where we "store" both knowledge and skills that have become automated through extensive practice—for instance, riding a bicycle, reading, or typing.

The task of composing places high demands on executive attention as well as both working and long-term memory. As Kellogg and Whiteford point out, the successful writer possesses numerous cognitive resources, including sufficient verbal ability to express ideational content; ability to manage high demands on working memory due to concurrent need for planning of ideas, generation of text, reviewing of ideas, rapid retrieval of domain-specific knowledge from long-term memory, maintenance of current planning/sentence generation/reviewing in working memory, simultaneous mental representations of author's intention, meaning of text, and possible meanings construed by audience (254).

For well-practiced writers, many of these resources are stored in long-term memory—that is, "automated"—leaving executive attention and working memory free to attend to the multiple cognitive demands of a specific writing situation. In contrast, the less practiced writer will have automated far fewer of the necessary resources, and whatever is not automated will make demands on working memory, diverting significant executive attention and slowing down the composing process. Thus, "for the skill as a whole to be well controlled, its component processes must become *relatively* automatic and effortless through practice" (Kellogg & Whiteford 251). (To quote the famous words of the late Duke Ellington: "Sure is easy when you know how!") The writer who does not "know how" in the sense of having stored multiple resources in long-term memory must instead engage in "effortful cognitive processing" (251), rendering the composing process both time-and labor-intensive.

In order to automate certain components of the writing task, then, Kellogg and Whiteford point out the necessity of "deliberate practice" that, they emphasize, takes place over many years, not merely fourteen weeks. "Deliberate practice" entails (a) effortful exertion to improve performance, (b) intrinsic motivation to engage in the task, (c) carefully tailored practice tasks, (d) feedback that provides knowledge of results, and (e) high levels of repetition over several years . . . .The term *deliberate* indicates that one must undertake the practice with an explicit goal of learning the skill and improving one's performance.

Practice in the sense of putting in the time, but just going through the motions, is not enough. The learner must be sufficiently interested to endure the effort required by deliberate practice (253-254).

For those of us who teach many reluctant writers, I would highlight the importance of "effortful exertion," "intrinsic motivation," and "sufficient interest"—key points to which I will later return. Writers who do not consciously try to improve, do not care, or are motivated primarily by the prospect of extrinsic reward are less likely to improve than those who exert significant, intrinsically motivated effort. Drawing on the work of Hattie and Timperley, Kellogg and Whiteford also note the importance of receiving formative feedback that helps the novice writer to approach target expectations more closely: "Feedback in educational environments is most effective when it informs the learner how to do the task better as opposed to providing praise for correct performance or punishment for mistakes" (260).

While quality of practice is crucial, quantity also matters; as stated by the power law of skill acquisition, "Performance improves as a power function of the amount of practice" (251). Skill development in any domain entails three stages: the early cognitive stage, in which the learner becomes acquainted with the targeted expectations; the intermediate associative stage, in which "specific inputs are associated with appropriate responses from the study of examples" (251); and the autonomous stage, in which the learner has sufficiently internalized the complex skill, "thus reducing the degree of attention and effort required" (251). Only through practice that is both repetitive (frequent and over time) and deliberate (high quality) can writers make the quantum shift from the early cognitive stage to the intermediate associative stage.

To make this shift also requires a further transition: from "declarative knowledge," or knowing *about* what a task entails, to "procedural knowledge," or knowing *how* to perform a task. (This distinction brings to mind the widespread "Monday morning quarterback" syndrome; many people know, or think they know, a fair amount about many things, without being able to do those things very well themselves.) In terms of writing, novice writers may have sufficient declarative knowledge to be able to recognize, say, a powerful argumentative strategy; yet without deliberate practice and formative feedback, writers will not build the procedural knowledge they need to deploy a similar strategy effectively themselves. Indeed, say Kellogg and Whiteford, we can expect that the initial attempts of novices to imitate expert examples will necessarily fall short—not necessarily because our students lack intelligence or because our teaching is poor, but because a time lag is built into our cognitive structures (250).

At first glance, the stages of improvement outlined by Kellogg and Whiteford would not appear to be "news"; we all recognize the familiar stages of "beginning," "intermediate," and "advanced," as well as the fact that declarative knowledge is much more easily achieved than procedural knowledge. What is less well understood by many, however, is the nature of learning curves: "Performance improvements are initially rapid and then gradually lessen with higher and higher amounts of practice" (251). In other words, the more a learner advances, the more slowly he or she will appear to make progress. Further, because the "complexity of the task increases as one develops" (260), progress may *appear* to slow down as a learner approaches expertise. Thus, those unfamiliar with the nature of learning curves may mistakenly see deterioration when a writer is actually progressing toward a higher level of mastery.

Further adding to the complexity of developing writing skills is the expectation that intermediate and advanced writers shift from "knowledge telling," or "communicating what one knows"—the kind of "book report" or summary writing engaged in by novices—toward "knowledge transformation," or "writing used to transform/actively constitute knowledge" (253). (Kellogg points out in his earlier work that a handful of advanced writers will progress even further, toward "knowledge crafting"—the level achieved by experts (Kellog 5).) Notably, as learners shift from knowledge telling to knowledge transformation, the speed of learning relative to massed practice will *slow down*, though such a transition "ultimately benefits long-term retention" (258). Once again, then, at the very moment when a student is making significant progress, he or she may *appear*, at least for a while, to be getting worse.

With any composite skill, then, we move more quickly from incompetent to basic than from basic to intermediate; we move more slowly from intermediate to advanced and most slowly of all from advanced to expert, with more hours of deliberate practice resulting in fewer immediately visible improvements (though paradoxically, as a writer advances, additional practice becomes even more vital). This finding, as I will discuss later, carries crucial implications for both instruction and assessment.

Into this already convoluted situation, Kellogg and Whiteford point out that we must consider the crucial role of domain-specific knowledge in reducing demands on executive attention. Superior writing skills—not surprisingly—correlate with "writing in the professionally relevant domain of greatest interest to the student" (258). This is because "demand reduction . . . occurs by learning domain-specific knowledge that can be rapidly retrieved from long-term memory rather than held in short-term working memory" (Kellogg 3). When a writer deeply understands the material he or she is writing about and is familiar with both the discursive norms held by the target audience and the expected features of the genre, he or she can "retrieve relevant knowledge from long-term memory at just the right moment" (3). Indeed, says Kellogg, "Writing about topics that students know well provides a scaffold to support the writers and to allow them to devote a higher degree of executive attention to the juggling of planning, generating, and reviewing" (15).

Here it is worth noting a point observed by numerous composition instructors: Many students write reasonably coherent personal essays but do not do as well when they attempt source-based research writing. Often, we are tempted to attribute this differential performance to student laziness or solipsism. The question of whether today's so-called "millennial generation" displays more narcissism than previous generations is highly debated (see, for example, Jean Twenge and Keith Campbell's *The Narcissism Epidemic* and Twenge's *Generation Me*, along with counter-arguments such as Eric H. Greenberg and Karl Weber's *Generation We* and Neil Howe, William Strauss, and R.J. Matson's *Millennials Rising*). But momentarily setting aside that discussion—and allowing for the fact that temporary narcissism is often a feature of adolescence, although one best outgrown eventually—it may be that students' superior performance on personal essays stems not so much from egocentricity as from domain familiarity. Bearing in mind the crucial role played by intrinsic motivation in the quality of practice, Kellogg and Whiteford further suggest that students are more likely to succeed when they have opportunities to write about issues on which they hold strong feelings and opinions. Of course those who can *only* write well when composing personal essays are unlikely to succeed as writers in upper-division college courses or in the workplace; thus it is vital that instructors introduce students to relevant disciplinary conventions and domain-specific conversations, and that colleges and universities continue to develop and expand WAC and WID programs rather than expecting first-year composition classes to "do all the work" singlehandedly. This, of course, is hardly news for composition teachers. David Bartholomae long ago pointed out in "Inventing the University" that students' unfamiliarity with discursive conventions will necessarily produce "amateur" performances that are imitative at best, and that learning to use academic language appropriately is one of the many demanding tasks placed on student writers. Again, Kellogg and Whiteford's work is not so much new information as *why* this is so: When writers are working within a familiar domain (whether that domain is considered properly "academic" or not), working memory and executive attention do not need to be diverted toward domain familiarization and away from the primary writing task (253).

Kellogg and Whiteford point out further possible factors adding to the complexity of college writing tasks—performance anxiety generated by high-stakes assignments, for example, or motor skills or technological know-how that may not be fully developed. Adding to the complexity of teaching younger writers is the fact that the regions of the brain most associated with executive attention—the prefrontal cortex and frontal lobe—are not fully developed in most individuals until the mid-twenties. (The slow maturation of the frontal lobe accounts for a good many of the challenges of adolescence, since this region of the brain governs self-regulation.) For all these reasons, then, it is unreasonable to expect most student writers to write at expert level. As Kellogg states, "Learning to become an accomplished writer is parallel to becoming an expert in other complex cognitive domains. It appears to require more than two decades of maturation, instruction, and training" (2).

The fact that the frontal lobes are still developing—and with them, the capacity for executive attention—means that analytical writing will be challenging enough for most students of traditional college age; those who have not automated key components of the composing process through extended deliberate practice during the K-12 years will take even longer to achieve expertise than their peers who have. Many entering college students will have engaged in few writing tasks more substantive than the standard five-paragraph essay, especially in this era of "No Child Left Behind" with so much writing instruction squeezed to fit the "box" of standardized testing. Meanwhile, in our hyper-technological age, more simultaneous demands are made on executive attention—for *all* of us—than, arguably, at any previous time in history. Last but hardly least, one must consider the wild cards of intrinsic motivation and effortful exertion; many students openly state that they are only in a writing class because it is required, and too many of them exert minimal or inconsistent effort. Furthermore—due at least in part to excessive teacher workloads—a good many of our students arrive at college having received primarily summative assessments in the form of reductive letter grades, rather than the formative assessment that is crucial in shaping deliberate practice.

IMPLICATIONS OF COGNITIVE PSYCHOLOGY FOR DESIGN OF WRITING INSTRUCTION

Given all this, some might suggest it is hopeless to try and teach college-level writing at all. Yet Kellogg and Whiteford—while certainly acknowledging the cognitive complexity of advanced composition tasks—do not make this claim; instead they emphasize the necessity of designing writing instruction that takes into account how cognitive processes actually work— "training" writers rather than merely "teaching" them. A "training" approach is grounded in awareness of cognitive processes and is similar in many ways to the way athletes and musicians are trained. The key to training is to provide learners with frequent—ideally, daily—opportunities to *use* the target skill over a lengthy period of time, receiving regular formative feedback, and being provided immediate opportunities to apply and assimilate that feedback. Expected progressions are built sequentially into the training materials, and assessments that take proper account of the nature of learning curves. The never-ending quest for additional expertise is at the same time balanced by realistic expectations of what a learner at any given level can be expected to achieve.

For those of us in composition studies, this approach suggests that much of what our field espouses has been appropriate all along—emphasis on formative feedback and revision, separation of drafting and revision tasks, WAC and WID programs that distribute writing tasks throughout the curriculum, initial assignments that focus on material already familiar to the writer, and so forth. Still, I would suggest that there are other aspects of pedagogy where the American educational system is lagging when it comes to training writers (though most likely there are "pockets" throughout the country in which appropriate training in writing is indeed taking place).

First, it is crucial that we *systematize* (by which I most emphatically do *not* mean "standardize") the concept that training should focus on helping novice writers to automate key aspects of the writing process during their developmental years by offering extensive opportunities for daily, deliberate practice. Second, schools at all levels need to incorporate these daily writing tasks into the curriculum in all disciplines, rather than relegating the teaching of writing solely to English faculty. This necessitates training faculty in other disciplines in how to instruct and assess writing—particularly making colleagues aware that to offer formative feedback and provide immediate revision opportunities does not constitute a "cop-out" or a "lowering of standards," but is a necessary aspect of a training program. At the college level, this means continuing and expanding our existing WAC and WID programs, distributing writing throughout the curriculum and at all levels. (Once again, this entails educating faculty about how best to teach and assess writing.) Finally—a point to which I will return—assessments should be both designed and analyzed so as to take account of the findings of cognitive psychology, bearing in mind the nature of learning curves, the difference between "knowledge-telling" and "knowledge transformation," and the importance of domain familiarity.

The time required to engage in formative assessment is, of course, one of the most formidable barriers to designing writing training in line with cognitive research, especially for colleagues in other disciplines who are not accustomed to grading writing. On this point Kellogg and Whiteford make an intriguing observation:

> Although regular formative feedback is generally thought of as beneficial, it is not widely appreciated that *providing feedback only intermittently can be beneficial*. . . . First, performance appraisals and grades can actually impair, as well as benefit, performance. . . . Second, less might be more when it comes to instructor evaluations of the written work of students. It is not entirely clear that students read, comprehend, and learn from extensive feedback . . . .Third, in a variety of tasks, intermittent feedback has been shown to slow the acquisition of a skill during training compared with continuous feedback, but

it has the benefit of enhancing long-term retention of the skill. (261 – Emphasis mine)

Kellogg also discusses the research of Alexander Astin, who found in 1993 that the two most crucial factors in writing improvement were the "number of writing-skills classes taken" and "amount of feedback given by instructors" (Kellogg 262). Yet interestingly, the amount of feedback turned out to be "substantially less important than the number of opportunities to compose in writing classes" (262). (For the statistically minded, the difference was a correlation of partialB = .31 for amount of writing done and partialB = .12 for amount of feedback given.)

While this finding may seem counter-intuitive to those of us who live by providing feedback, it makes sense if we consider how learners improve in other domains, such as sports or performing arts. Athletes and musicians never limit their efforts to high-stakes performances and games but practice/rehearse extensively. (An athlete who only engaged in his or her sport on "game day" would surely fail, as would a musician who only played when in front of audiences.) The finalized high-stakes writing product, geared toward an audience and likely written for a grade, may be analogized to the public performance of a musician or athlete. Certainly a good deal of practice takes place under the guidance and coaching of a professional—analogous to providing drafts for teachers who provide formative feedback. But highly skilled athletes and performers also practice a great deal *on their own, privately, without receiving feedback.* A musician, for example, typically attends lessons with an expert once per week but practices skills daily on his or her own, without receiving immediate feedback. Athletes typically engage in individual workouts and training sessions beyond formal practices under the coach's eye. As crucial as formative feedback is in helping learners improve, then, it also seems apparent that learners in any domain also need opportunities to practice their skill extensively, at times without an audience. This awareness might encourage all of us, across disciplines, to integrate writing more enthusiastically into the curriculum; if opportunities to write extensively ultimately matter more than feedback, we can be freed of the perceived obligation to read and respond to every single word and instead, just ask our students to do as athletes- and musicians-in-training do: engage as often as possible in the target skill.

Here it is further interesting to consider that while deliberate practice is crucial, even very advanced musicians and athletes also engage in warm-up activities—say, lay-up drills for basketball players, or musical scales for pianists. The corollary for a writing student, I will suggest, is freewriting.[2] At first glance it may appear that freewriting is at odds with some aspects of "deliberate practice" with its emphasis on conscious skills acquisition, and certainly writers are unlikely to progress toward advanced composition skills by engaging in freewriting and nothing else. Yet in cognitive terms, there are multiple ways in which freewriting can be a beneficial add-on to more deliberate practice and writing with the expectation of feedback.

First, freewriting allows a writer, especially the novice, to set aside concerns such as audience, purpose, or editing—all components that require extensive diversion of executive attention. While this may be less crucial for the advanced writer who has automated multiple processes in long-term memory, cognitive psychology suggests that the best way to assist novice writers is to separate the various components deliberately, allowing the writer to focus his or her executive attention on fewer tasks. (Once again, separating drafting from editing has long been a hallmark of composition theory; what is notable here is that while many have understood for decades *that* such separation works, cognitive research demonstrates *why* it works.) Freewriting as a heuristic tool may give writing students much-needed practice in generating text without the need to divert executive attention to editing concerns.

Second, freewriting offers yet another benefit: the greater effectiveness of "spaced practice" (regular, shorter writing sessions) as opposed to "massed practice" (also termed "binge writing"). Drawing upon the work of Robert Boice on writing blocks, Kellogg and Whiteford state: "A common mistake of developing writers is to compose in marathon sessions or binges of massed practice that can exhaust and frustrate the writer. Writing apprehension and even writer's block can result from this misconceived kind of practice" (257). Kellogg and Whiteford refer to the work of psychologists Richard Schmidt and Robert Bjork demonstrating that spaced practice "maximizes long-term learning" (258), suggesting there is much benefit from frequent yet shorter bursts of writing.

A third potential benefit of freewriting touches on that thorny issue of deliberation in practice—the need for "effortful exertion," "intrinsic motivation," and "sufficient interest" in generating improvement. The crucial question of how best to motivate disengaged students is often neglected in much public discourse regarding the "literacy crisis" (whether real, perceived, or some combination). A detailed discussion of how best to inspire the apathetic student is beyond the scope of this essay, and clearly, there are no panaceas. Yet I would suggest that freewriting offers one possibly helpful strategy. Students who have frequent opportunities to write about matters of concern to them, without fearing the response of a potentially hostile audience or the specter of an editorial red pen, may stand a better chance of coming to care intrinsically about producing a better written product. Arguably, much student passion for learning has been diminished by a K-12 education emphasizing successful performance on standardized tests over invention, or correct selection of prefabricated answers over critical thinking and exploration of ideas. Freewriting can offer students an opportunity to engage with subject matter of their choice, on their own terms, thereby increasing the odds that they may develop the intrinsic motivation so crucial for improvement.

Of course successful writers do not thrive on freewriting alone, and a well-designed approach to writing instruction will hardly stop there. What becomes apparent in light of cognitive research, however, is that even in this accountability-obsessed era, there is still a place for freewriting in the composition classroom. Using freewriting frequently and appropriately—in conjunction with other important elements of a training program, including domain familiarization, intermittent formative feedback, and appropriate task scaffolding—is also likely to generate more meaningful assessment results, not because we have tweaked the data to show what we want it to show but because students who have written extensively, focused their executive attention appropriately, and developed intrinsic motivation for writing are more likely to produce meaningful, audience-friendly texts that meet or exceed our expectations. Cognitive psychology suggests that regular freewriting can help writers gain in all these areas, ultimately contributing to their long-term success as writers.

IMPLICATIONS FOR DISSEMINATION, ASSESSMENT, AND INTERPRETATION

The hypothetical scenario with which I opened this essay is, for many of us, not so hypothetical. While some current cultural anxiety regarding student writing skills may be overblown—based on anecdote, a limited definition of what constitutes "good" writing, false nostalgia for an earlier (presumably Edenic) educational age, or studies that are methodologically and/or epistemologically problematic—many present concerns about the quality of student-writing are well-founded. Much anxiety is fueled by periodic reports—often widely touted in the media—bemoaning the poor writing skills of American students. The National Assessment of Educational Progress, for instance, reported in its 2011 "Nation's Report Card" that only 27% of high school seniors scored "proficient" or higher on its assessment measure, with 24% of these ranked as "proficient" and only 3% as "advanced"; 52% performed at the "basic" level ("Nation's Report Card" 30). Back in 2004, the National Writing Program's National Commission on Writing stated that American companies spend up to $3.1 billion per year on "remedying deficiencies in writing" ("Writing" 4), stating that one-third of the firms surveyed believe that "one-third or fewer of their employees, both current and new, possess the writing skills companies value" ("Writing" 13). Many faculty members express similar concern. For instance, in 2006, Alvin P. Sanoff reported in the *Chronicle of Higher Education* that 44% of college faculty surveyed believed the majority of their students were not well prepared for college-level writing; interestingly, only 10% of high school teachers surveyed believed they were sending poorly prepared high school seniors on to college, suggesting a perception gap between high school and college instructors (Sanoff).

Many constituencies have even gone so far as to question whether college students today are learning anything at all. Of recent note, Richard Arum and Josipa Roksa claimed in their 2011 study *Academically Adrift* that approximately 45% of the undergraduate students they studied did not make expected gains in complex reasoning, critical thinking, or writing. *Academically Adrift* in particular has garnered significant media attention, triggering a wave of performance and assessment-related anxiety at colleges and universities across the country.

Such claims, however, are debatable and open to criticism on a variety of fronts. The NAEP examination, for instance, depends solely on a thirty-minute timed writing sample, skewing the results in favor of those who can read and write quickly while meeting a set of arbitrary and limited expectations. The provocative claims made in *Academically Adrift* are based primarily on the Collegiate Learning Assessment, a timed and standardized test which has been subjected to numerous criticisms—among them an insightful 2008 critique by Mark D. Shermis, who presents multiple grounds for his claim that "the information on reliability and validity for the CLA is sketchy" (11).

What seems apparent despite these limitations, however, is that a good many people believe that "good" student writing is rare, and that this belief—while possibly overblown—is not entirely unfounded. Clearly there is much work to be done by those of us in composition studies, both with respect to helping our students improve *and* to dispelling potentially skewed public perceptions. Part of our task, then, is to educate not just colleagues in other disciplines but members of other constituencies we serve as well. This is especially crucial when it comes to questions surrounding accountability and assessment.

The increased pressure for academic "accountability" in recent years has not been wholeheartedly embraced by academia and has been rightly criticized on a number of fronts. Shermis, for instance, points out what he calls "an ambiguity" underlying the pressure for assessment first promulgated by the Bush administration (which, of course, continues despite the 2009 change in national administration):

> On the surface, it would seem that the secretary's push is simply a logical extension of the rhetoric associated with No Child Left Behind (that is, accountability for funds expended). Yet the fiscal role of the federal government in postsecondary education has traditionally been limited to underwriting costs for economically disadvantaged students and grant funding (for which a service is received). (10)

Many of us fear that the *true* motivation behind the accountability movement at the college level is to contain potential disruption of dominant discourses by forcing writing instruction into a "measurable," ostensibly "objective" container, in the process reinscribing hegemonic power and neutralizing the transformative possibilities of alternative discourses and counter-hegemonic voices. Since it is beyond the scope of this essay, however, to explore fully the ideological underpinnings of the current push for accountability, I will provisionally argue along with Monica Stitt-Bergh and Thomas Hilgers that since demands for assessment are presently here whether we like it or not, we are best served by taking the reins of our own assessment projects. As Stitt-Bergh and Hilgers put it, "The outsourcing of assessment carries a high price: it signals that the locus of responsibility for assessment

is some external organization instead of the program's stakeholders .
. . . On the other hand, when an institution in-sources assessment, it
has a greater chance of reaching assessment's ultimate goal of program
improvement" (Stitt-Bergh and Hilgers).

If assessment is inevitable, then, it is vital that we as faculty members take charge of the process, moving beyond a reluctant and perfunctory jump through accreditation hoops to develop methods that produce meaningful and illuminating results. The goal of assessment should not be to "standardize" instruction, but to garner meaningful evidence that is used to foster a cycle of continuous improvement (which in some cases may mean continuing to do what is already working well). Here the work of Kellogg and Whiteford becomes further useful for suggesting more nuanced, scientifically grounded methods of understanding how writing improvement actually occurs, and how it does (and does not) make sense to measure such improvement. For instance, studies such as *Academically Adrift* appear to be predicated on the assumption that writing and critical thinking skills should produce measurable gains within only four semesters. Yet for the eighteen and nineteen year-olds whom Arum and Roksa examined, multiple factors mitigate against their claim: the reduced speed of learning curves as learners advance, the slow maturation of the frontal lobes during late adolescence, the significant amount of time required for measurable improvement, the complexity inherent in shifting from knowledge-telling to knowledge-transformation, and the lack of domain-specific expertise on the part of the typical college freshman or sophomore. The findings of Kellogg and Whiteford suggest that in the course of one semester—or even two, three or four—it is likely that many assessments will indicate little to no improvement, and in some cases may even demonstrate a slight decline. Yet this hardly leads logically to the quantum-leap conclusion that the time students devoted to learning was wasted, that the instructors' teaching was ineffective, or even that the students really are failing to learn. While the results could possibly point toward such findings in at least some cases, *Academically Adrift* does not take full account of all these potential variables.

When designing and interpreting assessments, then, we must bear in mind that critical thinking and writing skills are likely to develop more rapidly for students who have delved into an area of specialty, rather than for those who have only been exposed superficially to a range of general education courses in fields they do not intend to pursue. Furthermore, the additional anxiety produced by a time-sensitive, high-stakes test such as the Collegiate Learning Assessment is likely to divert necessary executive attention, particularly for novice-to early-intermediate writers who have stored fewer cognitive resources in long-term memory. (Under such circumstances, one could argue that the fact that 55% of general education students *did* make measurable gains in the first two years of college would appear to be the more salient finding.)

Academically Adrift may be only one study (and the Collegiate Learning Assessment only one means of measurement), yet it provides a useful example for demonstrating the limits of externally imposed, standardized tests in assessing how well our students are learning to write. For assessments to be more meaningful, it is helpful to be aware of the cognitive processes entailed in learning to write, which are far more complex than can be gauged using superficial analysis. More insightful assessment design must account, for instance, for the apparent temporary downturns that often occur as a student moves toward increasing cognitive complexity; for the difference between knowledge-telling and knowledge transformation; and for the way in which lack of domain familiarity may mask actual writing skill.

Finally, meaningful assessments will look for gains that can be reasonably expected within the time period being assessed. At the college level, it is important to note that a K-12 education devoid of adequate deliberate practice cannot be compensated for in a few weeks, or even months; in addressing the importance of time and maturity in developing advanced writing skills, Kellogg and Whiteford mention the "lack of distributed writing tasks in the system" (254). In the absence of meaningful educational reform that replaces the current misguided emphasis on standardized testing with a writing-intensive K-12 experience focused on helping students to automate key components of the composition process, college instruction will not be able to conquer this limitation singlehandedly. This challenge is further exacerbated in the absence of intrinsic motivation: "Without sufficient motivational interest, one never moves beyond the stage of acclimating to the concepts of the domain and learning at a relatively shallow level" (Kellogg and Whiteford 254). As such, any meaningful assessment of student writing progress should find a way to correlate student interest and effort with the outcomes as well.

What Works? Process, Practice, Patience

When designing both writing instruction and assessment, four points seem clear: First, a one-semester (or even one-year) college composition course can hardly be expected to produce expert writers all by itself; those who perform best at the freshman level are likely to be those who automated multiple cognitive components of the writing task through deliberate practice during their formative years. Second, effective writing instruction will not stop after the freshman year; given the importance of domain familiarity, it is vital to maintain and further develop college-level WAC and WID programs that allow student writers to engage in deliberate and frequent writing practice in their target domains in subsequent years. Third, if assessments are to be meaningful and instructive rather than stand as perfunctory "hoops" through which we must jump, the nature of learning curves must be taken into account both when designing and analyzing assessment tools. Fourth, when we design both our writing instruction and our assessments, it is crucial to remember that measurable improvement in writing takes considerable effort over a long period of time, and that both learners and instructors need to be patient, persistent and consistent rather than expecting instantaneous results. Time and patience may be qualities in short supply in our fast-moving, instant-gratification-obsessed culture, but when it comes to the training of expert writers, the field of cognitive psychology reminds us that there are simply no shortcuts.

Deepening our awareness of the cognitive complexity inherent in composing can help us do a more effective job of guiding our students along the long and winding path toward writing expertise, as well as more accurately ascertaining the extent to which students are (or are not) succeeding. While the field of composition studies has done an excellent job of discovering and disseminating what works, cognitive psychology can tell us more about *why*—demonstrating the limitations of an "either/or" teaching philosophy and explaining why truly effective writing instruction and assessment should make use of a variety of approaches, drawing upon techniques often associated with process pedagogy (such as freewriting) as well as more social-epistemic emphases (such as the need to help students achieve mastery of discipline-specific discursive conventions). For all the "debates" that have taken place in composition studies over the past several decades, the findings of cognitive psychology suggest that all along, there is wisdom to be found at multiple points along the ideological spectrum.

NOTES

1. This is not to neglect the social dimension of composing; Kellogg and Whiteford point out that writing is at once both cognitive and social (253)

2. Here I am using the definition of "freewriting" specified by Peter Elbow, most recently in *Vernacular Eloquence*: Freewriting asks the writer to "write without stopping" and should be written "with the expectation of not sharing." Furthermore, the writer should not "worry about any standards for writing" during the course of the freewriting activity (148).

WORKS CITED

Arum, Richard, and Jospia Roksa. *Academically Adrift: Limited Learning on College Campuses.* University of Chicago Press: 2011. Print.

Bartholomae, David. "Inventing the University." *Cross-Talk in Comp Theory: A Reader.* Ed. Victor Villanueva and Kristin L. Arola. Urbana: NCTE, 2011. 523-553. Print.

Elbow, Peter. *Vernacular Eloquence: What Speech Can Bring to Writing.* New York: Oxford U.P., 2012. Print.

Greenberg, Eric H., and Karl Weber. *Generation We: How Millennial Youth Are Taking Over America and Changing Our World Forever.* Pachatusan Press: 2008. Print.

Howe, Neil, William Strauss, and R.J. Matson. *Millennials Rising: The Next Great Generation.* Vintage Press, 2000. Print.

Kellogg, Ronald T., and Alison P. Whiteford. "Training Advanced Writing Skills: The Case for Deliberate Practice." *Educational Psychologist* 44.4 (2011): 250-56. Print.

Kellogg, Ronald T. "Training Writing Skills: A Cognitive Developmental Perspective." *Journal of Writing Research* 1.1 (2009): 1-26. Print.

"The Nation's Report Card: Writing 2011." *National Assessment of Educational Progress at Grades 8 and 12.* Web.

Sanoff, Alvin P. "A Perception Gap Over Students' Preparation." *The Chronicle of Higher Education*: March 10, 2006. Web.

Shermis, Mark D. "The Collegiate Learning Assessment: A Critical Perspective." *Assessment Update* 20.2 (2008): 10-12. Print.

Stitt-Bergh, Monica, and Thomas Hilgers. "Program Assessment: Processes, Propagation, and Culture Change." *Across the Disciplines: A Journal of Language, Learning, and Academic Writing.* December 3, 2009. Web.

Twenge, Jean. *Generation Me: Why Today's Young Americans Are More Confident, Assertive, Entitled—and More Miserable Than Ever Before.* Free Press: 2007. Print.

—, and W. Keith Campbell. *The Narcissism Epidemic: Living in the Age of Entitlement*. Free Press: 2010. Print.

"Writing: A Ticket To Work . . . Or A Ticket Out." *National Writing Project*: September 1, 2004. Web.

KAIROS

Kairos is on the Web at http://www.kairos.technorhetoric.net/

Kairos is the longest-running online journal in writing studies. The journal was first published in 1996 and maintains its editorial and publishing independence through virtual collaboration by staff members across universities across the world. With no budget, the journal runs exclusively on in-kind donations and volunteer editorial and technical labor. The mission of *Kairos* has always been to publish scholarship that examines digital and multimodal composing practices, promoting work that enacts its scholarly argument through rhetorical and innovative uses of new media. We publish "webtexts," which are texts authored specifically for publication on the World Wide Web. Webtexts are scholarly examinations of topics related to technology in English Studies fields (e.g., rhetoric, composition, technical and professional communication, education, creative writing, language and literature) and related fields such as media studies, informatics, arts technology, and others. Besides scholarly webtexts, *Kairos* publishes teaching-with-technology narratives, reviews of print and digital media, extended interviews with leading scholars, interactive exchanges, "letters" to the editors, and news and announcements of interest.

Perspicuous Objects: Reading Comics and Writing Instructions

In this webtext, Fred Johnson puts theorists of visual rhetoric into conversation with comics theorists and practitioners in order to look closely at the use of comics and comics principles for teaching students about composition, meaning-making, and critical reading. His webtext, "Perspicuous Objects," is woven with three threads: his theoretical and practical discussion of comics, his rich reading of a particular comic called "Sonic Medicine" by Scott Kolbo, and other comics examples that are laced throughout. It's a beautiful piece to read and is an excellent example of the crossovers possible between literary/media studies and digital rhetorics/writing studies. Access the webtext here: http://kairos.technorhetoric.net/19.1/topoi/johnson/index.html

5 Perspicuous Objects: Reading Comics and Writing Instruction

Fred Johnson

"Perspicuous Objects" puts theorists of visual rhetoric into conversation with comics theorists and practitioners in order to consider the potential of comics and comics principles for teaching students about composition, meaning-making, and critical reading. As Robert Watkins (2008) suggested in *Kairos*'s 2008 "Manifesto" issue, the comics page, especially as described by Scott McCloud (1993/1994), is enticingly full of rhetorical gestures, and composition processes used by comics artists recall processes we tend to present in writing classes. Comics are a complex form with a long history, and they are full of wonderfully complicated sets of relationships between words and images and shapes and lines.[1] It can be challenging, however, to describe those relationships and their rhetorical power, and though we have language for naming the parts of a comics page, there is no obvious, generally established way of guiding students into close reading of comics. With that in mind, "Perspicuous Objects" goes in search of useful critical language for talking insightfully about specific comics texts and how they do what they do. I look particularly at cartoons as focused analytical images, the ways that drawn lines can take on meaning in context, and the extent to which the whole page is necessary to the communicated meaning of any specific visual gesture in a text. This is not an exhaustive look at comics, then, but a close look at important aspects of the comics page from which careful analytical readings may spring and out of which useful teaching exercises might be derived.

In *Understanding Rhetoric*, a writing textbook in the form of a graphic novel, Elizabeth Losh and Jonathan Alexander (with Kevin Cannon and Zander Cannon illustrating) (2014) have pointed out that comics are appearing more frequently in contemporary classrooms because they are "both textually and visually rich," demanding that readers decode images and text "in tandem" (p. vii). Craig Stroupe (2000) has pictured a "visualized English Studies" in which words on the page "don't simply talk to words, but to images, links, horizontal lines—to every feature of the iconographic page" (p. 618). In contemporary multimodal discourse, he argued, verbal literacy is frequently "layered into a more diverse amalgamation of literacies" (Stroupe, 2000, p. 608). Comics at their best are an extraordinary locus for such "amalgamated" literacy. Comics artists work with close attention to how the elements on their pages affect each other. Comics bring together image and word and representations of time and space and motion, and comics artists use all of those elements and more to achieve narration, poetry, argumentation, and other ends. In short, comics are ripe for reading in what Stroupe (2000) called the "elaborationist" tradition of English departments, wherein we "typically value complexity, irony, connotation, and deferred meanings, achieved through an awareness of the medium itself, whether visual or verbal" (p. 611). Yet to note the rhetorical and literary complexity of comics, or even to name the parts of the comics page, is not to analyze what any individual comic is doing—is adding up to—as literature or as rhetoric.

"Perspicuous Objects" has roots in my frustration with limits I have encountered during classroom discussions of comics. For example, I have read Chris Ware's (2000/2001) *Jimmy Corrigan—The Smartest Kid on Earth* with several groups of English majors. They always acknowledge the novel's complexity and are impressed with its formal beauty. We tend to do an acceptable job talking about the visual as we consider the novel. But I find myself searching for more effective ways to increase both our analytical rigor and the playfulness of our thinking about the comics form as integral to Ware's storytelling. For example, Ware does something interesting with repeated appearances of a bird in *Jimmy Corrigan*. That bird on the page is not the word "bird" but a drawing of a bird on a page full of carefully arranged images. What can we say about the drawing itself, about the details chosen or left out? There is a lot of sadness in *Jimmy Corrigan*, and somehow that bird is part of it, but there is nothing fundamentally sad about Ware's cartooning. Where does the sadness come from? How does the page convey or contribute to it? And can we be more specific than "sad"? Sad how?[2]

Based on our conversations about some of the teaching ideas elsewhere in "Perspicuous Objects," Scott Kolbo (whose art appears throughout this webtext) asked his art students to do a line-style project, drawing themselves in two different styles and observing the differences. Scott's students had some interesting success inventing new expressive modes for themselves by shifting out of their habitual line-style habits. Yet, much like my literature students talking about Chris Ware, when Scott's students wrote about their work they ran up against the limits of their vocabularies. They asserted that particular line styles exuded positivity or calm or melancholy or some other emotion. But how? What made those lines do that? Would they always do that, in any context? I don't want to demand that art students always explain exactly how an image gets at what they want it to get at. It's art; sometimes something just works. On the other hand, I nearly *always* want to burden my literature and writing students with explaining how a text does what it does. I nearly always want them to be able to say something insightful and precise about how their readings and their composition choices are justified and effective.

Put another way, I want my students (and myself) to move away from a comics version of what Rich Rice called "unremediated schmoozery" (Rice & Ball, 2006) and towards the *at* and *through* perspectives Richard Lanham (1993) has identified. Rice said that we might see rhetoric as "organized schmoozery," but, even so, he argued, "Students who use presentation or form" to win over audiences "but do not themselves understand…why they're presenting what they're presenting, limit their opportunity to learn" (Rice & Ball, 2005). As it pertains both to reading comics and to composing with comics-like visual effects, helping students avoid "unremediated schmoozery" means helping them understand and describe their own choices and the choices of comics artists so that students can take purposeful control of their own work and be more aware of how visual composers try to win them over. Lanham (1993) argues readers are conditioned to assume that books can convey thought transparently, containing but neither distorting nor otherwise affecting an author's thought. Thus, typical readers of traditional books have tended to try to look *through* texts without ever looking *at* them. Lanham showed how emerging electronic forms make it clear that all "production decisions" are actually "authorial" (p. 5), so that even a traditional codex-form book should be seen as "an act of extraordinary stylization," not only conveying a writer's thought but also affecting and shaping and shepherding it (p. 9). He described a "bi-stable oscillation" between contemplating conveyed thought (the *through* perspective) and contemplating the way thought has been organized and conveyed (the *at* perspective), and he suggested not only that both perspectives are important to understanding a given text, but also that both perspectives are crucial to understanding, fundamentally, "how knowledge is held" (p. 24). For Lanham, as for Rice, form must be chosen and deployed mindfully, and must be seen not as incidental to a text but as part of the text's meaning-making machinery.

Clearly texts with conspicuous visual elements lend themselves to discussion of the *at* and the *through* as well as the relationship between the two. But it is easy to simply name the visual bits and pieces, instead of looking thoroughly at them. Looking at visual design, we identify traits such as contrast, repetition, alignment, proximity (cf. Williams, 2008). Looking at movies, we identify cuts, pans, framing. In comics we identify frames and panels and (often using McCloud's 1994 definitions) panel-to-panel transitions. Naming the parts is useful to analysis, and experimenting with styles and effects and visual gestures can be a way to learn how those styles, effects, and gestures work. However, if students are to read any individual text in a way that sees not only the *at* or only the *through*, but that also sees the relationship between the two, then we need to do more than name parts and techniques.

No one has been a more skillful, compelling explainer of comics than McCloud, whose indispensable *Understanding Comics* has made a case for the depth and power of comics art while anatomizing typical comics elements. But *Understanding Comics* and the volumes that have followed it are not about *analyzing* comics texts, exactly; they are about appreciating the machinery of the comics form generally, and they are about instrumental processes used by comics artists. The difference matters, partly because McCloud's interest in practitioners means he is often coaching his readers about how to get *their* potential readers to look straight *through* a comics text, and partly because his focus on general rules and common denominators means he can skip looking closely at the sorts of idiosyncratic touches that give any *specific* comics text its style and voice. For example, McCloud identified a series of line styles and the kinds of emotional information they might generally express, but he did not closely analyze any specific line embedded in any specific comics text (pp. 124-126). In Scot Hanson's (2009) Kairos interview with McCloud, McCloud talked about his "endlessly reductive, formalist-wonky sensibility" and how he tends to look for context-neutral formulations that will "always be true." That tendency to seek the universal gives McCloud's work its profoundly useful heuristic power. On the other hand, the generalness of his comics commentary means his texts have not considered the difficulties of analyzing any specific comic closely, and it means he has potentially bypassed some concerns that someone teaching or learning in a literature or rhetoric studies context might find central.

McCloud's (1993/1994) "non-sequitur" panel-to-panel transition may be the most interesting specific example of this difference in perspective. His wonky, reductive, useful, admittedly "inexact" (p. 74) list of six panel-to-panel transitions includes clear categories, such as "moment-to-moment," but it ends with the "non-sequitur" transition, a transition between two images that have "no logical relationship" and which, McCloud noted, the mind tends to find ways to connect in spite of their apparent illogic (p. 72). The non-sequitur category keeps things manageable by keeping McCloud's anatomy of panel-to-panel transitions at that universal level rather than grappling with the many nonlogical ways panels might be connected. It points would-be practitioners toward clear, practical storytelling techniques, and though it does not exactly discourage abstract panel-to-panel transitions, it makes them an exception to be used sparingly. But percolating beneath the non-sequitur lid is the messy, idiosyncratic universe of visual figurative language, where a non-sequitur might turn out to be an instance of metonymy. In other words, McCloud has pushed several kinds of visual complexity to a backburner here at exactly the point where what Stroupe (2000) called elaborationism might begin to ask questions about complex rhetorical and poetic relationships linking together images. Where McCloud says these images have no logical relationship, an English teacher might see the roots of artful poetics and rhetorical wit.

Consider, for example, Madeleine Sorapure's (2006) suggestion that metaphor and metonymy might play a central role in our assessments of new media compositions. Sorapure argued that we might assess the degree to which student-made visuals make figurative turns away from associated written texts. That strategy is as surely a move into non-sequitur territory as it is a productive way to point students toward the complexity possible in image-text relationships. In a similar vein, Stroupe (2000) reflected on the rhetorically productive ways that visual and textual elements might be placed in tension, so that (for example) "the visuals zig where the verbal text zags" (p. 626). Stroupe (2004) associated this kind of composing and reading with what he calls the "rhetoric of irritation," a dialogical, polyvocal rhetoric in which seemingly mismatched terms and discourses and voices are brought together so that (as in Bakhtin's theory of the novel) tensions between them might produce or express new insights and ideas. These zigzagging tensions, Stroupe argued, are not "haphazardly inappropriate" but "coherent inappropriateness" (p. 251). Getting students to notice and analyze those productive mismatches becomes, in Stroupe's argument, a key task for English teachers, who must help students become not just users of language but aware interpreters and practitioners, able to consider not only how signs constitute a world but also how different signs might constitute a different world. In both Sorapure's and Stroupe's cases, we can see college composition teachers becoming interested in a place, this non-sequitur space, that McCloud has considered insightfully but only briefly.

This interest in figurative turnings and irritating discourse friction might enliven our engagements with comics texts. Where does a given comics page go beyond simple representation of the story or explanation of a point? Where are words in dialogic or figurative tension with images, and which image and design choices are in tension with each other? If students are producing comics or comics-like texts, are they moving into a composition space where, as Losh and Alexander (2014) have suggested, "the images and text must be read in tandem" (p. vii)? These are potentially productive questions. McCloud, for good reason, warned would-be comics practitioners against overdoing it: "I see it in comics, these thick, overly layered visual artifacts of style, inking styles, and compositional tropes that really contribute nothing whatsoever…except to clutter the page" (Hanson, 2009). McCloud also identified with Edward Tufte's (1983) fight against "chartjunk," irrelevant decoration used to "jazz up" visuals (p. 107) (as discussed in Hanson, 2009), and he and Tufte have offered good advice to practitioners whose goal is to help readers look *through*, not necessarily *at*, their work. If we follow the lead of Stroupe or Sorapure and talk with students about creating productive friction between the elements on their pages, if we encourage them to play with figurative turnings, we do risk having them produce chartjunk and extraneous markings. At some point, a talk about clarity and simplicity must be in order.

However, in urging students to experiment we also urge them to grasp the complex poetic and rhetorical possibilities of the page, rather than focusing on absolute clarity as the primary value. The potential reward in terms of learning is greater than the risk of chartjunk.

With all that in mind, "Perspicuous Objects" asks whether teachers and scholars in the disciplines are looking closely enough as we begin to unpack the tensions in a given comics text. How close can we press our noses to the glass? How much looking *through* are we doing when we think we're looking *at*? We can help students learn about the complexity possible in multimodal texts by having them seek out figurative turnings and discursive frictions, but, alone, those pedagogical moves do not wholly address my concerns about the limits of the discipline's vocabulary for talking about comics. There is more to say about the constitutive bits of the comics page. The interesting tensions and productive rhetorical moves in comics do not begin in the space where a visual is bumping its cartoon shoulders with alphabetic text, or at the point where an artist mixes different drawing styles. The rhetoric of comics begins at the level of the line and includes instinctual choices—including choices that leave behind visual clutter—that artists make as they form the cartoons that fill their pages. To notice that a bird has been brought to the page as a metaphorical representation of certain continuities between the generations of Jimmy Corrigan's family is interesting. But that bird is not the word "bird." It is a drawing, with particular drawn details. To ignore the bird itself, its particularities, is to look *through* the drawing, rather than at it. For that reason, "Perspicuous Objects" looks at these types of small pieces and considers how they do what they do, not as representatives of a general type of comics-page object but as constituent, idiosyncratic components of specific comics texts.

Comics will work most powerfully for teaching purposes when teachers are looking closely at what artists do with the texts' basic constituent components. Attention to comics fundamentals—line style, abstraction, image selection, and concatenation of images—is not by any means the only way to address complex multimodal rhetoric (or even complex comics rhetoric), but such attention is likely to pay off quickly for students learning to communicate visually. As we ask students to analyze the inner workings of any given multimodal text, whether professionally produced or peer-produced, we ought to give them tools to move beyond loose assertions about the emotions expressed by a line style. We ought to help them to see images as images and to avoid reducing visual artifacts like Ware's (2001) bird (or Scott Kolbo's birds) to words. We should offer them ways to grapple with a given text's subtle concatenation, or joining, of visual and verbal gestures. Comics texts, because they use line and image purposefully, offer excellent exemplars as well as opportunities for discussion. To study the ways that comics artists select their images—even their lines—and then activate those images by placing them into a context is to study how careful selection and juxtaposition can turn visual elements into perspicuous objects that contribute meaning to a composition. It is also to study invention, arrangement, analysis, and meaning-making, so that attention to comics fundamentals has the potential to not only supplement but also become integral to what writing students learn about authoring texts of all kinds. Finally, "Perspicuous Objects" aims to get closer to the *at* of comics, to build a stronger vocabulary for talking about what we see when we look closely at comics, and to offer some suggestions about how a closer look at the *at* of comics might lead to worthwhile teaching.

As explained in the sidebar, "Perspicuous Objects" follows three threads. One is the main argument, accessible using the dot navigation header, the "Jump To" menu, or the numbered links at the foot of each page. A second thread is Scott Kolbo's "Sonic Medicine" (2013b) broadside, a one-page comic which appears in embedded images throughout "Perspicuous Objects." The third thread explores both Scott's art and "Sonic Medicine" (Kolbo, 2013b) specifically. Readers might begin with any one of those threads, though my suggestions is that they begin with the "Sonic Medicine" (2013b) broadside, which makes a good mental warmup for the rest of "Perspicuous Objects."

1. DEFINING COMICS

In *Understanding Comics*, Scott McCloud (1993/1994) defined comics as "juxtaposed pictorial and other images in deliberate sequence" (p. 9), and his definition has become an important point of reference in comics theory. McCloud's definition highlights the way that comics feature the joining of multiple visual pieces assembled together for the purpose of sending messages to an audience. By this definition, comics artists are improvisatory signmakers, drawing deliberately on semiotic resources that will be understood by a given audience and combining those chosen resources in evocative ways for that audience.

One might question, for example, what amounts to a sequence for McCloud, or whether text-image combination should be more clearly a part of his definition, as McCloud himself has admitted (pp. 20-21). His definition is helpful but, inevitably, incomplete; there is no perfectly attenuated definition for comics as a form, any more than there is a perfect definition for any artistic form. On this point, comics scholar Joseph Witek (2009) has argued helpfully that definitive "comicsness" is not to be found in "the more-or-less arbitrary stipulation of some defining formal criteria (such as the presence of word balloons, the placement of verbal text within the picture plane, the creation of continuing characters, or the use of mechanical printing)" (p. 149). Instead, Witek wrote, comicsness is "a historically contingent and evolving set of reading protocols that are applied to texts" (p. 149). Those reading protocols depend, in part, on the attitudes of readers: "to be a comic text is to be read as a comic" (p. 149).[3] And the protocols shift over time, as Witek demonstrated in his analysis of how arrows, numbers, and grid lines in comics have developed. It may be impossible, then, to put forward an authoritative definition of "comics" or "comicsness," but two generally observed traits have been fundamental to modern comics and are more or less expected by all comics readers: that comics come to life through the concatenation of multiple visual signs (as McCloud has explained) and that comics tend to be built around cartoons. Though these two basic traits do not point us to every facet of comics as an artform, they can make a fine starting point for would-be visual composers looking to learn from comics.

2. Cartoons as Perspicuous Objects

Comics artists have been attracted to cartooning from the beginning, especially if we mark the start of modern comics with *Punch*'s (2014) nineteenth-century innovations in satirical magazine cartooning.[4] Comics have taken many forms since the mid-1800s, from single panel gags to four panel strips to full page newspaper layouts, pulp comic books, and perfect-bound graphic novels. These different forms offer artists different affordances, but cartooning has been integral to each, even as, in recent years, other kinds of image manufacturing have matched (or far exceeded) cartoons for ease of production and reproduction. By all accounts, one of the major assets of cartooning is the readability of cartoons, as compared to more detailed, less stylized visual forms. Comics artist Chris Ware (2004b) suggested that our responses to cartoons have the swiftness of reading, as when we interpret road signs and panicking swimmers: "you don't really spend a lot of time considering the esthetic value of an arrow telling you not to crash, or the gestural grace of a person drowning; you just read the signs and act appropriately" (p. 11). Seth, another respected contemporary comics artist, has said something similar: "The cartoonist is trying to boil down real life experience into an image that is capable of conveying the depth of life by only suggesting it.... To see a cartoonist suggest a winter day in just a couple of lines is to understand the beauty of a thing done right" (Ngui, 2006, p. 23).[5]

Abstraction, then, is key to cartooning, and is a major attraction of cartooning for comics artists. Scott McCloud (1993/1994) described cartooning as an artful use of abstraction to achieve the kind of swift readability that Ware (2004b) and Seth (Ngui, 2006) describe. He wrote that cartooning is "amplification through simplification" (McCloud, 1993/1994, p. 30), a mode of expression wherein the artist abstracts an object away from the real in order to emphasize a subset of its qualities. In this accounting, the readability of cartoons is rooted in the way that a cartoonist selects and emphasizes salient details, leaving out distracting details and quickly—instantly, if all goes well—focusing readers on the relevant attributes of the characters and situations depicted.

The act of cartooning, as Ware, Seth, and McCloud see it, exemplifies the sign-making process that Gunther Kress and Theo van Leeuwen (2006) described in *Reading Images*. Kress and van Leeuwen highlighted a five-year-old who depicts a car by drawing a series of circles, having selected the wheel as the "criterial aspect" of the car that is "adequately representative of the object" for his purposes (p. 7). (The dog pictured above demonstrates similar sign-making by my son.) In this accounting, visual representation results from a process in which the signmaker first selects (perhaps instinctively, as with the child artist) important "criterial aspects" of a thing and then finds a way to represent those aspects for a given audience and context (Kress & van Leeuwen, 2006, p. 8). When Seth (Ngui, 2006) talked about representing a winter day with a couple of aptly selected lines, he suggested such a process, and when Chris Ware (cf. 2004b) talks about the stripped down, instantly readable content of cartoons, he, too, sounds like the kind of signmaker Kress and van Leeuwen (2006) described. Further, because of the way cartoons tend to isolate and clearly emphasize certain qualities of their subjects, they may be understood as fundamentally analytical images. Such images, Kress and van Leeuwen (2006) argued, are a kind of visual "this is" (p. 91), directing the viewer's attention toward specific "Possessive Attributes" of a depicted object (p. 87). As an example, they point to the image of an arctic explorer (a "Carrier" of analysis, in this case) whose specialized clothing has been labeled in a textbook (p. 51, pp. 88–89); this is a clear case of an image being used to present a whole (the explorer/"Carrier") and direct attention to its parts (the selected "Possessive Attributes"). But explicit labels are not necessary for an image to enact an analytical process. It is only necessary that the image be presented in such a way that certain possessive attributes are made clear to an attentive (or intended) viewer.

The labeled image ("Jeremiah's Entrance"), above left, highlights a few—although only a few—of the possessive attributes Scott Kolbo emphasized in this depiction of Jeremiah. The image looks like an exercise students might do themselves with their own work, with the work of peers, or with the work of a comics artist: Label attributes and consider what has been emphasized. Elsewhere, I've described how visual inventory-taking exercises might work in a classroom, and how they might help raise students' awareness of the way images can be designed to carry particular analytical messages. Here, I want to dwell briefly on an irresistible (to me) resonance between visual and textual composing. When writers work, no matter the medium, they are faced with choices about which details to include and which details to leave out based on their communication goals and audiences. When readers decode messages, especially when they are reading closely, they often find themselves focusing on the fine details of a text and on the ways a text's meaning may have been skewed by one element or another in the mix. Cartoons not only share that quality with written texts, they also manifest that quality in a way that makes a question like "What is this writer showing us?" more literal than in a written text. Cartoons can vividly illustrate what it means to analytically select and emphasize certain details. Or, flipped around, consideration of a richly detailed prose paragraph can show students how hard it is to convey with prose what comics artists convey almost instantly through their cartoon drawings. All students, even those who do not consider themselves artistically gifted, can experiment with making images that express or emphasize something, and their artistic and communicative failures and missteps with images may be as instructive and worth talking about as their successes, just as an ambitious prose composition that does not fully succeed can be a better learning tool than a dull composition that is clear but attempts to say very little.

Both Ware (2004b) and Seth (Ngui, 2006) have suggested it is possible for a cartoonist to fail as an analyst, to add too much detail to a cartoon—to do, in essence, too little selection of the relevant possessive attributes of the person, object, or idea he intends to represent, and so to fail at the cartoonist's task of choosing a limited set of criterial aspects for any given object. Said Ware (2004b): "the more detailed and refined a cartoon, the less it seems to 'work,' and the more resistant to reading it becomes" (p. 11). Said Seth: "The more detailed the drawing—the more it attempts to capture 'reality'—the more it slows down the story telling and deadens the cartoon language" (Ngui, 2006, p. 22). Kress and van Leeuwen (2006), remarkably, sounded a lot like Ware and Seth when they talked about the problem of adding too much detail to images that are meant to provide analysis: "Too much life-likeness, too much detail, would distract from their analytical purpose. Only the essential features of the possessive attributes are shown, and for this reason drawings of various degrees of schematization are often preferred over photographs or highly detailed artwork" (p. 88). While cartoons can be used to enact many of the semiotic processes Kress and van Leeuwen (2006) explored in *Reading Images*, it is clear that they are born of a kind of analytical abstraction process—an "amplification through simplification" (McCloud, 1993/1994, p. 30)—nicely suited to fostering the swift readability that artists like Ware and Seth and McCloud try to achieve.

Brianne Bilsky (2012) has underscored this point in an interesting way. In her analysis of both Art Spiegelman's (1986 & 1991/1996) *Maus* and Alison Bechdel's (2006) *Fun Home* as representations of history, she noted that "the analog" (comics-style cartooning) does not "hold out the promise of precision" in truth-telling in the same way as "the digital" (e.g., digital photographs) (p. 134). Yet further thought (and close analysis of the comics in question) shows that there is a "loss of the real" in both photographs and comics (Bilsky, 2012, p. 133).[6]

In Bilsky's reading, cartooning became one way for storytellers to own the ambiguity of storytelling and consciously call into question the ability of a given narrative to tell unfiltered, unmediated truth. That is, Bilsky nicely made the case that all storytelling images are analytical, focused by an artist, and in need, themselves, of close analysis.

McCloud has had much to say about the kinds of choices artists make as they abstract their subjects into cartoon form. They draw on a range of stylistic choices, from the realistic (as in a simple photograph) to the purely iconic (as in a simple smiley face). Cartoon drawings on the iconic end of the spectrum require less interpretation because their meanings have been made quite clear by the abstraction process. That is, more complicated drawings offer less sharply defined analysis because they are constituted without such clearly focused selection of criterial aspects—and that means more work for the reader, just as cluttered prose (or highly sophisticated prose) can mean more work for a reader. McCloud (1993/1994) has built this realistic-to-iconic continuum into a third dimension, eventually offering up a two-page pyramid full of stylistic options, from complex "reality" at the lower left corner to simple icons with clear meaning (akin to simple words) in the lower right corner, and then up to pure lines (think Mondrian) at the top of the pyramid (pp. 49–57). Isolated from any other complicating factors (e.g., other cartoons, text, or a storyline), the most iconic (lower right) cartoons are easiest to interpret swiftly, though not necessarily richest in meaning; artful and meaningful cartooning can happen at all points inside McCloud's ingenious pyramid except (he has implied) at the lower left corner, where "reality" resides. (I asked Scott Kolbo to demonstrate Scott McCloud's idea using variously abstracted images of himself, and he sent me his version of McCloud's stylistic pyramid, included at right.)

Comics critic Douglas Wolk (2007) has contended that a cartoonist's freedom to distort reality has "one hard limit": The cartooning "has to be legible—the reader has to be able to recognize everything and everyone in the image very quickly" (p. 124). Wolk's (2007) remark here lines up generally with Witek's (2009) notion that "to be a comic text is to be read as a comic" (p. 149), but Wolk's (2007) vague invocation of "the reader" deserves a second look, in light of both McCloud's (1993/1994) pyramid and Kress and van Leeuwen's (2006) conception of signmaking. From a social semiotic point of view, Kress and van Leeuwen explained, signmakers make meaning using "the semiotic resources available for communicative action to a specific social group" (p. 10).[7] Communicators aiming for a broad audience might choose to use a series of easily decoded cartoons to transmit straightforward stories and messages. Consider typical newspaper comic strips, or airplane safety cards. Where the joke's punchline (or the safety card's meaning) must be instantly understood by a large (and not highly attentive) audience, easy-to-decode cartoons can be an effective rhetorical tool, built from semiotic resources available to many potential readers. But not all cartoonists want their images to be as easy to decode as the Sunday funnies. Wolk (2007) is no doubt correct that in many cases "nothing turns off a reader faster than not being able to tell what she's looking at" (p. 124), but what turns away one reader may be just the thing to attract a different reader. It is easy to imagine a devoted reader of hero comics who would be irritated by cartooning that departs substantially from the hero comic norm. But more literary-minded author–artists like Ware and Seth, along with a whole range of more radical cartoon stylists (no matter what their content), certainly do find audiences, much as independent films find audiences, though summer blockbusters always demand and receive more popular attention. McCloud's (1993/1994) strength, in the context of this discussion, is that he has authorized the whole of his pyramid for use. He has acknowledged the whole universe of cartooning style and, implicitly, the many different kinds of audience that sign-making cartoonists, freed from narrow production and content limits, may have in mind as they work.

In fact, the endless variety of cartooning styles coming to print today recapitulates the enduring tension in art and literature between work that yields up its meaning easily and work that demands (or invites or repays) extensive attention and contemplation.[8] Some cartoons (and the comics they populate) are meant, as Ware (2004b) suggested, to be no more difficult to interpret than road signs or than the waving arms of a drowning man; some comics (and the cartoons that populate them) are meant to rival the poetry of T. S. Eliot or the art of Joseph Cornell in aggregate complexity and difficulty. There is plenty of artistic space between the drowning man and abstract Modernism, of course, and plenty of space outside of that bracketed territory, for that matter. McCloud's (1993/1994) pyramid literally illustrates the point: Many kinds of abstraction are possible, and cartoonists may design their cartoons for many different rhetorical situations and draw upon different semiotic resources, depending in part on their intended audiences. An artist employing the analytical powers of artful abstraction may produce cartoons that, for a given readership, act as perspicuous objects imbued with comprehensible significance. Those cartoons may yield up their meanings as easily as roadsigns, or they may be deployed in more complicated ways so that they resist instant reading and, perhaps, offer richer literary and aesthetic rewards for attentive audiences. In turn, a student studying the analytical powers of artful abstraction may learn a great deal both from looking at a wide variety of work by skillful cartoonists and by experimenting with their own drawings and images, adding and subtracting details in order to make different statements. Doing so, they will have the chance to learn more about both visual and nonvisual composing, and they will have the chance to become more aware as interpreters of visual rhetoric.

Above, Scott shows the moment when he feels he's overworked a panel, putting in so much detail that the panel begins to do more (or maybe less) than he wants it to do. That is to say, for Scott, the crossed-out work on the right shows the end of perspicuity and the beginnings of confusion, for his purposes.

3. Three Cartoon Voices (The Integration of Cartoon and Comic)

Best American Comics 2010, edited by Neil Gaiman (2010), is a useful tour through a variety of cartoon-driven storytelling styles.[9] Among many fine choices, Gaiman (2010) included an excerpt from Bryan Lee O'Malley's (2009/2010) popular comic *Scott Pilgrim Versus The Universe*, populated with big-eyed, shaggy-haired kids, drawn clearly and appealingly in thick black lines. These cartoons lack the slick conformity of mainstream hero comics, but average readers are nevertheless likely to find them visually welcoming. Jason Heller (2007), introducing an *Onion A.V. Club* interview of O'Malley, noted that O'Malley's

Scott Pilgrim comics "[dovetail] romance, comedy, martial arts, and science fiction with a cartoony style that draws from manga and video games"; they are built around Scott Pilgrim, "a hapless twentysomething who must battle his girlfriend's evil ex-boyfriends while learning to cope with a gay roommate, a struggling band, and the looming responsibilities of adulthood." The comic is fittingly set in diners and living rooms and other crucibles for the romantic confusion of twenty-somethings in rock bands. This is a comic that exists toward the right-hand, iconic, swift-reading side of Scott McCloud's (1993/1994) stylistic pyramid (discussed in the "Cartoons as Perspicuous Objects" section). The cartoons (see below) are uniform and clear but also unfussy and loose; the aesthetic of *Scott Pilgrim* is one of affected and effective casualness, a comics equivalent to Scott Pilgrim's own self-consciously messy (but not too messy) hair. The panels are uncrowded, and special effects in the panels—abstract dots and lines and grey-outs and so on—tend to signpost the emotional states of the characters. It looks like the comic is going to be lighthearted and energetic, maybe the comics equivalent of a smart summertime comedy on film, and that is what it is. The drawings and the story are artfully blended.

Bryan Lee O'Malley, from *Scott Pilgrim vs. The Universe* (2009/2010, p. 269).

Also in *Best American Comics* 2010 (BAC10), Theo Ellsworth's (2009/2010) strange, clever story, "Norman Eight's Left Arm," features robots (pictured in the header above, and below at right, in a scrollable box) that look as if they were kludged together from left-over bric-a-brac in a madman's workshop. They sit across from one another at a formal dinner table in the middle of a woods; they make a wager that involves (no surprise) Norman Eight's detachable left arm. Woodland critters peek out of the underbrush. Compared to O'Malley's (2009/2010) drawings for Scott Pilgrim, Ellsworth's (2009/2010) playful drawings for "Norman Eight" are less inviting and familiar-feeling, more intricate but also less careful, controlled, and refined. The backgrounds are both more full and more full of things that do not immediately make sense, iconic or not. Before the robots speak, their stilted robot speech is foreshadowed not only by their posture but also by the linework from which they are formed and by the ways their setting surrounds them. The comic, like *Scott Pilgrim*, features mostly big panels, and the panels in this case are fairly uniform, often six-to-a-page in a grid, suggesting (accurately) that the story will be evenly paced and easy to follow. As with *Scott Pilgrim*, the drawing here fits on the right-hand side of McCloud's (1993/1994) stylistic pyramid. However, it inhabits a space further left (and further up) in the pyramid, and, as McCloud's (1993/1994) pyramid suggests is likely, the drawing style itself is less immediately accessible than O'Malley's (2009/2010) *Scott Pilgrim* drawing. Still, "Norman Eight" looks quirky and funny and not prohibitively difficult to read, and it is quirky and funny and readable. Like *Scott Pilgrim*, "Norman Eight" is drawn in a style that is nicely fitted to its humor and perspective. More than that: Scott and "Norman" are drawn in styles that are integral to their content. Cartooning style, for these comics, does not just fit or amplify the stories. For comics like these, narrative voice is inseparable from visual style.

   To be clear, swiftly read, iconic cartooning does not guarantee an easily accessible, straightforward comic. *BAC10* also includes an excerpt from Chris Ware's (2008/2010) developing *Rusty Brown* comic (originally published in Ware's *Acme Novelty Library #19*). Art Spiegelman has said that Ware's much-praised *Jimmy Corrigan—The Smartest Kid on Earth* "seems to . . . have a kind of formal, Joycean complexity that shows what a really visually literate comic can be. And what's more amazing is that it actually does have an emotional strength, that it's not just some kind of formal experiment. It's a rather moving literary work" (Peeters, 2004). The *Rusty Brown* excerpt in *BAC10* is similar in form, style, and complexity to *Jimmy Corrigan*. It contains many panels, often quite small, carefully designed into each page. Ware's drawing is economical and clear, almost architectural (as critics commonly point out), suggesting no wasted or meaningless mark. His concerned-looking cartoon figures are frequently overwhelmed physically, not only by their environments but also by the ways the page itself closes in on them. Together, the style of Ware's pages and the look of his cartoons suggest that this will be a story about Rusty Brown's unhappiness, and so it is. The drawing style is more iconic than "Norman Eight" or (arguably) *Scott Pilgrim*, yet Ware's visual text is much more dense, his meaning less accessible. There are more objects on the page. Their relationships to one another are sometimes obscure. Even the design of these pages announces the story's relative complexity. At times, the panels seem to demand simultaneous or recursive reading, rather than unidirectional sequential reading. A look at a Chris Ware page suggests that sometimes the iconic, readily interpretable images on the right-hand side of McCloud's (1993/1994) pyramid can be deployed in dazzlingly complex ways.

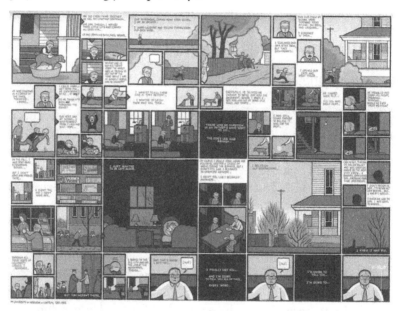

Chris Ware, from *Acme Novelty Library #19* (2008/2010, p. 145).

Those who have seen work by O'Malley, Ellsworth, or Ware will know that my textual descriptions barely begin to describe their artwork. In a well-made comic, the drawing style announces something significant about the comic's content, even before anyone reads a word, and the drawing itself—from the cartoons down to the lines that comprise them—is always a significant part of the content and voice of a comic.[10] These perspicuous cartoon objects may be produced instinctively by talented comics artists, but they are nevertheless analytical images, abstracted from the real in ways that draw readers' attention to relevant possessive attributes of the things they depict. For comics, effective cartoons are significance-laden signs. They are gathered and sequenced on the page for their intended audiences. They draw on semiotic resources likely to speak to those audiences. As others have said, cartoons in comics are not simply illustrations of the words in the speech bubbles. Just as in Ware's (2004b) drowning man example, attentive reading of a cartoon image does not necessarily result in (or need to result in) a translation of the image into words, and no such translation is required either to establish or to convey the cartoon's significance. Sometimes no such translation is possible. To read the words in a comic without also attending to the images is to fail to read the comic—is to fail to pay attention to all that the comic is communicating. It is at best a kind of weak skim reading that ignores the commentary and analysis embedded in the cartooning. Every object on the page contributes to the voice of the comic and is part of the comic's content; everything on the page speaks.

4. Visual Analytical Focus

A comics page, like a page of traditional prose, can be too complicated for its own good. The clarity of images at the far right corner of Scott McCloud's (1993/1994) stylistic pyramid is partly a result of their simplicity; there are no confusing internal juxtapositions, no pen strokes that raise questions about meaning or might cause a reader to pause and ponder. Yet even a simple, highly iconic drawing style can be deployed in complex ways, as in much of Chris Ware's work. Conversely, a complicated cartooning style, or a style that aims for some variety of realism, may be so detailed that, in the context of a given narrative, it is unfocused and distracting (as Ware, Seth, and McCloud—along with Gunther Kress and Theo van Leeuwen—all, in their own ways, indicate). This might be a matter of making the images less analytical by making them more fussy, or a matter of sublimating swift, clear communication to an aesthetic ideal; it is certainly a matter of lacking focus, of drawing in a style that sends stray signals without contributing artfully to the concatenation of signs that makes up the text. Such lack of focus might be said to lead to the comics equivalent of what, in prose writing, we sometimes call purple prose, or overwriting. For students, learning to to talk about the level of detail in a visual composition can be a bridge to talking about the same in any kind of composition. What details are chosen? How do the included details change the meaning of a text or help it achieve its purpose? Do they ever get in the way? How does the level of detail, or the emphasis given to any one element of the text, contribute to the voice of the text as well as the content? How is the voice of the text, its actual form, inseparable from its content? Comics make visible those elements of style that writing teachers often work to make clear to their students.

McCloud's (1993/1994) pyramid is useful here, again, for thinking about how any given signmaking choice made by a cartoonist contributes to a given text. While the pyramid appears at first to gauge a cartoon's level of abstraction, that is not exactly what it does. Part of what makes the pyramid a helpful illustration is the way it eliminates (or at least complicates) the notion that one image is more or less abstract than another. In the right-hand corner, a basic smiley face communicates instantaneously because it is abstracted in a way that makes its meaning nearly unambiguous. Any drawing anywhere to the left of the right-hand corner may contain, within itself, complicating juxtapositions—details and quirks of style that are at least the beginnings of readable significance. But that does not make the more complicated image less abstract, exactly. McCloud (1993/1994) has suggested that as a cartoon's style approaches that right-hand corner (or any other corner), we should see the artist as having focused her work in a chosen way, rather than as having eliminated details or as having made a simpler statement (p. 57). In this sense, the images at the far right are not the most abstract; they are the most precisely focused, the most straightforward as analytical images, and maybe the least nuanced. Images in other parts of the pyramid are not more abstract but differently abstracted, less focused, and more subject to potentially poetic ambiguities. Drawings that land in the pyramid's middle—like Theo Ellsworth's drawings, for example, or even drawings from some out-of-the-ordinary superhero comics—are abstract in ways that say more and maybe take longer to unpack than images at the far right. That complication may make reading the images a less instantaneous experience than reading road signs but still lend itself to a smooth and satisfactory reading experience for a given comic's audience. Less focused lines may be perfectly fitted to a comic's content, providing commentary and analysis that simpler cartooning would not provide. Or the complication may be complication for its own sake, tending to distract readers rather than contribute to the text's meaning. For some artists the latter might be a desirable end. Comics show vividly how style results in part from choices about what to include as well as how to present it.

Many well known cartoonists choose a simplified style that communicates quickly, though few choose anything like the absolute focus of McCloud's (1993/1994) right corner. As I explore in "La Ligne Juste…," Charles Schulz's (1950/2004) *Peanuts* presented a clear example of a simple style that is in some ways quite iconic but is also enlivened by its creator's personal touch. Randall Munroe's (2014) web comic *XKCD* (see images above and below), built primarily with stick figures, pushes almost all the way into McCloud's (1993/1994) right corner. Munroe's stick figures are injected with a small dose of gestural meaning but, on the whole, they tend to pose so little obstacle to reading that they point reader attention in the direction of Munroe's clever text. Munroe's stick figures have some expressive power and some nuance, though; they do not exist in the far right corner of McCloud's (1993/1994) pyramid, exactly, and the context provided by Munroe's words and settings gives them verve.

On the other hand, an artist like underground comics legend R. Crumb has created cartoons that are so uniquely stylized—so aptly fitted to the expression of his abundant personal idiosyncrasies—that they do, no doubt, pose a kind of obstacle to readers. And that is certainly the intent; much of Crumb's meaning-making depends on his arresting (sometimes alarming) style and subject matter. Not to put too fine a point on it, Crumb's drawing demonstrates a different and richer kind of abstraction than does Munroe's straightforward stick-figuring for *XKCD*. It makes little sense to call Crumb's work "less abstract" than *XKCD*, but it does make sense to note that Crumb focuses reader attention in unique ways, drawing attention to more and quite different possessive attributes of its subjects. Crumb's content would not work (or would work very differently) in *XKCD*'s style, and *XKCD* would not work (or would work very differently) in Crumb's style. Where *XKCD*'s concatenation of significant elements relies heavily on text, R. Crumb's concatenation of meanings owes much more to Crumb's unique cartooning than to what we read in his speech and thought bubbles.

In other words, if Crumb's work were rendered in *XKCD*'s style, it would not say what it says. But also, tellingly, it seems impossible that if *XKCD* were drawn in Crumb's style, Crumb's style would still express the neuroses that it expresses; the rest of the content, beyond the style, is still relevant—still part of the concatenation of signs. When Crumb's graphic adaptation of the the biblical book of Genesis was to be released in 2009, there was some anticipation of the scandal it would no doubt inspire. For example, Susan Jane Gilman (2009), reviewing for National Public Radio (NPR) and familiar with Crumb's work and reputation, "assumed" his Genesis "would . . . be the funniest, most subversive, most profane ever." It was not; it was Crumb's best attempt to illustrate, literally, the words of the text. Said Gilman:

> You expect it to be sardonic, but it is not. You may expect it to be psychedelically spiritual—it's not that, either. Rather, it's humanizing. Crumb takes the sacred and makes it more accessible, more down-to-earth, less idealized. And this may be a blessing, or it may be subversion itself.

Married to this new content (and with some restraint on Crumb's part), Crumb's style *means* differently, so that rather than raising questions about blasphemy and disrespect, it raises questions about what is gained and lost by rendering the stories of Genesis in an almost pedestrian way, with no attempts at transcendent grandeur. In contrast, Michelangelo's graphic adaptation of Genesis (at the Sistine Chapel, and available for viewing in a Vatican-approved online edition, not to scale) looks different than Crumb's and indisputably gets at different aspects of the stories than does Crumb's (2009) illustrated Genesis. Meaning emerges from the concatenation of style, focus, and other narrative elements, in this case in a way that defuses some of the scandal that R. Crumb's followers might have expected from his work.

In *Reading Comics*, Douglas Wolk (2007) took a swipe at the work of comics artist Alex Ross by, essentially, accusing Ross of including too much detail—working too far toward the left-hand, perceived-reality corner of McCloud's (1993/1994) pyramid—in a way that Wolk (2007) said did not particularly serve the stories Ross was telling. Ross's very popular painted comics render superheroes in a superglossy romanticized hyperrealism, much praised by fans for its detail and inspired by the more idealistic elements of socialist realism. (He may be the Norman Rockwell of superhero comics.)[11] Unimpressed, Wolk characterized Ross's work as "painted upgrades of standard superhero-comics imagery" that "exude grand seriousness" but "are stiff and glossy," like "inspirational office posters starring Batman or Wonder Woman" (p. 123). He argued that Ross's paintings "leave too little to the imagination" (p. 123), as if Ross's paintings were actually photo-realistic renderings of superfolk. They are not that, exactly, but they do have an orderly, scrubbed-clean quality that calls to mind things like propaganda posters, promotional pamphlets, romance novels, and televangelist hair. The detailed faces of Ross's characters look like the faces of specific people, groomed for a photo shoot (in part because Ross painted them based on staged photographs of models). The aging Batman that Ross featured in his *Kingdom Come* mini-series (co-written with Mark Waid, 1996) may be angry, but he sure is a handsome old fellow, captured in a nice soft focus that highlights his weathered face without making it scary (Waid & Ross, 1996/1998).

The contrast between Ross's attractive Batman in *Kingdom Come* (Waid & Ross, 1996/1998) and Frank Miller's (1986/2002) Batman in *The Dark Knight Returns*—grim, somehow out of focus, less closely detailed, sometimes oddly contorted and imbued with pain—illustrates what Wolk (2007) found objectionable in Ross, I think. Where the linework in Miller's (1986/2002) Batman comics works as a visual analytical commentary on his version of the character and the fictional world the character inhabits, Ross's (Waid & Ross, 1996/1998) renderings are focused on the grandeur and power of the superfolk he depicts, regardless of the story they inhabit. (An Alex Ross-illustrated Genesis, we can speculate, would not be noted for revealing the pedestrian humanity of its characters.) For a reader like Wolk, who admires the textured authorial voice present in messier drawings, Ross's images are about as engaging as the images of happy, well-groomed college students in college brochures. They are studio-scrubbed popstar voices when what Wolk wanted was the interesting grain of a folk singer's voice or the emotive sloppiness of punk rock. Gauged as analytical images, Miller's Batman cartoons highlight the character's psychological trauma. Ross's, even when they reveal the character's pain or weakness, somehow point to Batman's physical strength and poise, placing a glossy, hyper-realistic aesthetic above the thematic concerns of the story. Because of his commitment to a style inspired by social realism, Ross's paintings include detail work that critics call excessive, especially for the comics medium (which depends so much on the swift readability of its images). Why, detractors might ask, does Ross paint characters in a way that makes me pause to consider whether their facial expressions ring true? Sales and critical recognition in the comics industry attest to the success of Ross's work for many readers of superhero comics; for supporters, he is drawing on just the set of semiotic resources they want him to draw on, adding just the kinds of details they want to see. But for Wolk and those who share his view of Ross, the pedantic detail embedded in Ross's characters makes the artwork weak as cartooning—an oddly unfocused distraction from the story, in something like the way high definition television, by revealing too many fine details on actor's faces, can distract. For Wolk, Ross's Batman is a visual carrier of possessive attributes that detract from his stories. For writing students (whether they side with Wolk or Ross in this particular disagreement), the exploration of questions like these about visual voice may easily be linked to lessons about noting and assessing connections between voice, style, content, and form in other kinds of composition.

5. La Ligne Juste, Formal Traits, and Concatenation

'La Ligne Juste'

It will always be difficult to convey in words the qualities that make a cartoon's style—from its characters all the way down to its lines—unique or compelling or demanding or uniquely suited to a particular kind of content.[12] For example, both Chris Ware (2004a) and designer/author Chip Kidd (2001) have tried to explain what they value in Charles Schulz's Charlie Brown comics. Both Ware and Kidd began by looking at the cartoons themselves, and even at the lines that make up the cartoons, attempting to explain how Schulz so aptly matched and mixed style and story. And both appealed, implicitly, to our vision: They claimed we needed only to look attentively to see Schulz's voice in his lines and to see how others fail to bring Charlie to life. Ware pointed to unfinished sketches left behind by Schulz, just scribbles on notebook pages that even in their unfinished state (Ware argued) evoke the style and spirit of Schulz's *Peanuts* gang (p. 67). Drawn by anyone other than Schulz, Ware said, Charlie "always comes out looking so *wrong*, a lurid joke, like someone dressed up at a costume party" (p. 66). Kidd made much the same point about reprinted pages from a 1950s *Tip Top Comics* version of Charlie Brown that was not drawn by Schulz. Kidd said that the manifest failures of that comic illustrate "how deceptively simple Schulz's style is" and also that Schulz's style is "impossible to copy."[13] Something about Schulz's lines, from Schulz's hands, both men have argued, is essential to making Charlie Brown be who he is and mean what he means. The motivated sign-making begins, they have suggested, with the impossible-to-capture qualities of the cartoonist's lines.

In search of further insight into the power of Schulz's lines, Kidd's (2001) richly visual *Peanuts: The Art of Charles Schulz* had done what many fans of many kinds of artists do: It has looked into the artist's processes and toolbox. Kidd's book explained what kind of drawing paper Schulz worked on, how he scripted, when the lettering went on, when the cartoons went on. The book even included this charming bit of trivia about Schulz's exact tools:

> He used a 914 Radio, and relied on these pen nibs so much that when the company announced it was going out of business, he bought the entire remaining stock. The hundreds of boxes saw him through the rest of his career. (n.p.).

Over the course of his book, Kidd suggested at least three loose periods in Schulz's *Peanuts* drawing: an early period, which Schulz himself said had a "harshness" and lacked "warmth" (n.p.); a middle period of development and maturity; and a late period in which Schulz, because of shaking hands, began to draw more slowly and less cleanly. Kidd praised even the final period: "Rather than harming the strip, this actually made the linework even more expressive. . . . Due to Schulz's discipline and mastery of technique, the gradually wavier lines never looked like a mistake—they were a natural, effective design choice" (n.p.). Kidd included a Schulz quote suggesting that Schulz himself took something like a fan's pleasure in seeing his lines emerge from those 914 Radio nibs: "I am still waiting for that wonderful pen line," Schulz said,

> that comes down when you are drawing Linus standing there, and you start with the pen up near the back of his neck, and you bring it down and bring it out, and the pen point fans a little bit, and you come down here and draw the lines this way for the marks on his sweater. (qtd. in Kidd, n.p.)

All of this interest in penwork suggests, again, how important even a line can be to a comic—so important that, Kidd (2001) implied, as the line style of Charlie Brown's world changed, so did the character of that world. The distinctive voice in a line is that irreplaceable quality of the hand that is drawing, joined to the pen, joined to the paper, and so on down to the day and hour when the drawing was made.

Kidd (2001) and Ware (2004a), in their appreciation of Schulz, have written of his lines in the way that some writers speak of *le mot juste*. Schulz's linework may not be the best linework for all contexts. It would be the wrong linework in some contexts. He probably even had weak line days, and, like everyone, his set of available semiotic resources must have been bounded in part by his own artistic limitations. But in the world of Charlie Brown, Kidd and Ware (and many others) have told us, Schulz's linework is just right—essentially *la ligne juste*, a visual storytelling analog for *le mot juste*. Scott McCloud (1993/1994) has said that all lines (not just Schulz's lines) have "expressive potential," that

> by direction alone, a line may go from passive and timeless—
> to proud and strong—to dynamic and changing! By its shape
> it can be unwelcoming and severe—or warm and gentle—or
> rational and conservative. By its character it may seem savage
> and deadly—or weak and unstable—or honest and direct.
> (pp. 124–125)[14]

And McCloud (1993/1994) drew these different lines along with his explanatory text, then showed their deployment in several comics, persuasively demonstrating how line styles can fit and amplify the content of a comic. Even so, he is only partially correct. *La ligne juste* does what it does only in context; there is no fundamental meaning to a line style. To get "savage and deadly" lines (McCloud, p. 125), the artist must join those lines to content that evokes the savage and the deadly. Wedded to other content, those same lines might read as whimsical and awkward, or bland and pedestrian. Theo Ellsworth's (2010) robots would not be nearly so strange if they did not live in the woods. Bryan Lee O'Malley's (2010) hipsters would take on different kinds of significance if they were working in corporate cubicles and attending business seminars. A line style itself, or a cartooning style itself, can provide crucial elements of meaning for comics, but lines and cartoons on their own mean little (or nothing) until they are activated by and in context. Significance begins at the level of the line, but only if the line is given a context in which to signify. As McCloud (1993/1994) himself has said, comics come to life through the juxtaposition and ordering of multiple bits of visual data that have been brought together so that they can communicate together (p. 9).

Formal Traits

Because significance in comics emerges from the whole set of juxtaposed images and not from any single image alone, it is important to avoid the mistake of assigning meaning to a line style or drawing style without considering the full context in which it is deployed. Other narrative-driven media similarly tempt critics into the kind of reductive reading that turns formal traits into automatic ciphers for narrative meaning. Film studies students, for example, learn that a high angle shot (looking down from above on a subject) tends to suggest that the subject of the shot is vulnerable, whereas a low angle shot (looking up at the subject) tends to dignify or empower a subject. Yet those shots do not always mean those things, any more than a jagged line in a comic will always evoke danger.

Dave Monahan's (2006) excellent "Camera Angles" tutorial (from his *Looking at Movies* DVD) made this point clear by examining a scene from Stanley Kubrick's (1980) *The Shining*. The wife, Wendy (played by Shelly Duvall), is in danger from the husband, Jack (played by Jack Nicholson), but Monahan showed how, in the scene where Wendy discovers her danger, Kubrick used a combination of low angle shots, lack of information about the environment, and story context to evoke Wendy's vulnerability to Jack's madness. This is roughly opposite of the conventional wisdom about low angle shots, but Monahan's reading is undeniably correct (and a testament to Kubrick's skill and style as a filmmaker). Because conventional shot-angle wisdom says Wendy must be empowered in a low angle shot, an inexperienced critic might tax his brain mightily trying to find a way to explain how Wendy is empowered in the scene. But he would be making the mistake of reading the formal trait as if it were a clue for decoding, rather than considering how the formal trait operates in—is activated by and in—the context of the scene.

Similarly, beginning literature students (often aided and abetted by imagination-killing reliance on *Spark Notes*) sometimes want to assign symbolic meanings mechanically, without reference to story context. Green must mean money. Or maybe springtime. Yellow must mean money (gold!). Or maybe sickness. In a much discussed scene from F. Scott Fitzgerald's (1925/1995) *The Great Gatsby*, the narrator espies Jay

Gatsby standing in his yard at night, reaching out across the water and toward a green light that turns out to be shining at the end of the dock belonging to his long lost love, Daisy Buchanan. *Spark Notes* (2013) reductively opines:

> Situated at the end of Daisy's East Egg dock and barely vis-ible from Gatsby's West Egg lawn, the green light represents Gatsby's hopes and dreams for the future. Gatsby associates it with Daisy, and in Chapter 1 he reaches toward it in the darkness as a guiding light to lead him to his goal. Because Gatsby's quest for Daisy is broadly associated with the Ameri-can dream, the green light also symbolizes that more general-ized ideal. In Chapter 9, Nick compares the green light to how America, rising out of the ocean, must have looked to early settlers of the new nation.

When students rely on this kind of gloss, they end up asserting, with-out adequate (or, sometimes, any) proof and logic, that the scene where Gatsby reaches for the light has some ill-defined something to do with the hopes and dreams of Americans, as if that vague, unsupported (by them) assertion explains anything about the novel, its characters, or the scene. The *Spark Notes* (2013) gloss on the text makes the entire context of the scene just drop away, so that any of the light's possessive attributes being highlighted by Fitzgerald (1925/1995) are submerged beneath speculation about the possessive attributes he *might* be high-lighting. What is it about trembling toward a dock light that is sup-posed to evoke the early European colonists? How is that metaphor interesting and complex and embedded into the narrative, if that is the metaphor Fitzgerald has given us? In what sense is this dock light supposed to be "guiding" Gatsby, and toward what possible end? If we restore the context, we get the nosy, nosy narrator spying on his neighbor, his neighbor acting quite strange, and—in the context of the larger narrative—a scene from the life of an awfully creepy stalker. How warped must a man be to reach trembling toward an estranged lover's house in the middle of the night? How scary is a guy who buys a palace across from his ex-lover's estate under an assumed identity with the explicit goal of homewrecking the ex-lover's family? The scene becomes much more interesting in context, and, with context in mind, it becomes much harder to assert that the green of the light must obviously symbolize something as nebulous as every man's hope for prosperity.

Concatenation

Charles Schulz's lines (or Ellsworth's or O'Malley's or your favorite toddler's) are more interesting in context, too. Roland Barthes (1961/1996), who normally wrote about images in isolation (even when he was writing about film), noted in passing how some meanings emerge only in the composite: "Naturally, several photographs can come together to form a sequence . . . ; the signifier of connotation is then no longer to be found at the level of any one of the fragments of the sequence but at that . . . of the concatenation" (p. 24). In another text, Barthes (1964/1996) pointed specifically to the importance of concatenation for "cartoons and comic strips," in which individual words and images are part of "a more general syntagm and the unity of the message is realized at a higher level, that of the story, the anecdote, the diegesis" (p. 41). This notion that meaning arises from concatenation (a notion which can be profitably extended to any complex narrative) is fundamental for interpreters of sequential media like film and comics. Encountered outside of Peanuts, observed without foreknowledge of the strip or of Charlie Brown's place in culture, neither Charlie nor Schulz's lines would contain the significance that Kidd (2001) and Ware (2004a) assign them. Even setting aside the significance that accrues to Charlie because of his fame, the meaning of Charlie is established not by the linework alone but by the linework joined to Charles Schulz's sensibilities as a storyteller, gag writer, and character designer. Charlie's significance emerges from the concatenation of Charlie (a "chronically depressed child," as Lev Grossman (2004) once called him)[15] with the formulaic restraints of the newspaper strip, the chosen settings, the child's-eye point of view, the repeating gags (the kite tree, the football, the baseball games, the little red-haired girl), and the other characters (the preternatural dog, the bully, the losing baseball team, the kid with the blanket, the filthy kid, the frustrated musician), and (no doubt) the linework. Significance emerges when Charlie (looking and acting as he does) meets Linus (looking and acting as he does) on the pitcher's mound at the end of another lost game. It is even fair to say that the significance of Charlie begins to emerge, pretty strongly, by the end of the first Peanuts strip, with the punchline "Good ol' Charlie Brown. . . . How

I hate him!" (Schulz, 1950/2004, p. 1). But that significance does not come from the line style alone, as significant as the lines certainly are.

The first *Peanuts* comic, and the beginnings of Charlie Brown's significance, not in the lines alone, but in the lines joined to the concatenation of significant words and images on the page. (My reading of Scott Kolbo's (2013b) "Sonic Medicine" looks in more detail at how the meaning of *his* comic arises from a concatenation of signs.)

If the first necessary point in an analysis of how comics say what they say is that the figures and lines on the page all speak, the second is that nothing on the page speaks alone.[16] Elsewhere, I have included several straightforward teaching exercises, and all of these, in a sense, are designed to help students experiment with and talk about the juxtaposition of visual elements. All of them are meant to prompt thinking about the complex ways that even subtle juxtapositions can alter the meaning of concatenated bits and pieces in a composition. Meaning for comics (and films and novels and other complex texts) arises, as Barthes (1961/1996) suggested, at the level of concatenation. As the meaning of a film angle emerges from its use in the context of the film, and as the significance of a literary symbol depends on how it is used inside the text itself, the meaning of Charlie is not in Charlie's lines alone but in the concatenation of elements that makes up Charlie's world (and Charlie's relationship to readers).

As I have argued above, the style of the images matters, without a doubt. Style is integral to the work's voice and meaning and focus. But the meaning of the visual style arises from its integration into the work (or from audience expectations), not from its intrinsic qualities alone.[17] The complexity of the whole page (rather than of the individual image) is one important reason why Ware's (2008) Rusty Brown comics are more demanding than Theo Ellsworth's (2009) "Norman Eight," even though Ware's drawing style (somewhere further to the right than Ellsworth's style on McCloud's stylistic pyramid) is arguably simpler than Ellsworth's. Ware's comics tend to include a greater number and complexity of juxtapositions, even in single panels, and he creates a more complicated reading experience by integrating his iconic figures into emotionally fraught situations and building his panels into visually rich pages that contribute significantly to his storytelling.[18] La ligne juste gets its power from integration into the cartoon, which gets its power from integration into the comic; concatenation is key. Everything on the page speaks, all at once, and comics can help students enter into a conversation about how that rule might be applicable not only to visual compositions but also to a complex composition of any kind.

6. Teaching Comics, Teaching Writing

Below, I describe a small set of straightforward classroom exercises that might (all together or not) follow from and reinforce study of the comics-related ideas explored throughout "Perspicuous Objects." Each builds on comics and comics theory, and each is designed to ease students into close analysis of visual rhetoric. Each in its own way is meant to help students learn to describe their own visual work and the visual work of others, in part by learning to look more closely at what Richard Lanham (1993) might have called the *at* of comics, and to avoid or grow past what Rich Rice and Cheryl E. Ball (2006) called "unremediated schmoozery" in the use of visuals.

Stylistic Inventories

The personal voices and perspectives of comics artists tend to be expressed more or less clearly in their visual work (as I argue in other sections of "Perspicuous Objects"); for teaching visual communication, the blatant presence of personal voices is one important advantage that comics have over many other common visual forms. It rarely seems that a cartoonist is trying even a little bit to be objective; the form itself, as Scott McCloud (1993/1994) has argued, demands the use of telling distortions and simplifications. With cartoons, there is rarely the problematic sense, as with photographs, that the image *ought* to be telling the unfiltered truth; all cartoonists are fabricators and embellishers—consciously, obviously so. For that reason, it is not difficult to place the work of several cartoonists side by side and stage a discussion about the different kinds of possessive attributes the cartoonists are highlighting in the subjects and objects they choose to draw. It is relatively simple to ask students to look at how one artist's depiction of human beings differs from another's—how the focus of one artist's visual analysis of the world differs from the focus of another artist's. Such a discussion might easily expand to include not only human figures but also the visual qualities of spaces and settings, and of the objects in those spaces; the discussion should certainly touch on the ways that texts, lines, and other objects on the page affect the meaning of the drawn figures. It may be relatively difficult to put the key differences into words, but beginning with *a written inventory* of what is actually on the page—images and lines and traits of images and lines, along with key written elements—will give students the raw data they need to make a case based on very specific evidence, and, if all goes well, to begin to talk about how specific sets of stylistic choices serve the unique texts in which they appear. Ideally, these sorts of lessons could carry over to analysis of visuals in more mundane documents, where overall context and deployment can be just as subjective, though not so *obviously* subjective.

Doodled Self Portraits

To help students think further about the selective, analytical nature of cartoons and comics, teachers might ask them to try building their own analytical images—by drawing, by staging photographs, by altering images with photo-editing software. Those images might be deliberately focused and analytical, aimed at conveying specific ideas, somehow, but it is also possible to ask students to create less *deliberately* focused analytical images and then to try to explain what they have done. For example, students might draw themselves in whatever doodling styles they have developed during their years of scribbling in the margins of notebooks. (This will be easier for some students than others, and—especially if done in class—the best artists in the group will need to be given a time limit and a reminder that this is their habitual doodle drawing, not their most accomplished portraiture.) After sketching, either in small groups or as a class, students can look at the different kinds of possessive attributes emphasized in their different drawing styles, and they can speculate about how this drawn style might fit into a narrative. That step is important: It asks students both to notice the embedded analytical traits of their own doodling styles and to see how, even at the level of doodling, drawing can analyze and present the world in quite different ways.

Second Portraits

A productive next step for the doodling exercise might ask students to draw themselves using a second, different line style—maybe choosing one of the line styles McCloud (1993/1994) suggested in *Understanding Comics*, maybe simply choosing a different point on McCloud's stylistic pyramid, maybe imitating the line style of a classmate, maybe imitating a comics artist the class has considered, or maybe using some combination of the above. The second style will often be much harder to produce, but it will result from the conscious, current choices of the image maker. The second set of drawings will provide not only another group of images to analyze but also a practical experience trying to invent effective expression with visuals. Trying to draw in a second style may also make students aware of the limits of their own semiotic resources—of how their limited experience with drawing and looking at drawings and trying to express anything through drawing means, naturally, that there are few visual moves they can make easily (unless they have rare and well-developed artistic skills). This is a chance for students to more fully appreciate the complexity and difficulty of the work done by visual communicators of all kinds, and it is at the same time a chance to understand that they can, within limits, begin using some of the tools deployed by more sophisticated visual communicators.

Other Drawings

One potential drawback to self portraiture can be the sense that the portrait (and its followup) ought to be doing some serious self-expression, or that self-drawing is too uncomfortably revealing of self-image. That might add a welcome layer of complexity, in some cases, but it might also be a distraction. For that reason, a teacher might choose to ask students to draw someone else in the class, or someone fictional, or just *anyone*. A teacher might also ask students to draw human figures (or personified human-like figures) representing specific states of mind or specific situations or specific ideas. The variations are practically limitless, each with its own potentially productive (but potentially distracting) complications.

Staged and Altered Photographs

Close study of comics and cartoons may also work as useful scaffolding for studying the rhetoric of photography and other less obviously subjective visual forms. If we can ask how Charlie Brown is affected by his immediate context, we can also ask how a front page news photo is affected by its context—the headlines, the stories, other images, the visual design, even the paper's reputation. If we can talk about how cartoonists choose details to include and emphasize, then we can talk about how photographers do the same. As in comics, there are perspicuous objects in news photos and billboards and all sorts of visual messages; all photographers and designers are amplifying by simplifying, though often in more subtle ways than comics artists. As a result, students can apply what they have learned from the careful reading of comics to the staging of photographs. Some students may find camerawork less intimidating and personal than cartooning, in fact, but such work can still demand that they mindfully select what will be seen in their images—how, in effect, their images will function as focused, analytical compositions. Students might experiment with amplification through simplification in a photograph, controlling what their viewers see, and how much of it, in order to imbue an image with deliberate focus and analytical commentary. Students might also experiment with changing the meaning of a photograph using even the simplest tools provided by photo editing software—subtle color shifts, added lines or highlights, cropping, and so on. What happens, they can ask, with the change of an angle, the movement or substitution of an object, the alteration of facial expressions? How can one squiggly line, one added object, one subtle shift change everything?[19]

Text-and-Image Juxtapositions

Staging, manipulating, and then purposefully juxtaposing photographs to other texts can be a manageable way to experiment with the power of context to change the meaning of an image (and the power of an image to change the meaning of its context). For example, students could consider the ways that different kinds of images would add different kinds of meaning to a given essay (one of their own, or maybe one that the class has read together). Building from an understanding of the analytical, focus-making qualities of cartoons, such a discussion can look closely at what a given image is saying in the context of an essay—how it is supporting or supplementing or even pushing

back against the essay's argument.[20] Students can use the critical vocabulary they acquire while studying comics to explain how their own
images are contributing (or not) to their own writing; they need not
fall back on the vague assertion that images accompanying essays are
good to include because they give readers something exciting to see on
the page.

Image-and-Image Juxtapositions

Students might also do some purely visual juxtaposition and concatenation, combining a single image with a series of second images in
order to produce different concatenated meanings. A child playing
in one image, joined to an explosion in the second, suggests danger.
That same child joined to a picture of a graduating senior suggests
the process of growing up. Students might experiment, as Madeleine
Sorapure (2006) has suggested, with specific visual figurative language
by making, for example, metaphorical or metonymic juxtapositions.
And they might try some more ambitious concatenation, using more
than two images, whether those images are produced by themselves
or provided by someone else—as with David Staley's (2010) "visual
chord". They might start with a series of images illustrating an action
or a moment in a story and then add, subtract, or rearrange images to
alter the apparent meaning of the sequence. This kind of assignment
might be designed to teach Scott McCloud's (1993/1994) six standard
comics transitions, which can all be approximated with a camera, but
it will gain even more power if students are required to unpack and
experiment with what McCloud called non sequiturs—which are the
domain of visual figurative language.

Self Analysis

More traditional writing assignments can be built around the tension
between the visual and the textual, of course. Most obviously, if our
goal is to make students more comfortable explaining what is happening in their visual compositions, then it makes sense to have them try
to write about what they meant to communicate in their own partly
(or mostly) visual compositions. Meta-accounts of the work they do
with visuals will give them a chance to explain their intentions and to
exercise their new vocabulary for visual analysis. Actually requiring
students to deploy concepts like *concatenation* and *criterial aspect* in

their writing invites them to think hard about what those concepts have meant to their visual composing process.

Analysis of Others, Translation of Others.

Similarly, students can show (and increase) their grasp of visual analysis by writing analytical essays about the synergy of visual style and other types of content in other people's work, not just their own work. For example, they might be asked to use their new vocabulary in service of an analysis of a published comic, at the level of the panel or a series of panels or a page or the whole work. And we might ask our students to attempt a translation of a portion of a comic—a page or a few panels—into prose. The translation would require close attention to all the details used in the comic and to the style of the comic, and the completion of the translation would ask students to confront the sorts of meanings that comics visuals convey easily but that prose may say only with difficulty and at length. They would have to grapple in such essays with the way some comics artists pack paragraphs worth of significance into a few concatenated images.

7. IN CONCLUSION

A discussion of what makes comics tick that does not explicitly consider the visual language choices of the artist will always be an incomplete discussion. In fact, the words on the page are sometimes the least interesting place to start a reading of a comic. However, it isn't always obvious to readers that they ought to be reading well-made comics with the kind of rigor they might bring to the reading of a well-made traditional text. The English majors I teach tend to be trained to think about the juxtaposition of textual images and the importance of small details in a poem, but they often need a nudge to think in the same way about the images inside a graphic novel. Or maybe they just need permission to bring the full range of their literary and rhetorical tools and sensibilities to the reading of images in the comics form. Whatever the case, when I assign a graphic novel or comic, even and especially to English majors, I always remind my students to look at the pictures, which are not just illustrations of the words but are instead visual language that is as much text as the traditional text on the page. I ask them to notice how the images are made, how their very form can be analytical, how they can draw the mind in certain directions. I ask them to notice how the meanings of images on the page arise in the aggregate, rather than alone, with every mark on the page meaning something and no mark on the page meaning what it means when taken by itself.

In many cases, a discussion of the comics grotesque might be a great place to start: How are these figures attenuated? What kinds of amplification by simplification are going on? How do the images work together with juxtaposed images and texts to establish characters and places? This is close reading that takes into account visual details in the ways that close readers of poetry and fiction are trained to take into account imagery rendered in text. What were my first impressions? What's concatenated visually here in support of my first impressions? Is there anything that contradicts my initial response? How has looking closely at the more granular details deepened or altered my reading of the whole piece? In reading comics, then, what we add to the text-on-a-page paradigm is this: Look at the pictures, and look at the pictures next to the pictures. They are full of information. They are also imagery, and they are doing all the amazing things that imagery does, and they are doing it in complex ways worth examining. But you have to look to see it.

The discussions of cartooning and concatenation throughout "Perspicuous Objects" leave much still unsaid about the virtually endless set of rhetorical tools used by comics artists, and especially about the poetics of joining images and designing pages. But as a whole the framework suggested by "Perspicuous Objects" provides a way to look at the constituent elements of a specific visual narrative and to begin analyzing the rhetorical and literary work being done by its lines, abstractions, image selections, and juxtapositions. The webtext focuses on terminology and ideas that can help along critical thinking about how images can be analytical by design, how they can be inflected by their context and placement, and how they can rise above straight-forward illustration of what a composition is already saying with words alone. With a useful vocabulary for talking about how formal, visual qualities of a comic are integral to its meaning-making, students can begin their analytical work by looking closely at specific images as focused, analytical images contributing to a narrative, rather than by loosely translating images into words. They can move beyond discussing visual narratives as if they are traditional stories or essays that happen to be illustrated, and they can look more closely at the relationship between a visual narrative's *at* and *through* states, as Richard Lanham (1993) suggested they should.

That is to say, the ideas presented here can help an analytical reader avoid, for example, treating a cartoon bird as if it is little different than the word "bird." Further, if students learn to describe and analyze the rhetorical situation of cartoons in the context of comics, then that analytical outlook should help them begin to see and analyze the constructedness of all kinds of images deployed in all kinds of multimodal discourses. Moreover, if they can make a case about how context affects even what a stray squiggly line means, then they are becoming more sensitive to the ways all extended arguments are crafted out of many small, connected pieces. Other strategies can move students toward this kind of analytical outlook, too, of course; my case here is that comics can provide an excellent starting point for conversations and lessons about the dynamics and difficulties of not only multimodal communication, specifically, but also meaning construction and analysis, generally.

Comics often make their way into classrooms in much the same way that film does—as a form teachers expect students to somehow connect with better than they connect with print, whatever that means. A comic like Marjane Satrapi's (2007) *Persepolis*, chronicling Satrapi's experiences with religious and political extremism, might become the anchor for classroom discussions of religious and political extremism. Leaving aside the dubious assumption that students will always find a comic more congenial than simple prose, there is surely value in many such discussions, but just as surely these discussions tend to consider the comics form of the narrative only in passing, if at all—skipping over looking *at* the text in order to look right *through* it.

But to ignore the form is to ignore much of what a highly visual text means. To ignore the form is also to miss an opportunity to teach students something about how visual rhetoric works, much as ignoring the form and style of a film—or the form and style of traditional prose texts—means sacrificing opportunities to talk about how communication works. Cartoons and comics can be used to show how every mark on a page contributes something to the page's meaning, how all the marks depend on each other for their significance, how images can be analytically focused, how abstraction itself is a sort of analysis, how style matters, how the arrangement of elements can be significant—how created images can be literate and literary, in short.

Not only can students become sharper readers of comics, their study of accumulated, concatenated meaning in comics may become the study of how selection and arrangement are crucial to composing and expression of ideas, period.

NOTES

1. McCloud (1993/1994) pointed to comics-like art appearing in ancient and early modern cultures (pp. 9-19), and Franny Howes (2010) has argued convincingly that we might talk about a "visual rhetorical tradition" that includes forms and techniques appearing and reappearing throughout history, with or without any assistance from Europeans or Americans.

2. Another famous example is Art Spiegelman's (1986 & 1991/1996) *Maus*, in which the choice to make Germans cats and Jews mice becomes more interesting when we ask not just "Why are the Germans cats?" but, instead, "Why are the Germans *these* cats, drawn *this* way, surrounded by *these* other drawn objects?"

3. Witek's (2009) formula might be reversed to focus on the intentions of creators: To be a comic is to be produced as a comic. And it could happen that a text intended as a comic is not received as a comic, or that a text not intended as a comic is received as a comic. But Witek's statement is helpful as a starting point in that it identifies comics-ness rhetorically, in a sender–text–receiver relationship.

4. *Punch* (2014) was published from 1841 to 2002. Its cartoons, available unofficially all over the Web, are currently archived and searchable (and licensable) at an official *Punch* site online.

5. Seth (with no surname) is the pen name of Gregory Gallant.

6. Similarly, Kress and van Leeuwen (2006) allow that certain photographs can serve an analytical purpose, especially if they are less complicated than unfiltered reality—controlled in some way by the photographer's choices, as all photographs are, especially if taken by professional photographers (p. 89).

7. This is how they define and limit *langue*, rather than defining it as the language used by a master language user whose grasp of the language's affordances transcends all social usages/limits (Kress & van Leeuwen, 2006).

8. Consider, for example, the contrast between the poetic styles (and intentions) of Carl Sandburg and T. S. Eliot. Both are highly image driven, both chronicle city life, and both are writing during the early decades of the 20th century. But Sandburg prides himself on swift readability and Eliot would be unhappy if readers thought "The Love Song of J. Alfred Prufrock" was a one-read-and-done poem. To favor the complexity of Eliot is to favor

what Craig Stroupe (2000) called the "elaborationist" bent in English department pedagogy (p. 611).

9. Since 2006, the Best American series has been releasing annual comics anthologies, curated by interesting practitioner–editors (in order, 2006–2013: Harvey Pekar, Chris Ware, Lynda Barry, Charles Burns, Neil Gaiman, Alison Bechdel, Françoise Mouly, Jeff Smith). Offerings in the series can be useful as affordable introductions to several different comics artists and their styles.

10. This point about comics page style has an imperfect parallel in paragraphing style. An academic article simply looks, at first glance, different than a textbook page or a newspaper. The page signals something about its content before the reader begins to decode the words on the page, and that initial visual signaling is, in fact, one piece of the document's content, significance, and rhetorical effort. This is not to say that first impressions—of paragraphing or cartooning—cannot be dead wrong; but first impressions are always part of the meaning-making effort.

11. The folks at the Norman Rockwell Museum (2012) are open to that idea, and in late 2012 they hosted "Heroes and Villains: The Comic Book Art of Alex Ross," the first gallery exhibition of Alex Ross's work (originally curated for a 2011 exhibition at the Andy Warhol Museum). The exhibition featured Ross's work alongside work by Norman Rockwell, Andrew Loomis, J.C. Leyendecker, and Andy Warhol, and the Rockwell Museum's promotional materials note Ross's reputation as "the Norman Rockwell of the Comics World."

12. It's like dancing about architecture. It's like singing about cake. It can be done, but it's not quite the building. It's not quite the cake. It is also why looking *at* a comic's form is so difficult.

13. Kidd uses no page numbers in this volume.

14. The unusual punctuation for McCloud's (1993/1994) quote is the end result of combining text from several sequenced comics panels.

15. Grossman (2004) on *The Complete Peanuts*: "The first volume (1950–52) confronts us afresh with what a brilliant, truly modern and totally weird idea it was to create a comic strip about a chronically depressed child" (p. 72). (*The Complete Peanuts* is a reprinting of all of Schulz's work, designed by Seth and scheduled to be published volume by volume over more than a decade.)

16. A metaphor for the concept: Water is water everywhere, but it takes on a meaning it would not otherwise have when it is part of a glass of water. The glass is a glass. The water is water. But they mean something different when they are a glass of water, together. Significance depends on concatenation.

17. I argue above with McCloud's (1993/1994) suggestion that certain line styles just intrinsically mean something, even when divorced from con-

text. I might similarly have argued with the way Will Eisner (1985/2008), in *Comics and Sequential Art*, suggested that certain visual moves will necessarily express certain meanings. See, for example, his "Micro-Dictionary of Gestures," which featured a number of poses, in silhouette, labeled as anger, fear, joy, and so on (p. 102). These would be useful for a practitioner trying to think about the significance of poses, for certain, yet they are not certain to mean, in every context, what Eisner said they mean, any more than a high angle shot, in cinema, always means that the featured character is in danger. Gunther Kress and Theo van Leeuwen (2006) ran a similar (and similarly worthwhile) risk of overgeneralizing when they explored the significance of visual composition. When they discussed the way new information tends to appear at the right, for example, they established some good, general rules (pp. 179ff), yet those rules will be of only limited value in decoding something like Chris Ware's most complex pages.

18. Ellsworth, in his other works, has produced some dazzlingly complicated images and pages, and it pays to look closely at his details. Yet, even at his most complex, Ellsworth's pages (like most comics pages compared to Ware) do not demand the same kind of close attention as Ware's do on first reading.

19. It is beyond the scope of "Perspicuous Objects," but the language of filmmaking and film studies—especially its grammar of camera angles and distances—can be useful for this sort of photo-based exercise.

20. Craig Stroupe modeled something like this in his "Visualizing English" (2000) and "Rhetoric of Irritation" (2004) articles, particularly in his reading of Gregory Ulmer's (1992) "Metaphoric Rocks" essay on Florida tourism.

ACKNOWLEDGMENTS

Scott Kolbo's art adds a depth to this webtext that I couldn't have achieved on my own, and he was extremely patient with my funny, random requests. (What about a "Heavy Charlie Brown?"; "Here's a link to a kid's Batman mask. What if Heavy Man wore that?"; "Make me a visual nonsequitur.") It's an honor that he agreed to collaborate with me on this project.

Lauren Pangborn, as an undergraduate double-major in computer science and art, agreed to take on the initial construction of the "Perspicuous Objects" webtext as a course project. She deserves credit for a lot of the best visual features of the site design, including the parallax scrolling. She and her mentor, **Brytton Bjorngaard**, gave me a basis to work from and helped me work through coding and design issues I couldn't have solved without them.

Bryan Lee O'Malley, Theo Ellsworth, and Nelson Kahikina each generously gave permission for the use of their art in "Perspicuous Objects."

Charles Andrews, Hannah Lee Crawford, Amy Evans, Shannon Kelly, Jacob Martin, Danny Parker, John Pell, Kaitlin Schmidt, Nicole Sheets, Doug Sugano, and Alex Wiese all willingly and helpfully provided annotated versions of "Sonic Medicine" (Kolbo, 2013b) for the People Reading 'Sonic Medicine' page.

Kiri Evanson, Haley Larson, and Andie Taylor, students of Scott Kolbo at Seattle Pacific University, all contributed images to the Teaching Comics, Teaching Writing section.

Sarah Berentson, Sam Cooper, Brittany Kirkpatrick, Maegan McClanahan, Alyssa Olds, Delsey Olds, Kayla Strahm, Kent Ueland, students I taught at Whitworth University, also contributed their work to Teaching Comics, Teaching Writing.

REFERENCES

Anderson, Sherwood. (1992). The book of the grotesque. *Winesburg, Ohio* (pp. 22–24). New York: Penguin. (Original work published 1919)

Barthes, Roland. (1996). The photographic message. *Image–Music–Text* (Stephen Heath, Trans.) (pp. 15–31). New York: Hill and Wang. (Original work published 1961)

Barthes, Roland. (1996). Rhetoric of the image. *Image–Music–Text* (Stephen Heath, Trans.) (pp. 32–51). New York: Hill and Wang. (Original work published 1964)

Bechdel, Alison. (2006). *Fun home: A family tragicomic.* New York: Mariner Books/Houghton Mifflin.

Bilsky, Brianne. (2012). *The page redux : American literature in the information age.* (Unpublished doctoral dissertation). Stanford University, Stanford, CA.

Crumb, R. (2009). *The book of Genesis illustrated.* New York: Norton.

Eisner, Will. (2008). *Comics and sequential art: Principles and practices from the legendary cartoonist.* Rev. ed. New York: Norton. (Original work published 1985)

Ellsworth, Theo. (2010). Norman Eight's left arm. In Neil Gaiman (Ed.), *The best American comics 2010* (pp. 229–243). New York: Houghton Mifflin Harcourt. (Reprinted from *Sleeper car*, by Theo Ellsworth, 2009, Jackson Heights, New York: Secret Acres)

Fitzgerald, F. Scott. (1995). *The great Gatsby.* New York: Scribner. (Original work published 1925)

Gaiman, Neil. (Ed.). (2010). *The best American comics 2010.* New York: Houghton Mifflin Harcourt.

Gilman, Susan Jane. (2009, October 19). R. Crumb's awesome, affecting take on Genesis. *NPR.org*. Retrieved August 20, 2013, from http://www.npr.org/2009/10/16/113802982/r-crumbs-awesome-affecting-take-on-genesis

Grossman, Lev. (2004, May 3). Books: Suffer the little children. *Time*, 72–73.

Hanson, Scot. (2009). A comics-format interview with Scott McCloud. *Kairos: A Journal of Rhetoric, Technology, and Pedagogy*, 14(1). Retrieved August 19, 2013, from http://kairos.technorhetoric.net/14.1/interviews/hanson/index.html

Heller, Jason. (2007, November 9). Interview: Bryan Lee O'Malley. *The Onion A.V. Club*. Retrieved August 20, 2013, from http://www.avclub.com/articles/bryan-lee-omalley,14171/

Howes, Franny. (2010). Imagining a multiplicity of visual rhetorical traditions: Comics lessons from rhetoric histories. *ImageTexT: Interdisciplinary Comics Studies*, 5(3). Retrieved August 19, 2013, from http://www.english.ufl.edu/imagetext/archives/v5_3/howes/

Kidd, Chip. (Ed.). (2001). *Peanuts: The art of Charles Schulz*. New York, NY, Pantheon.

Kolbo, Scott. (2009). The Heavy Man. *Ruminate Magazine*, 14. Retrieved April 20, 2014, from http://www.ruminatemagazine.com/issue-14-with-earnest-jest/

Kolbo, Scott. (2013a). Artist's statement. Retrieved April 20, 2014, from http://scottkolbo.com/About.html

Kolbo, Scott. (2013b). Sonic medicine broadside. *Scott Kolbo 2013 portfolio*. Retrieved April 20, 2014, from http://scottkolbo.com/Portfolio/2013%20Portfolio/pages/kolbo.2013.001.htm

Kress, Gunther, & van Leeuwen, Theo. (2006). *Reading images* (2nd ed.). New York: Routledge.

Kubrick, Stanley (Director & Producer). (1980). *The shining* [Motion picture]. USA: Warner Bros.

Lanham, Richard. (1993). *The electronic word: Democracy, technology, and the arts*. Chicago, IL: University of Chicago Press.

Losh, Elizabeth; Alexander, Jonathan; Cannon, Kevin; & Cannon, Zander. (2014). *Understanding rhetoric: A graphic guide to writing*. Boston, MA: Bedford/St. Martin's.

McCloud, Scott. (1994). *Understanding comics: The invisible art*. New York: HarperPerennial. (Original work published 1993)

Miller, Frank. (2002). *Batman: The dark knight returns*. New York: DC Comics.

Monahan, Dave (Producer, Director, & Writer). (2006). Camera angles. *Looking at movies* [DVD]. USA: Norton.

Munroe, Randall. (2014). *XKCD: A webcomic of romance, sarcasm, math, and language*. Retrieved January 1, 2014, from http://xkcd.com

Ngui, Marc. (2006). Poetry, design, and comics: An interview with Seth. *Carousel*, 19, 17–24.

Norman Rockwell Museum. (2012). About the Exhibition. *Heroes and villains: The comic book art of Alex Ross*. Retrieved August 20, 2013, from http://www.nrm.org/alexross/about/

O'Malley, Bryan Lee. (2010). *Scott Pilgrim vs. the universe* (Excerpt). In Neil Gaiman (Ed.), *The best American comics 2010* (pp. 259–269). New York: Houghton Mifflin Harcourt. (Reprinted from *Scott Pilgrim vs. the universe*, pp. 68–77, by Bryan Lee O'Malley, 2009, Portland, OR: Oni)

Peeters, Benoît (Director). (2004). *Chris Ware: The art of memory* [Motion picture]. France: Arte France.

Punch. (2014). Retrieved August 20, 2013 from http://punch.photoshelter.com/

Rice, Rich, & Ball, Cheryl. (2006). Reading the text: Remediating the text. *Kairos: A Journal of Rhetoric, Technology, and Pedagogy*, 10(2). Retrieved August 19, 2013, from http://kairos.technorhetoric.net/10.2/binder2.html?coverweb/riceball/index.html

Satrapi, Marjane. (2007). *The complete Persepolis*. New York: Pantheon. (Original work published 2000 and 2001)

Schulz, Charles. (2004) In Gary Groth (Ed.), *The Complete Peanuts* (Vol. 1). Design: Seth. Seattle, WA: Fantagraphics. (Original work published 1950)

Sorapure, Madeleine. (2006). Between modes: Assessing student new media compositions. *Kairos: A Journal of Rhetoric, Technology, and Pedagogy*, 10(2). Retrieved August 19, 2013, from http://kairos.technorhetoric.net/10.2/binder2.html?coverweb/sorapure/index.html

SparkNotes. (2013). *The great Gatsby*: Themes, motifs, and symbols. *SparkNotes*. Retrieved August 20, 2013, from http://www.sparknotes.com/lit/gatsby/themes.html

Spiegelman, Art. (1996). *The complete Maus*. New York: Penguin. (Original work published 1986 and 1991)

Staley, David. (2010). On violence against objects: A visual chord. *Kairos: A Journal of Rhetoric, Technology, and Pedagogy*, 14(2). Retrieved August 1, 2014, from http://kairos.technorhetoric.net/14.2/topoi/staley/index.htm

Stroupe, Craig. (2000). Visualizing English: Recognizing the hybrid literacy of visual and verbal authorship on the web. *College English*, 62(5), 607–632.

Stroupe, Craig. (2004). The rhetoric of irritation: Inappropriateness of visual/literate practice. In Charles A. Hill & Marguerite Helmers (Eds.), *Defining visual rhetorics* (pp. 243–258). Mahwah, NJ: Lawrence Erlbaum.

Tufte, Edward R. (1983). *The visual display of quantitative information*. Cheshire, CT: Graphics Press.

Ulmer, Gregory. (1992). Metaphoric rocks: A psychogeography of tourism and monumentality. In Christoph Gerozissis (Ed.), *The Florida landscape: Revisited*. Lakeland, FL: Polk Museum.

Waid, Mark, & Ross, Alex. (1998.) *Kingdom come*. New York: DC Comics. (Original work published 1996)

Ware, Chris. (2001). *Jimmy Corrigan, the smartest kid on earth*. London: Jonathan Cape. (Original work published 2000)

Ware, Chris. (2004a). Charles Schulz's preliminary drawings. In Chris Ware (Ed.), *McSweeney's quarterly concern 13: An assorted sampler of North American comic drawings, strips, and illustrated stories, &c* (pp. 66–71). New York: McSweeney's.

Ware, Chris. (2004b). Introduction. In Chris Ware (Ed.), *McSweeney's quarterly concern 13: An assorted sampler of North American comic drawings, strips, and illustrated stories, &c* (pp. 8–12). New York: McSweeney's.

Ware, Chris. (2010). *Acme novelty library #19* (Excerpt). In Neil Gaiman (Ed.), *The best American comics 2010* (pp. 126–148). New York: Houghton Mifflin Harcourt. (Reprinted from *Acme Novelty Library #19*, no page numbers, by Chris Ware, 2008, Malaysia: Tien Wah)

Watkins, Robert. (2008). Words are the ultimate abstraction. *Kairos: A Journal of Rhetoric, Technology, and Pedagogy*, 12(3). Retrieved August 20, 2013, from http://www.technorhetoric.net/12.3/topoi/watkins/index.html

Williams, Robin. (2008). *The non-designer's design book* (3rd ed.). Berkeley, CA: Peachpit.

Witek, Joseph. (2009). The arrow and the grid. In Jeet Heer & Kent Worcester (Eds.), *A comics studies reader* (pp. 149–156). Jackson, MI: University Press of Mississippi.

Wolk, Douglas. (2007). *Reading comics: How graphic novels work and what they mean*. Philadelphia, PA: De Capo.

IMAGE CREDITS & FAIR USE JUSTIFICATIONS

Scott Kolbo made most of the images included in this webtext. Scott's work can also be found online at ScottKolbo.com. Retrieved August 20, 2013, from http://www.ScottKolbo.com

Student Images. Kiri Evanson, Haley Larson, and Andie Taylor, students of Scott Kolbo at Seattle Pacific University, all contributed images to the Teaching Comics, Teaching Writing section. Sarah Berentson, Sam Cooper, Brittany Kirkpatrick, Maegan McClanahan, Alyssa Olds, Delsey Olds, Kayla Strahm, Kent Ueland, all students of mine at Whitworth University, also contributed to Teaching Comics, Teaching Writing.

Kate Beaton's "Great Gatsbys" strip is from her *Hark! A Vagrant* webcomic, and she has given general permission for the use of her work in academic contexts. "Great Gatsbys" retrieved August 20, 2013, from http://www.harkavagrant.com/?id=259

R. Crumb's 1969 Self Portrait, and the cover of his *Genesis*. **Fair Use Rationale:** The copyright for these images is most likely owned by either the publisher of Crumb's *Genesis* or R. Crumb himself. However, these low resolution (72 pixels/inch) images are unsuitable to use for high-end reproduction. The images are used to illustrate specific points in this academic webtext. The "Self Portrait," in particular, is significant as a representation both of the artist himself and of the artist's distinctive style. As the subject is protected by trademark or copyright, a free use alternative does not exist. Any other uses of these images may be copyright infringement.

Theo Ellsworth's drawings from "Norman Eight's Left Arm" are used by express permission of the artist, as is his "First Contact."

Nelson Kahikina's untitled painting is used by express permission of the artist. Also, I bought it from him when we were wide-eyed kids back at Ball State in Muncie, Indiana. It's from my personal collection of wonderful things.

"Frank Miller's Batman from *The Dark Knight Returns*," from *The Dark Knight Returns, #2* (April 1986); Frank Miller (Penciller), Klaus Janson (Inker), & Lynn Varley (Colourist). **Fair Use Rationale:** The copyright for this image from the interior of a comic book is most likely owned by either the publisher of the comic or the writer(s) and/or artist(s) who produced the comic in question. However. this low resolution (72 pixels/inch) panel from *The Dark Knight Returns, #2* is unsuitable to use for high-end reproduction. The image is used to illustrate a specific point in this academic webtext. As the subject is protected by trademark or copyright, a free use alternative does not exist. All DC Comics characters and the distinctive likeness(es) thereof are Trademarks & Copyright © 1938-2014 DC Comics, Inc. ALL RIGHTS RESERVED. Any other uses of this image may be copyright infringement.

Randall Munroe's *XKCD: A Webcomic of Romance, Sarcasm, Math, and Language* webcomics appear online under a Creative Commons license. "Fall Foliage" (2009, October 12), Retrieved August 20, 2013, from http://xkcd.com/648/; "Batman" (2012, January 16), Retrieved August 20, 2013, from http://xkcd.com/1004/

Bryan Lee O'Malley's drawings from *Scott Pilgrim vs. The Universe* are used by express permission of the artist.

"Alex Ross's Batman (Out of Costume) from *Kingdom Come*," from *Kingdom Come, #3* (July 1996); Alex Ross (Penciller, Inker, Colourist). **Fair Use Rationale:** The copyright for this image from the interior of a comic book is most likely owned by either the publisher of the comic or the writer(s) and/or artist(s) who produced the comic in question. However, this low resolution (72 pixels/inch) panel from *Kingdom Come, #3* is unsuitable to use for high-end reproduction. The image is used to illustrate a specific point in this academic webtext. As the subject is protected by trademark or copyright, a free use alternative does not exist. All DC Comics characters and the distinctive likeness(es) thereof are Trademarks & Copyright © 1938-2014 DC Comics, Inc. ALL RIGHTS RESERVED. Any other uses of this image may be copyright infringement.

Charles Schulz's first *Peanuts* strip, by Charles Schulz (1950, October 2). **Fair Use Rationale:** The copyright for this image from the interior of a comic book (*The Complete Peanuts*, Volume 1) is most likely owned by Peanuts Worldwide, LLC. However, this low resolution (72 pixels/inch) scan of the first *Peanuts* strip is unsuitable to use for high-end reproduction. Its appearance here at a low resolution does not limit the copyright owner's rights to sell the comic in any way. The image is used to illustrate a specific point in this academic webtext. The image is significant as the first appearance of a notable comic strip by a notable comics artist. It is the first published *Peanuts* strip, and the first appearance of the Charlie Brown character. As the subject is protected by trademark or copyright, a free use alternative does not exist. All Peanuts characters and the distinctive likeness(es) thereof are Trademarks & Copyright © 1950-2014 Peanuts Worldwide, LLC. ALL RIGHTS RESERVED. Any other uses of this image may be copyright infringement.

Images from Chris Ware's *Acme Novelty Library #19* (2008). **Fair Use Rationale:** The copyright images from the interior of this comic book (*Acme Novelty Library #19*) is most likely owned by either the publisher of the comic or Chris Ware himself. However, these low resolution (72 pixels/inch) scans of pages from the comic is unsuitable to use for high-end reproduction. Its appearance here at a low resolution does not limit the copyright owner's rights to sell the comic in any way. The image is used to illustrate specific points in this academic webtext. The image is significant as an illustration of Chris Ware's distinctive style. As the subject is protected by trademark or copyright, a free use alternative does not exist. Any other uses of this image may be copyright infringement.

Winesburg, Ohio Map by Harold Toksvig. The map of the town Winesburg, Ohio, from the first edition of Sherwood Anderson's *Winesburg, Ohio* was published in 1919 and is therefore in the public domain in the United States.

LITERACY IN
COMPOSITION STUDIES

Literacy in Composition Studies is on the Web at http://licsjournal.org

Literacy in Composition Studies is a refereed open access online journal sponsoring scholarly activity at the nexus of Literacy and Composition Studies. With *literacy* and *composition* as our keywords we denote practices that are deeply context-bound and always ideological and recognize the institutional, disciplinary, and historical contexts surrounding the range of writing courses offered at the college level. Literacy is often a metaphor for the ability to navigate systems, cultures, and situations. At its heart, literacy is linked to interpretation—to reading the social environment and engaging and remaking that environment through communication. Orienting a Composition Studies journal around literacy prompts us to analyze the connections and disconnections among writing, reading and interpretation, inviting us to examine the ways in which literacy constitutes writer, context, and act.

Understanding Computer Programming as a Literacy

In "Understanding Computer Programming as a Literacy" Annette Vee demonstrates what is at stake once we move beyond surface-level analogies between computer programming and literacy. The editors nominated Vee's piece because of the new and meaningful way Vee draws on literacy scholarship to direct our attention to the importance of the social contexts of programming as writing. Annette Vee was interviewed for—and "Understanding Computer Programming as Literacy" was linked to—in an article in *Mother Jones*.

6 Understanding Computer Programming as a Literacy

Annette Vee

Abstract: Since the 1960s, computer scientists and enthusiasts have paralleled computer programming to literacy, arguing it is a generalizable skill that should be more widely taught and held. Launching from that premise, this article leverages historical and social findings from literacy studies to frame computer programming as "computational literacy." I argue that programming and writing have followed similar historical trajectories as material technologies and explain how they are intertwined in contemporary composition environments. A concept of "computational literacy" helps us to better understand the social, technical and cultural dynamics of programming, but it also enriches our vision of twenty-first century composition.

> *We compare mass ability to read and write software with mass literacy, and predict equally pervasive changes to society. Hardware is now sufficiently fast and cheap to make mass computer education possible: the next big change will happen when most computer users have the knowledge and power to create and modify software.*—Guido van Rossum, from a 1999 DARPA grant application to support the teaching of computer programming.

In his DARPA grant application, Guido van Rossum, the designer of the Python programming language,[1] almost certainly hoped to tap into the positive cultural associations of literacy in order to secure funding for his project. While invoking "literacy" is rhetorically opportunistic because it is a trigger for funding, says Cynthia Selfe, the comparison between programming and literacy has been echoed so frequently that it is more than just rhetorical flourish. This parallel between programming and literacy began almost as soon as programmable computers were invented. Since the 1960s, computer enthusiasts have employed the concept of "literacy" to underscore the importance, flexibility, and power of writing for and with computers. Computer scientist Alan Perlis argued in 1961 that all undergraduates should be taught programming, just as they are taught writing in first year composition courses. At Dartmouth University in the 1960s, mathematicians John Kemeny and Thomas Kurtz designed the Basic programming language for students and non-specialists. Later, Kemeny wrote: "Someday computer literacy will be a condition for employment, possibly for survival, because the computer illiterate will be cut off from most sources of information" (216).

The parallel between programming and literacy has now made its way into popular commentary: Douglas Rushkoff says that learning programming gives people "access to the control panel of civilization" (1) and Marc Prensky argues "[a]s programming becomes more important, it will leave the back room and become a key skill and attribute of our top intellectual and social classes, just as reading and writing did in the past." Code.org, a non-profit started up in 2013 and supported by Mark Zuckerberg and Bill Gates, showcases on their website a litany of quotes from educators, technologists and public figures claiming that learning to code is a issue of "civil rights," the "4th literacy," and a way to "[c]ontrol your destiny, help your family, your community, and your country."

The promotion of computer programming as a type of writing appropriate for the masses is present in many more places than I have listed here.[2] But, unfortunately, when "literacy" is connected to programming, it is often in unsophisticated ways: literacy as limited to reading and writing text; literacy divorced from social or historical context; literacy as an unmitigated form of progress. Despite these anemic uses of the concept of literacy, however, I argue that these computer specialists are on to something. What does this persistent linking of programming to writing mean for literacy specialists?

Computer programming has a lot in common with textual literacy—historical trajectory, social shaping, affordances for communication, and connections to civic discourse. In this article, I argue that the refrain of "literacy" in reference to computer programming is not only apt because of these parallels, but that our definitions of literacy must shift to accommodate this new form of digital writing. Whether or not computer programming will be a mass literacy remains to be seen. But as code and computers have become central to our daily lives, programming has certainly become a powerful mode of written communication. Literacy studies may help us to better understand the social, technical and cultural dynamics of this important composition technology.

My approach to the link between programming and literacy moves beyond these brief, comparative gestures and leverages these historical and social findings from literacy studies:

- Historically, literacy became important when text became important to governance (Clanchy) and literacy became infrastructural when everyday life depended on it (Gilmore).
- Literacy is not simply the technical processes of reading and writing but is also shaped by social factors and ideologies (Street; diSessa).
- Which kinds of literate identities are available to people can shape how they learn literacy (Heath; Purcell-Gates; Banks).

These tenets of contemporary literacy studies provide useful perspectives on the ways that computer programming has become central to our communication practices over the last 60 years, and what that might mean for 21st century writing.

I first define and review claims about "computational literacy" and outline some salient features of code, including how it became a kind of writing. I then draw on precedents in the history of literacy in order to help us consider the future of literacy as intersecting with the writing of code. Next, I provide an overview of some of the social contexts of computer programming that bear a resemblance to the social contexts of literacy. Finally, I argue that literacy educators might want to help shape the values and approaches to programming because of programming's central role in our contemporary writing environments. Values espoused in computer science, while productive in professional contexts, are too narrow for a future where programming might become a generalized rather than specialized practice—a *literacy*. Given these stakes, I contend that literacy scholars must cultivate a deeper understanding of the complex relationship between textual and computational literacy.

COMPUTATIONAL LITERACY

Arguments for what we should consider a "literacy" have proliferated over the last two decades. Beyond the literacy of reading and writing text, scholars have proposed visual literacy (Kress and van Leeuwen), design literacy (Cope and Kalantzis), quantitative literacy (Wolfe), and video game literacy (Squire), among many other kinds of "literacies." Frameworks offer to help teachers manage the demand of integrating these new literacies into composition classes (Selber; Cope and Kalantzis; DeVoss, McKee and Selfe). This raft of new literacies and pedagogical approaches suggests the power of "literacy" as a descriptive term that implies urgency, but it also gestures toward the increasing complexity of contemporary information representation and communication. Fearing a dilution of literacy's explanatory power, Anne Frances Wysocki and Johndan Johnson-Eilola warned us against using the term to describe any and all systems of skills. Consequently, I want to be cautious about overusing the term *literacy* as well as piling on yet another skill considered essential to 21st century composition. So, what exactly is literacy? And why might it be useful to stretch its conceptual apparatus to describe computer programming?

Defining "computational literacy"

I define "literacy" as a human facility with a symbolic and infrastructural technology—such as a textual writing system—that can be used for creative, communicative and rhetorical purposes. Literacy enables people to represent their ideas in texts that can travel away from immediate, interpersonal contexts (to write) and also to interpret texts produced by others (to read).

The critical difference between a *literacy* and a system of technology-dependent communicative skills—what Andrea diSessa called a "material intelligence"—is in the positioning of the technologies that those skills employ: the technologies undergirding literacies are more central to life than those for material intelligences (5). While people *benefit* from material intelligences, they *need* literacies to intelligence to become a literacy, then, a material component or technology must first become central, or *infrastructural*, to a society's communication practices.[3] Next, the ability to interpret or compose with that technology must become central and widespread, which critically depends on the technology's ease of use (diSessa). In the case of textual literacy, the timing of these two events varies considerably with the society under discussion. In Britain, for instance, written texts became central to society centuries before the ability to read and write them did. And in more isolated societies, the ability to interpret texts may not yet be a literacy because it is not widespread or because texts are not important.

Extending diSessa's schema, I propose that: *a determination of whether or not a system of skills is a literacy depends on its societal context.* One can be skilled at leveraging specific technologies to communicate, but a *literacy* leverages *infrastructural* symbolic technologies and is necessary for everyday life. Although many material intelligences are dubbed "literacies," this definition of literacy narrows its field and allows the term to retain its potency.

Like textual literacy, computer programmingisalsoahuman facility witha symbolic technology—code—that allows people to represent and interpret ideas at a distance. Throughout much of the world, code is now infrastructural. Layered over and under the technology of writing, computer code now structures much of our contemporary communications, including word processing, email, the World Wide Web, social networking, digital video production, and mobile phone technology. Our employment, health records, and citizenship status— once recorded solely in text—are catalogued in computer code databases. But while the technology of code is now infrastructural to our society, the ability to read and write it is not yet widespread. By the definition above, then, computer programming is a *material intelligence*, not yet a *literacy*. However, as code becomes more infrastructural and as more people learn to write it, computer programming is looking more and more like a literacy. As I describe in more detail below, programming is leaving the exclusive domain of computer science and becoming more central to professions like journalism, biology, design—and, through the digital humanities, even the study of literature and history.

The way that programming is flowing out of the specialized domain of computer science and into other fields suggests that it is becoming a literacy—that is, a widely held ability to compose and interpret symbolic and communicative texts in an infrastructural medium. Computer science and education scholars have used several terms to describe the form of literacy that programming might represent, including "procedural literacy" (Bogost; Mateas), "computational literacy" (diSessa), and "computational thinking" (Wing). In the field of rhetoric and composition, the terms "source literacy" (Stolley) and "proceduracy" (Vee) have also been employed. Here, I use the term "computational literacy" because it links the theoretical apparatus of literacy with the computation that is central to computer programming; however, I depart from these scholars in several key ways.

"Procedural literacy," for Ian Bogost, "entails the ability to reconfigure concepts and rules to understand processes, not just on the computer, but in general" (245). In this definition, Bogost equates literacy more with reading than writing—the "understand[ing]" of processes rather than the representation of them. He ascribes the "authoring [of] arguments through processes" to the concept of "procedural rhetoric" (29). For Bogost, understanding the procedures of digital artifacts or recombining blocks of meaning can be procedural literacy, too—not just the learning of programming (257). I differ from Bogost in my greater interest in writing as central to literacy practices, but also in my focus on social contexts and programming itself. While I agree that digital artifacts such as games can offer a window on the processes that underwrite software, I believe this turn away from programming sidesteps the powerful social and historical dynamics of composing code.

In another discussion of "procedural literacy," computer scientist Michael Mateas focuses on new media practitioners and attends to code-writing more specifically; however, his treatment of "literacy" is brief and leaves room for more exploration. Jeannette Wing focuses on her field of computer science (CS) rather than programming per se, arguing that "computational thinking ... is a fundamental skill for everyone, not just for computer scientists" (33). She explicitly relates her concept of "computational thinking" to reading, writing and arithmetic. I differ from Wing in that I think CS is but one—albeit important—guide to thinking about this new form of potential literacy. As programming moves beyond CS, we must broaden the conceptual apparatus we use to understand its functions in the world.

Education scholar Andrea diSessa's model of the social, cognitive and material "pillars" that support literacy is compatible with my definition of computational literacy. His term and concept of "computational literacy" acknowledges the computer as the material basis of the literacy, yet also breaks with the skills-based term "computer literacy" that limited educational theory in the 1980s and 1990s. Computation is, of course, the core function of the computer. But as computation becomes more deeply embedded in digital devices, programming is diversifying beyond what we might traditionally consider a "computer." This literacy will change as computing changes, just as textual literacy has changed with the affordances of new inscription technologies. Therefore, we need a concept of programming-as-literacy that abstracts it away from its current technologies. I favor diSessa's term "computational literacy" in this discussion because it points to the underlying mechanisms of the literacy of computer programming—computation—and yet also gestures beyond any specific instrument.

Influenced by Bogost, Mateas, Wing and diSessa, I define "computational literacy" as the constellation of abilities to break a complex process down into small procedures and then express—or "write"—those procedures using the technology of code that may be "read" by a non-human entity such as a computer. In order to write code, a person must be able to express a process in terms and procedures that can be evaluated by recourse to explicit rules. In order to read code, a person must be able to translate those hyper-explicit directions into a working model of what the computer is doing. My use of the term "literacy" here is strategic; by the definition of "literacy" above, this ability is still just a "material intelligence." However, "literacy" is suggestive of the role that this ability will take in the future, it evokes the frequent parallels made between programming and writing, and it opens up access to theories of literacy.

Computational literacy builds on textual literacy because it entails textual writing and reading, but it is also quite distinct from textual literacy. In programming, one must build structures out of explicitly defined components. As Wittgenstein argued, human language works differently: not through explicit definitions, but through use and exchange. This property of language-in-use facilitates literature and human communication as we know it. But it also makes language susceptible to failure: as JL Austin reminds us, a reader or listener can have too little information or may not want to be persuaded, which renders an action in speech "infelicitous." The explicitness required in programming is a source of critique from scholars in the humanities because it forces discrete definitions (e.g., Haefner). But code's discreteness also enables one to build complex and chained procedures with the confidence that the computer will interpret them as precisely as one writes them. Code can scale up and perform the same operation millions of times in a row—a perfect perlocutionary affordance that is impossible in human language. For these reasons, computational literacy is not simply a literacy *practice*—a subset of textual literacy. It is instead a (potential) literacy on its own, with a complex relationship to textual literacy.

The evolution of programming from engineering to writing

Programming has a complex relationship with writing; it *is* writing, but its connection to the technology of code and computers[4] also distinguishes it from textual writing. At the same time, the writing system of code distinguishes computers from other infrastructural technologies, such as cars.[5] This merging of text and technology was not always the case for computers, however; the earliest mechanical and electrical computers relied on engineering rather than writing to program them. To name one example: Harvard's Mark I, completed in 1944, was programmed by switching circuits or physically plugging wires into vacuum tubes. Each new calculation required rewiring the machine, essentially making the computer a special purpose machine for each new situation. With the development in 1945 of the "stored program concept,"[6] the computer's program could be stored in memory in the same way that it stored its data. While simple in hindsight, this design was revelatory—it moved the concept of "programming" from physical engineering to symbolic representation. Programming became the manipulation of *code*, a symbolic text that was part of a writing system. In this way, computers became technologies of writing as well as engineering.

In subsequent years, control of the computer through code has continued to trend away from the materiality of the device and towards the abstraction of the processes that control it (Graham). To illustrate: each new revision of Digital Equipment Corporation's popular PDP computer in the 1960s required a new programming language because the hardware had changed, but by the 1990s, the Java programming language's "virtual machine" offered an effectively platform-independent programming environment. Over the last 60 years, many designers of programming languages have attempted to make more writer-friendly languages that increase the semantic value of code and release writers from needing to know details about the computer's hardware. Some important changes along this path in programming language design include: the use of words rather than numbers; automatic memory management; structured program organization; code comments; and the development of programming environments to enhance the legibility of code. As the syntax of computer code has grown to resemble human language (especially English), the requirements for precise expression in programming have been changed—but not eliminated.

These language developments have led many to believe that programming will soon be obsolete—that is, once the computer can respond to natural human language, there will be no need to write code. As early as 1961, Peter Elias claimed that training in programming languages would soon cease because "undergraduates will face the console with such a natural keyboard and such a natural language that there will be little left, if anything, to the teaching of programming. [At this point, we] should hope that it would have disappeared from the curricula of all but a moderate group of specialists" (qtd. in Perlis 203). At first glance, Elias's claim appears to be supported by modern interfaces such as the iPad's. Thousands of apps, menus, and interfaces promise to deliver the power of programming to those who do not know how to write code. Collectively, they suggest that we can drag and drop our way to problem solving in software.

Elias's argument is perhaps the most persuasive against the idea that programming will become a literacy: computer interfaces and languages will evolve to be so sophisticated that very few people will need to know how to compose code. But, at least so far, that hasn't happened. While programming languages have continued to evolve since 1961, they still have a long way to go to be "natural language." Highly-readable languages such as Python, Ruby and Javascript still require logical thinking and attention to explicit expressions of procedures. Stripped-down interfaces and templates such as the iPad's can accommodate only limited design choices. They are built for the consumption rather than production of software. This means that the programmers and software designers (or the companies they work for) still call the shots.

Thus, the historical trajectory of programming language development I've outlined here suggests that the central importance of programming is unlikely to dwindle with the increasing sophistication of computer languages. In fact, if the history of literacy is any model—and in the next section I argue it is—then the development of more accessible programming languages might *increase* rather than decrease pressures on computational literacy. More sophisticated and more widely distributed writing technologies actually seem to have put more pressure on individual literacy, ratcheting up the level of skill needed for one to be considered "literate" (diSessa; Brandt). As a technology supporting a "material intelligence" becomes easier to master, that ability becomes more important to the workplace and more integrated into everyday life; it becomes more like a *literacy*. In this same way, as computers have become more accessible and languages easier to learn and use, programming appears to be moving *away* from the domain of specialists—contrary to Elias's hope.

HISTORIES OF TEXTUAL AND COMPUTATIONAL LITERACY

As Guido van Rossum suggested in his application for funding from DARPA (quoted above), we may be able to understand some of the ways that programming will function in society by turning to the history of literacy. In this section, we visit two key transitional periods in the history of literacy: the first is *when texts became infrastructural* to people's everyday lives, and the second is *when literacy began*. During the first transition, which we visit medieval England to observe, texts became central to people's lives because they aided developing institutions—government bureaucracy, written contract law and the enterprise of publishing—to scale up and accommodate population and information growth. In the second transition—the long nineteenth century in the West—institutions such as the postal service, written tax bills, public signage and mass education were built on the assumption that a majority of citizens could read and write. Below, I provide a broad-brush comparative history of these transitions to illustrate what we might learn about the trajectory of computational literacy.

When texts became infrastructural

We can see a similar historical pattern in the ways that the literacy technologies of text and code have spread throughout society: first emerging from central government initiatives, they expanded to other large institutions and businesses, and finally rippled out to restructure domestic life. Although texts had been present for ages, during the 11th-13th centuries in England, texts became commonplace in government, social organization, and commerce, enacting a gradual but profound change in the everyday life of average people. Writing evolved from an occasional tool into a highly useful and infrastructural practice for the communication and recording of information. As historian Brian Stock writes, during this time "people began to live texts" (4). This transition put a premium on skills that were once possessed only by scribes and clerks, and those who could read and write began to acquire a special status apart from other craftspeople. In a similar way, American government initiatives in computational technology prefigured the use of computers in business and education and domestic life.

For both text and code, the shift into societal infrastructure began with the central government's struggle to manage a sharp increase in information. In 11th century England, the Norman invaders to England struggled to control a vast and strange land and, consequently, the new ruler ordered a census to be taken—what became known as the "Domesday Book." Although the Domesday Book never became a comprehensive census, it required local authorities to produce written text in response to the crown's request, which encouraged and forced the adoption of text to record information in the provinces (Clanchy). In the same way that the Domesday Book attempted to catalogue the newly conquered English population, the late eighteenth century American census helped to recruit soldiers and tax citizens of the new United States. But just as memory could no longer catalogue early medieval England, human-implemented writing and mathematics reached their limit in late nineteenth century America. As the United States grew in population and the census grew in ambition, a new way of tabulating information was required. Herman Hollerith, a Census Office mechanical engineer and statistician, devised an analog, electronic computer anticipating the 1890 census information. Variations of the "Hollerith machine" were used until the 1950 census, which was the first to use a digital computer—the UNIVAC I (U.S. Census Bureau). Once again, the census was an impetus for a more sophisticated literacy technology.

After these and other centralized initiatives, both text and code made their way into other large information management projects. The ENIAC computer, created to produce firing tables for Americans in World War II, was finished too late to help the war effort; however, this research paved the way for computers to be taken up by large-scale industries and institutions such as airlines and universities in the 1950s and 1960s (Campbell-Kelly and Aspray). In a similar way, the English government prompted the adoption of writing in the provinces through new laws and policies. By the late 13th century, land laws had begun to favor written contracts over personal witnesses. To participate in this new documentary society, individuals needed to be able to sign their names or use seals to indicate their acquiescence to the contracts (Clanchy). The spread of the texts from the central government to the provinces is echoed in the way that the programmers who cut their teeth on major government-funded software projects then circulated out into smaller industries, disseminating their knowledge of code writing further. Computer historian Martin Campbell-Kelly suggests that American central government projects were essentially training grounds for programmers and incubators for computer technology, both of which soon became central to areas such as banking, airline travel, and office work. We might be reminded of what historian Michael Clanchy calls the shift "from memory to written record"—in the 1960s and 1970s, the United States experienced a shift from written to *computational* record.

Not until the 1980s did computers became cheap enough for most people to become familiar with them. At this point, the tipping point with computers was reached, "so that people of ordinary skill would be able to use them and want to use them" (Campbell-Kelly and Aspray 231). Here we see the final stage in the spread of text and code—its expansion from centralized government and commerce into domestic life. Prior to the 11th century, when writing was only occasional and not powerfully central to business or legal transactions, the ability to read and write was a craft not so different from the ability to carve wood or make pottery; the concept of "literacy" did not exist because knowing how to read and write were specialized skills, or "material intelligences" in diSessa's terms. But as the technology of writing became infrastructural, that is, when it became central to institutions such as government and commerce, the ability to manipulate that technology could no longer be relegated to a specialized class. Laypeople living in England in the 13th century became familiar with the ways texts could record actions, could make promises, and could define their place in society (Clanchy). At this time, those who could not read text began to be recast as "illiterate" and power began to shift towards those who could.

In the same way that the technology of text began to impinge on everyday life in early medieval England, people's lives are now being circumscribed by code. To borrow Brian Stock's phrase, we have begun to "live code." Many centers of commercial and economic power are connected to code— the founders of Google, Microsoft and Facebook are just several of the people who have restructured our work and personal lives through their ability to program computers. In smaller but aggregately profound ways, our course management systems, mobile phone apps and productivity software shape the way we now teach, communicate, and even understand ourselves. Behind all of this software are programmers—people who do this work as a profession. Since the beginning of software, there have never been enough programmers to satisfy society's need for them. We are in a perpetual "software crisis," as computer historian Nathan Ensmenger notes, and as the recent Code.org promotional video reminds us. Although code is everywhere, few—too few—can read or write it. What if those few became many? What if we're not short *programmers*, but instead *people who can program*?

When literacy began

As computers and code become more central to how we are constructed as citizens and to our communication, education, and commercial practices, computer programming is moving from a specialized to a generalized skill, or from a "material intelligence" to a literacy. We can see parallels to this moment in the ways that reading and writing became central to employment and citizenship in the nineteenth and twentieth centuries.

Beginning in the late eighteenth century United States, the ability to write and especially to read grew more common as a result of mass literacy campaigns, the rhetoric of building the new republic, vigorous economic activity, and personal motivation. The dramatic rise in literacy levels in the nineteenth century was tied to the increased importance of texts—newspapers that catalogued both local and global events, almanacs that offered advice to farmers, letters circulated by the post, and accounts that kept track of debts. Texts became a central conduit for culture and knowledge among certain groups in nineteenth century rural Vermont, for example, such that "reading became a necessity of life," according to historian William Gilmore. The ubiquity of text also affected democratic governance as printed ballots and changes in contract law put pressure on literacy (Stevens). These shifts in governance helped to justify the campaigns for mass schooling in the nineteenth-century United States (Soltow and Stevens) and rhetorically framed the work of mothers to pass literacy on to their children as citizens of the new republic (Gilmore 49). In the nineteenth and twentieth centuries the need for literacy accelerated: as literacy became common, it became more necessary and therefore became even more prevalent. Historian Lawrence Cremin commented on this period: "in an expanding literacy environment, literacy tends to create a demand for more literacy" (493).

In this same way, as computer code and the ability to write it becomes more prevalent, it is becoming an essential skill in professions outside of computer science. Clay Shirky describes this general pressure of programming on employment as "downsourcing," or the generalizing of this formerly specialized practice: "though all the attention is going to outsourcing, there's also a lot of downsourcing going on, the movement of programming from a job description to a more widely practiced skill." Although the need to *use* software has permeated almost all job description lists, trailing behind it is the need to program computers. Currently, scientists, economists, statisticians, media producers or journalists who know something about programming can streamline or enrich their research and production.

The pressure of computational literacy on the field of journalism merits a more detailed sketch because it illustrates some of the most interesting ways that writing is permeated with programming. Composition for online journalism—whether on blogs or traditional news organizations' websites— now involves the integration of visual, audio and programmatic elements. Alongside traditional writing, we see interactive graphics and information displays on websites such as the *New York Times*, *OK Cupid* and *Five-Thirty-Eight*. These ubiquitous multimodal compositions are leading the way toward a code-based approach to conveying the news. The press industry, anxiously experiencing as well as reporting on their own state of affairs, has picked up on this shift in information conveyance from alphabetic text to code-based digital media. A writer for the Web magazine *Gawker* describes the "Rise of the Journalist Programmer:"

> Your typical professional blogger might juggle tasks requiring functional knowledge of HTML, Photoshop, video recording, video editing, video capture, podcasting, and CSS, all to complete tasks that used to be other people's problems, if they existed at all [...] Coding is the logical next step down this

road [...] You don't have to look far to see how programming can grow naturally out of writing. (Tate)

In other words, the tasks that once belonged to other people's job descriptions have now been "downsourced" into the daily routines of today's typical journalist. The compositions *Gawker* lists differ in their technical requirements (e.g., HTML is "mark-up language," rather than a full programming language) but they all press on computational skills in some way. Responding to this shift in the profession, journalism schools have focused attention on training a new crop of journalists to be writers of code as well as text. For example, Columbia University recently announced a new Master of Science Program in Computer Science and Journalism that would integrate their traditional journalism program with computer programming (van Buskirk) and Northwestern's Medill School of Journalism has been offering scholarships to master's students with computer science or programming backgrounds for several years (Medill).

Several recent examples of computational literacy leveraged for civic applications also illustrate how it is bumping into writing, as well as into the traditional concerns of literacy educators. In "crisis camps" set up in major world cities after the 2010 earthquake in Haiti, teams of programmers used geographical data available from Google maps and NASA to write a Craigslist-style database that would match donations with needs and help locate missing persons (American Public Media). Launched in 2009, the organization Code for America uses the Teach for America model to embed programmers within local city governments to help streamline some of their specific bureaucratic processes ("About," *Code for America*). At the community level, Michele Simmons and Jeff Grabill present a case study of a citizen action group's website and database that reveal the dangers of PCBs in a local water supply, which demonstrates how community groups can struggle and succeed with code-based technology to get their messages out. Because of its centrality to civic rhetoric, Simmons and Grabill claimed this kind of programmatic database manipulation can no longer be relegated to technical disciplines: "writing at and through complex computer interfaces is a required literacy for citizenship in the twenty-first century" (441). Most of these civic activities do not require extensive skills in programming, but still draw on basic concepts of database construction and code-based computation, what might be considered basic computational literacy. This knowledge allows a writer to know when and where programming is best integrated, even if the writer does not compose the program herself.

In these civic spaces, programming supports writing that can make a difference in the world. Perhaps for these reasons, justifications for teaching programming as a generalized skill are often pronounced along civic lines, rather than the moral and religious forces behind textual literacy campaigns in the nineteenth century. Bonnie Nardi argues that it is important for end users to know how to program "so that the many decisions a democratic society faces about the use of computers, including difficult issues of privacy, freedom of speech, and civil liberties, can be approached by ordinary citizens from a more knowledgeable standpoint" (3-4). In moments like the Congressional debates on anti-spam laws for email in the mid 1990s (Graham) and the proposed Stop Online Piracy Act (SOPA) of 2012, we saw what happens when United States public officials do not have the general knowledge Nardi argued for. In those cases, fundamental misunderstandings of computer programming obscured the terms of debate and nearly led to crippling or unenforceable laws.

In this burgeoning need for journalists, everyday citizens and public officials to know something about programming, we can see a layering of literacy technologies such as Deborah Brandt described in her ethnographic study of literacy practices in twentieth century America. Somewhat paradoxically, the increased importance of literacy accompanied an increased *complexity* of literacy. Brandt's interviewees saw their workplaces change to require more sophisticated written communication, extensive legal knowledge, and the ability to compose with computers. As new literacy technologies became more accessible and prevalent, they were folded into previously established communication practices, thereby ratcheting up the complexity of required literate practices. It appears that the increased ease of use of digital technologies has multiplied literacy again: programming is now in that complex workplace literacy mix.

COMPUTATIONAL LITERACY FROM THE PERSPECTIVE OF LITERACY STUDIES

The historical trajectory I outlined above suggests that literacy in the twenty-first century is an increasingly complex phenomenon that includes skills with both textual and computational technologies.

Although apps and templates can help individuals and organizations pursue their interests in software without needing to know how to program, the specific information and communication requirements of businesses as well as governmental and social organizations are pushing software to be more customized. Consumer-focused services are often not flexible enough to accommodate local concerns, such as those that Simmons and Grabill describe. Additionally, leaving important decisions about software design up to the small (and relatively homogenous) population who can program disempowers those who only consume rather than produce software.

While Harvey Graff's historical findings indicate that the possession of literacy does not, independent of other factors, empower people or lift them out of lower incomes or social classes, *illiteracy* can be an impediment in a world where text and literacy is infrastructural to everyday life. In the same way, it appears that people who are not *computationally literate* must, in growing numbers of cases, rely on others to help them navigate their professional, civic and personal lives. In computation as well as text, the illiterate person is "less the maker of his destiny than the literate person," as Edward Stevens observes about colonial New England (64). As more communication, social organization, government functions and commerce are being conducted through code—and as computational literacy becomes more infrastructural—the power balance is once again shifting toward those who are skilled in this new literacy technology.

This shifting power balance should alert socially attuned educators to the importance of integrating computational literacy practices into their writing and rhetoric courses. These courses are already overburdened by teaching the surfeit of literacies I mentioned at the beginning of this article. However, we can begin to think about how our writing classes might incorporate computational understanding and expression. A specific design for how this could work is beyond the scope of this article, but web design and programming in composition classes is a good start. To be clear, teaching some aspects of computational literacy in composition classes does not mean that English departments should be teaching computer science. Just as computer scientists often stress that programming is just one aspect of their discipline (Wing; Denning), we can think of computer science as an important but incomplete perspective on computational literacy. Below, I offer some perspectives on computational literacy as a social phenomenon *outside* of computer science and argue that literacy educators can provide valuable pedagogical perspectives on programming.

Social aspects of computational literacy

Emphasizing the social factors of literacy that intersect with and exceed its technological affordances, Brian Street writes: "literacy, of course, is more than just the 'technology' in which it is manifest. No one material feature serves to define literacy itself. It is a social process, in which particular socially constructed technologies are used within particular institutional frameworks for specific social purposes" (97). Street's "ideological model" synthesizes the technological and social aspects of literacy and reminds us of their complex interactions. This techno-social lens from literacy studies can help us understand the material affordances of code and computers as well as the ways that programming's social values, contexts and communities shape practices of computational literacy and the identities associated with those practices.

Because the computer is a technological object and because programming requires explicitness in a way that human communication generally does not, computer programming is often portrayed as asocial, or purely technological. As work in the history of technology has demonstrated, however, computers are social technologies in their design and deployment (Ensmenger; Campbell-Kelly and Aspray). Programming languages are written by people, and programmers write code not only for computers but also for other programmers. Although code is *often* written *primarily* for its function (as read by the computer) rather than its aesthetic value (as read by other programmers), the dual audiences for code introduce a tension in values surrounding its composition. The computer requires precise expression, but human programmers need legibility and want aesthetically pleasing code. Emphasizing the aesthetic value of code for human audiences, the influential computer scientist Donald Knuth famously conceived of "literate programming," arguing "[l]iterature of the program genre is performable by machines, but that is not its main purpose. The computer programs that are truly beautiful, useful and profitable must be readable by people" (ix). Knuth's concept of "literate programming" is only possible because programming is done in social spaces with human audiences.

To understand some of these social influences on programming, we must disentangle them from the real and technical demands of the computer. Strictures such as how to control the program flow, how to name variables, how long functions should be, and how much code to write per line are established socially to help programmers work together, especially in very large teams, but they matter little to the computer. In other words, there are ways of organizing code that the computer understands perfectly well, but that are eschewed by certain human value systems in programming. Denigrated aspects of code are sometimes described with the affective term "code smells" (Atwood,

"Code Smells"), which highlights the tension between code's human and computer audiences.[7]

We might think of the fallacy of right-or-wrong code as similar to that of literacy's mechanistic misrepresentation—that reading and writing are simply a matter of proper grammar and accurate decoding. Indeed, textual writing generally requires some adherence to standards in order to facilitate its reading. While concision, clear transitions and active verbs may constitute good style in certain contexts for writing, these values are socially shaped (Prendergast). They depend greatly on genre, audience and context, and a description of writing as *merely* adherence to standards ignores the complex social spaces in which it is produced and interpreted. Programming requires adherence to more explicit standards than textual writing, but also cannot be reduced to them or removed from its social contexts. For example, a programmer working by himself on a smallscale app need not attend to "proper" commenting, code formatting and variable naming, just as Strunk and White-defined "proper grammar" is often inappropriate for non-academic or creative contexts. In other words, value systems for code can fail when applied outside of the social contexts in which they developed.

As programming becomes more relevant to fields outside of computer science and software engineering, we can see the unfolding of this tension between the values for code written in those traditional contexts and values for code written outside of them. In the sciences, where code and algorithms have enabled researchers to process massive and complex datasets, this tension of what is "proper code" is quite marked. For example, a recent *Scientific American* story reported that code is not being released along with the rest of the methods used in scientific experiments, in part because scientists may be "embarrassed by the 'ugly' code they write for their own research" (Hsu). A discussion of the article on *Hacker News*, a popular online forum for programmers, encapsulates some of the key tensions in applying software engineering values to scientific code. As one commenter argued, the context for which code is written matters: "There's a huge difference between the disposable one-off code produced by a scientist trying to test a hypothesis, and production code produced by an engineer to serve in a commercial capacity" (jordanb, *Hacker News*). Code that might be fine for a one-off experiment—that contains, say, some overly-long functions, duplication, or other kinds of "code smells"—might not be appropriate for commercial software that is, say, composed by a large team of programmers or maintained for decades across multiple operating systems. Although dominant values of programming may denigrate it, it could be just fine for a scientific context..

The practice of "obfuscating" code—rendering code illegible to humans while still parsable to the computer—also highlights the values that different contexts bring to bear on programming. Programmers will obfuscate code when they want to release working software but do not want people to read (and potentially copy or modify) its code. Obfuscation can also be used in playful ways, such as in the "Underhanded C Contest," where people write code that is deliberately deceptive—it appears (to humans) to perform one function, but actually (to the computer) performs another (Mateas and Montfort). Underhanded C contests have asked programmers to write code that misroutes luggage or mis-tallies votes while appearing to verify them. Another context for obfuscated code is in "weird languages," which are often meant to comment ironically on language design and implementation. Although they could technically be used to write software, these languages are intended more for play than use. For example, the aptly named Brainfuck language plays with obfuscation of code by taking away white space and using only a few symbolic characters rather than letters (Mateas and Montfort). If we think about code as written in social contexts and for other programmers, it makes sense that code can be creative, even playful, for the benefit of that human audience. Obfuscated code and weird languages suggest that the aesthetic value of programming varies with its context—just as it does for writing.

The specific forms and history of programming language technologies shape the value and uses of computational literacy, just as

Street claims they do for textual literacy (96). Indeed, as Mateas and Montfort argue regarding obfuscated and weird languages, their inherent "play refutes the idea that the programmer's task is automatic, value-neutral, and disconnected from the meanings of words in the world." This connection of code to "words in the world" suggests that its attendant literacy is imbricated in the world where programmers learn and practice their craft. Put another way, computational literacy encompasses not only the technical skills of reading and writing code, but is best understood as coupled with its social contexts.

Literate identities

Because reading is an interpretive act that draws on knowledge acquired in specific social contexts, Street argues, "the acquisition of literacy is, in fact, a socialisation process rather than a technical process" (180). In Street's ideological model of literacy, someone who has acquired literacy in one context may not be functionally literate in another context because literacy cannot be extricated from its ideology. According to Shirley Brice Heath's canonical ethnographic study of literacy, who literacy-learners see using and valuing literacy can impact the way they take it up, or if they take it up. Children growing up in environments where text is absent and literacy is marginalized have few ways to assimilate literacy into their lives, as suggested by Victoria Purcell-Gates's work with cycles of low literacy.

The impact of available identities on the development of literacy practices also appears to hold true for computational literacy. As demonstrated in the examples above about scientific and creative programming, the identities that computer science makes available for programming are too limited if it is to become computational literacy—a generalized rather than specialized skill. Problematically, historically disadvantaged groups in the domain of textual literacy are also finding themselves disadvantaged in computational literacy. For instance, in the 2011 account from the Bureau of Labor Statistics, only 20.8% of computer programmers were women.[8] Although programming was initially a female dominated field, it tipped toward male domination when it became more powerful and complex (Ensmenger), and has resisted a more general trend of increased participation rates of women evidenced in previously male-dominated fields such as law and medicine. Because programming is a potentially generalizable and powerful form of writing, who programs and who is computationally literate should be a concern of literacy educators.

Stereotypes for programmers appear to have been baked into the profession early on: Ensmenger notes that personality profiling was used in the 1960s to select for "anti-social, mathematically inclined male" programmers (79). Although it is no longer practiced explicitly, this personality profiling still influences the perception of programmers as stereotypically white, male, and socially awkward (Ensmenger). Even recent publications by professional organizations such as the ACM (Association for Computing Machinery) feature sexist images: a stylized illustration accompanying Peter Denning's 2008 article about the many facets of computer science (CS) shows five (seemingly white) males representing programming, engineering, math, etc. alongside one (seemingly white) female representing a computer *user*. High-profile sexism exhibited at tech conferences and fast-paced start-ups now appears to be compounding the problem—although countless men and women in tech have spoken out against it (Raja). The recent use of the term "brogrammer," associated with start-up culture only partially in jest, suggests a new kind of identity for programmers—as "bros," or, young, male, highly social and risk-taking fratboys (Raja). The so-called "rise of the brogrammer" suggests that programming *can* accommodate a broader set of identities, but these identities are still severely limited.

In addition to the narrow and lingering stereotypes of computer programmers, confining programming to its profession can constrain the styles and contexts of "acceptable" programming and discourage new learners. We can see this in the discussion about "ugly" scientific code above. The conflation of professional programming with the more generalized skill of programming is also evident in such recent critiques of the "learn to code" movement as Jeff Atwood's. Atwood, the co-founder of the popular online programming forum *Stack Overflow* and a prominent blogger, claimed we do not need a new crop of people who think they can code professional software —people such as New York City Mayor Bloomberg, who pledged in 2012 to participate in Codecademy's weekly learn-to-code emails: "To those who argue programming is an essential skill we should be teaching our children, right up there with reading, writing, and arithmetic: **can you explain to me how Michael Bloomberg would be better at his day to day job of leading the largest city in the USA if he woke up one**

morning as a crack Java coder?" ("Please Don't," emphasis in original)[9]. As several of Atwood's commenters pointed out, his argument presents programming as a tool only for the profession, and discounts the potential benefits of knowing aspects of programming in other professions or activities. In paradigms such as Atwood's, programming would be necessarily and problematically limited to the types of people already welcome in a professional context.

In contrast to these narrow perceptions of who should program, a concept of computational literacy teaches us that just as writing can be useful to those who are not professional writers, programming can be useful and enriching to many different groups of people. We can think about what Adam Banks calls "transformative access" to computational literacy—the access that allows people "*to both* change the interfaces of that system *and* fundamentally change the codes that determine how the system works" (45, emphasis in original). Changing the "interface" of programming might entail more widespread education of programming, perhaps even in our composition classes.

But changing "how the system works" would move beyond material access to education and into a critical examination of the ideologies embedded in that education. Programming as defined by computer science or software engineering is bound to echo the ideologies of those contexts. Peeling programming away from these ideologies reveals that the webmaster, gamemaker, tinkerer, scientist and citizen activist can also benefit from programming as a means to achieve their goals. Countless recent initiatives at colleges such as Harvey Mudd (Alvarado and Dodds), websites such as Codecademy.com and Code.org, and local organizations like Girl Develop It aim to teach programming in new contexts, as a more generalized skill than CS courses normally encourage. We might say they are all working toward "transformative access" (Banks) to programming. One major payoff of a concept of computational literacy is that it frames programming as a literacy practice with diverse applications rather than as a profession defined by a limited set of values.

CONCLUSION

Just as writing gradually worked its way into government and social infrastructures in the West, programming is moving into many of the domains previously dominated by writing. Similar patterns in these trajectories suggest that programming could eventually become the foundation of a new, computational literacy. But regardless of programming's future path, it is already a material intelligence and a powerful form of composition. Because of code's central role in governance, education, business and citizenship—because code is infrastructural—its writing practices concern literacy educators. This is the reactionary argument for paying attention to computational literacy—as Douglas Rushkoff says, "program or be programmed." This is also the logic behind some of the calls to teach programming to elementary school kids: my learning the Logo programming language in the United States in the 1980s was supposed to help us beat those Russians, just as programmer training in the 1960s had successfully done.

But a concept of computational literacy offers us more than Cold War technology training strategies. It also helps us to understand the ways in which composition is changing. Programming is not replacing writing, but is rather interlacing with it, augmenting it. Programming plays a supportive role in traditional writing (including for this essay, composed on a computer with word processing software), and facilitates new forms of written communication such as tweets, texts, Facebook posts, emails and instant messages. Examples I have named above from journalism, literary work and civic applications demonstrate some of the changes this new hybrid writing technology has brought. Looking at the writing of code through a concept of computational literacy allows us to focus on the writing practices that undergird our complex, contemporary composition environments. It enables us to more critically engage with our software because it highlights the people who write it as well as the historical patterns that precede it.

Finally, understanding computer programming as computational literacy leads the way forward towards a more comprehensive and inclusive writing pedagogy. It is important to widen access to programming because of its power and diversity of applications, which means that programming cannot be relegated to the exclusive domain of computer science. It is also important to open up our concepts of writing to include programming. Together, images, sound and other modes of composition have already shifted the way we communicate and how we can express and process information. Consequently, literacy scholars have added these modes of writing to our concept of literacy, and have debated how to incorporate them in composition classrooms. But programming enables *all* forms of digital composition. We must now shift our models of literacy to account for it.[10]

NOTES

1. Python is a popular language engineered to be broadly accessible and used often in education.

2. For a more comprehensive list, see my annotated bibliography, available here: http://www.scribd.com/ doc/96309313/ Computer-Programming-and-Literacy-An-Annotated-Bibliography

3. Here, I am drawing on Susan Leigh Star's framework, which describes infrastructure as embedded, transparent until it breaks down, has broad reach, is shaped by standards, and is difficult to change (381-2).

4. When I write "computers," I mean the general class of machines that can perform computations, not simply mainframes, laptops, etc.

5. Most modern cars contain computers, so, in some ways, I have artificially separated these two technologies. However, the car seems to be the most commonly invoked infrastructural technology to refute the unique importance of computers, and so it is the technology I choose to engage with here.

6. This is sometimes referred to as "von Neumann architecture," after John von Neumann, a member of the ENIAC team at the University of Pennsylvania, and the named author of the groundbreaking "First Draft of a Report on the EDVAC." Because the origin of this design was collaborative and complicated, I do not refer to it as "von Neumann architecture" here.

7. Another example of commonly denigrated code is the *goto* statement, famously derided and "considered harmful" by computer scientist Edsger Dijkstra because it allows programs to jump out of sequence ad hoc and therefore violates rules of clean program flow. Although few modern languages still technically support the goto statement's ability to circumvent formal program structure, it remains a touchstone for this clash in values.

8. In software development and applications, 19% were women, and in web development, 38.6% were women.

9. Atwood's invocation of Java—the language that dominates professional software contexts—is another indication of his assumptions that the "'everyone should learn programming' meme," as he calls it, is referring to professional and not casual programming contexts.

10. I would like to thank Tim Laquintano, Kate Vieira, Deborah Brandt, Steve Carr, Don Bialostosky, Michael Bernard-Donals and the anonymous peer reviewers for helpful comments on drafts of this article.

WORKS CITED

"About." *Code for America*. Code for America Labs, Inc., n.d. Web. 30 Jun. 2012.

Alvarado, Christine, and Zachary Dodds. "Women in CS: An Evaluation of Three Promising Practices." *Proceedings of the 41st ACM Technical Symposium on Computer Science Education*, 2010. 57–61. Web. ACM Digital Library. 30 Jun. 2012.

American Public Media. "Devising Aid Programs on Their Laptops." *Marketplace*. 18 Jan. 2010. Web. 31 Jan. 2010.

Atwood, Jeff. "Code Smells" *Coding Horror Blog*. 18 May 2006. Web. 20 Jun. 2012.

-----. "Please Don't Learn to Code." *Coding Horror Blog*. 15 May 2012. Web. 15 May 2012.

Austin, John Langshaw. *How to Do Things with Words*. Cambridge: Harvard UP, 1962. Print.

Banks, Adam. *Race, Rhetoric, and Technology*. Mahwah: Lawrence Erlbaum, 2006. Print.

Bogost, Ian. *Persuasive Games: The Expressive Power of Videogames*. Cambridge: MIT P, 2007. Print.

Brandt, Deborah. *Literacy in American Lives*. Cambridge, UK: Cambridge UP, 2001. Print.

Bureau of Labor Statistics, United States Department of Labor. "Labor Force Statistics from the Current Population Survey." 1 Mar. 2012. Web. 26 Jun. 2012. <http://www.bls.gov/cps/cpsaat11.htm>

Campbell-Kelly, Martin. *From Airline Reservations to Sonic the Hedgehog: A History of the Software Industry*. Cambridge: MIT P, 2004. Print.

Campbell-Kelly, Martin, and William Aspray. *Computer: A History of the Information Machine*. The Sloan Technology Series. 2nd ed. Boulder: Westview P, 2004. Print.

Clanchy, Michael. *From Memory to Written Record: England 1066-1307.* Malden: Blackwell Publishing, 1993. Print.

Code.org. Code.org. n.d. Web. 7 April 2013. <http://www.code.org/>

Codecademy. Codecademy. n.d. Web. 7 April 2013. <http://www.codecademy.com>

Cope, Bill, and Mary Kalantzis, eds. *Multiliteracies: Literacy Learning and the Design of Social Futures*. London: Routledge, 2000. Print.

Cremin, Lawrence. *American Education: The National Experience, 1783-1876*. New York: Harper and Row, 1982. Print.

Denning, Peter J. "The Profession of IT: Voices of Computing." *Communications of the ACM* 51.8 (2008): 19-21. *ACM Digital Portal*. Web. 10 Apr. 2013.

DeVoss, Danielle Nicole, Heidi A. McKee, and Richard (Dickie) Selfe. *Technological Ecologies and Sustainability*. Logan: Computers and Composition Digital P. 2009. Web. 17 Jul. 2013.

Dijkstra, Edsger. "Go to Statement Considered Harmful." *Communications of the ACM* 11.3 (1968): 147-48. *ACM Digital Portal*. Web. 23 Apr. 2010.

diSessa, Andrea. *Changing Minds: Computers, Learning and Literacy*. Cambridge: MIT P, 2000. Print.

Ensmenger, Nathan. *The Computer Boys Take Over: Computers, Programmers, and the Politics of Technical Expertise*. Cambridge: MIT P, 2010. Print.

Gilmore, William J. *Reading Becomes a Necessity of Life: Material and Cultural Life in Rural New England, 1780-1835*. Knoxville: U of Tennessee P, 1989. Print.

Graff, Harvey. *The Literacy Myth: Cultural Integration and Social Structure in the Nineteenth Century*. 1979. New Brunswick: Transaction Publishers, 1991. Print.

Graham, Paul. *Hackers & Painters: Big Ideas from the Computer Age*. Sebastopol: O'Reilly, 2004. Print.

Hacker News. "Secret Computer Code Threatens Science (scientificamerican)" 13 Apr. 2012. Web. 17 Apr. 2012. < https://news.ycombinator.com/item?id=3844910>

Haefner, Joel. "The Politics of the Code." *Computers and Composition* 16.3 (1999): 325-39. *ScienceDirect*. Web. 19 Aug. 2008.

Heath, Shirley Brice. *Ways with Words: Language, Life and Work in Communities and Classroom*. New York: Cambridge UP, 1983. Print.

Hsu, Jeremy, and Innovation News Daily. "Secret Computer Code Threatens Science." *Scientific American*. Scientific American, Inc.,13 Apr. 2012. Web. 17 Apr. 2012.

Kemeny, John. "The Case for Computer Literacy." *Daedalus* 112.2 (1983): 211-30. *JStor*. Web. 13 Jan. 2013.

Knuth, Donald. *Literate Programming*. CSLI Lecture Notes. United States: Center for the Study of Language and Information, 1992. Print.

Kress, Gunther, and Theo van Leeuwen. *Reading Images: The Grammar of Visual Design*. 1996. 2nd ed. London: Routledge, 2006. Print.

Mateas, Michael. "Procedural Literacy: Educating the New Media Practitioner." *Future of Games, Simulations and Interactive Media in Learning Contexts*. Spec. issue of *On The Horizon* 13.1 (2005): 110-11. Print.

Mateas, Michael, and Nick Montfort. "A Box, Darkly: Obfuscation, Weird Languages, and Code Aesthetics." *Proceedings of the 6th Digital Arts and Culture Conference, IT University of Copenhagen* (2005): 144-53. *NickM.com*. Web. 1 Mar. 2009.

Medill School of Journalism. "Admissions." Northwestern U, n.d. Web. 24 Apr. 2010.

Nardi, Bonnie. *A Small Matter of Programming: Perspectives on End User Computing*. Cambridge: MIT P, 1993. Print.

Perlis, Alan. "The Computer and the University." *Computers and the World of the Future*. Ed. Martin Greenberger. Cambridge: MIT P, 1964. Print.

Prendergast, Catherine. "The Fighting Style: Reading the Unabomber's Strunk and White." *College English* 71.1 (2009): 10-28. Print.

Prensky, Marc. "Programming is the New Literacy." *Edutopia*. 2008. Web. 23 Apr. 2010. <http://www.edutopia. org/literacy-computer-programming>

Purcell-Gates, Victoria. *Other People's Words: The Cycle of Low Literacy*. 1995. First paperback ed. Cambridge: Harvard UP, 1997. Print.

Raja, Tasneem. "'Gangbang Interviews' and 'Bikini Shots': Silicon Valley's Brogrammer Problem." *Mother Jones* (26 Apr. 2012). Web. 18 Jun. 2012.

Rushkoff, Douglas. *Program or Be Programmed: Ten Commands for a Digital Age*. N.p.: OR Books, 2010. Kindle file.

Selber, Stuart A. *Multiliteracies for a Digital Age*. Carbondale: Southern Illinois UP, 2004. Print. Studies in Writing and Rhetoric Series.

Selfe, Cynthia. *Technology and Literacy in the 21st Century: The Importance of Paying Attention*. Carbondale: Southern Illinois UP, 1999. Print. Studies in Writing and Rhetoric Series.

Shirky, Clay. "Situated Software." *Clay Shirky's Writings about the Internet*. 2004. Web. 15 Jan 2010.

Simmons, W. Michelle, and Jeffrey Grabill. "Toward a Civic Rhetoric for Technologically and Scientifically Complex Places: Invention, Performance, and Participation." *College Composition and Communication* 58.3 (2007): 419-48. Print.

Soltow, Lee and Edward Stevens. *The Rise of Literacy and the Common School in the United States: A Socioeconomic Analysis to 1870*. Chicago: U of Chicago P, 1981. Print.

Squire, Kurt D. "Video Game Literacy: A Literacy of Expertise." *Handbook of Research on New Literacies*. Eds. Julie Coiro, Michele Knobel, Colin Lankshear, and Donald J. Leu. New York: Lawrence Erlbaum, 2008. 635-70. Print.

Star, Susan Leigh. "The Ethnography of Infrastructure." *American Behavioral Scientist* 43.3 (1999): 377–91. *Sage Journals*. Web. 3 Jul. 2013.

Stevens, Edward W., Jr. *Literacy, Law, and Social Order*. DeKalb: Northern Illinois UP, 1988. Print.

Stock, Brian. *The Implications of Literacy*. Princeton: Princeton UP, 1983. Print.

Stolley, Karl. "Source Literacy: A Vision of Craft." *Enculturation*. 10 Oct. 2012. Web. 11 Apr. 2013. < http://enculturation.gmu.edu/node/5271>

Street, Brian. *Literacy in Theory and Practice*. Cambridge, UK: Cambridge UP, 1984. Print.

Tate, Ryan. "Hack to Hacker: Rise of the Journalist-Programmer." *Gawker: Valleywag.* 14 Jan. 2010. Web. 20 Jan. 2010.

U.S. Census Bureau. "History: Overview," "History: Univac I." 10 Dec. 2009. Web. 5 Jan. 2010.

van Buskirk, Eliot. "Will Columbia-Trained, Code-Savvy Journalists Bridge the Media/Tech Divide?" *Wired.* 7 Apr. 2010. Web. 20 Apr. 2010.

van Rossum, Guido. "Computer Programming for Everybody (Revised Proposal)." Corporation for National Research Initiatives, Jul 1999. Web. 23 Apr. 2010.

Vee, Annette. "Ideologies of a New Mass Literacy." Conference on College Composition and Communication Convention. The Riviera, Las Vegas. 14 Mar. 2013. Address.

Wing, Jeannette. "Computational Thinking." *Communications of the ACM* 49.3 (2006): 33-35. ACM Digital Library. Web. 7 Apr. 2007.

Wittgenstein, Ludwig. *Philosophical Investigations.* Trans. G.E.M. Anscombe. 2nd ed. Cambridge: Blackwell, 1997. Print.

Wolfe, Joanna. "Rhetorical Numbers: A Case for Quantitative Writing in the Composition Classroom." *College Composition and Communication* 61.3 (2010): 452-75. Print.

Wysocki, Anne Frances, and Johndan Johnson-Eilola. "Blinded by the Letter: Why Are We Using Literacy as a Metaphor for Everything Else?" *Passions, Pedagogies, and Twenty-First Century Technologies.* Ed. Gail Hawisher and Cynthia Selfe. Logan: Utah State UP, 1999. 349-68. Print.

PEDAGOGY

Pedagogy is on the Web at
http://pedagogy.dukejournals.org/

Pedagogy seeks to create a new discourse surrounding teaching in English studies by fusing theoretical approaches and practical realities. As a journal devoted exclusively to pedagogical issues, it is intended as a forum for critical reflection as well as a site for spirited and informed debate from a multiplicity of positions and perspectives. The journal strives to reverse the long-standing marginalization of teaching and the scholarship produced around it and instead to assert the centrality of teaching to our work as scholars and professionals.

Fighting Words: Instrumentalism, Pragmatism, and the Necessity of Politics in Composition

In Kurt Spellmeyer's commentary, entitled "Fighting Words: Instrumentalism, Pragmatism, and the Necessity of Politics in Composition," he argues that in a university increasingly shaped by commercial interests promoting "skills" at the expense of knowledge, composition has the opportunity to cooperate with the new order. But the field might choose to play an opposing role, revitalizing the humanities by placing politics where it belongs—at the very center of learning.

7 Fighting Words: Instrumentalism, Pragmatism, and the Necessity of Politics in Composition

Kurt Spellmeyer

Composition has come into its own just as the university is witnessing a period of unprecedented change that keeps pushing the humanities closer and closer to the margins. One sign of the shift under way is the decline of literary studies and the corresponding growth of a curriculum devoted to the practice of writing. This might be interpreted as yet another step in the relentless ascendancy of an instrumentalist paradigm that devalues "content" for the sake of "skills." Many in university management look on these changes approvingly, but scholars in the field of writing are likely to feel more ambivalent. After all, the history of their discipline can be understood as one long debate about whether writing properly belongs within a literary-critical tradition or whether it should reinvent itself as something like a social science, one that might be more at ease with an increasingly vocation-driven university. The storied history of tension between writing programs and English departments has only made the debate more complex. Time will decide the outcome, one assumes, but if writing studies elects to remain within the humanities, it will need to resist the pressure to assume a stance of professional detachment. In the context of this pressure, Gerald Graff's injunction "Teach the conflicts" (1992: 3 – 15) has a special salience. Instead of undermining our legitimacy, as Stanley Fish (2008: esp. 10 – 59) has charged, a renewed commitment to politics is the only way that writing studies can avoid losing its bearings as well as its soul.

Staying within the humanities might not seem like a smart move for a young field on the rise, and we should be honest about what the choice will eventually entail: wading straight into controversy when we could play it safe. But *eudaimonia*, human flourishing, has long been understood to follow from the right kind of political involvements. We could describe Plato's *Symposium* as a discourse on the unbreakable link between education, human flourishing, and the proper conduct of the polis (1961: esp. 218a – 21c). The same might be said of Aristotle's *Nicomachean Ethics*, which conceives of individual happiness as a collective achievement (1984: 1099b30 – 32). Outside the Western canon as well, we see a similar conjunction of self-cultivation and the social. Even while its narrative culminates in a mystical encounter with God in the form of Krishna, the *Bhagavad Gita* can be read as a discourse on civil responsibility (Devji 2010), while portions of the *Tao Te Ching* not only address potential rulers but also urge popular resistance to the goals of a militarizing state (Chen 1989: 128 – 35). What distinguishes our society today from its classical forebears, East and West, is the decoupling of *eudaimonia* from the category of politics. Within education this decoupling has had the effect of diminishing the importance of self-cultivation (*paideia*), as well as social knowledge (*phronesis*), in the name of accommodation to economic "laws" represented as value neutral. What have replaced *arete*, the excellence that is *paideia*'s goal, are objective "proficiencies" whose attainment must be assessed by an "education industry."

That an instrumentalist paradigm is on the ascendant seems most obvious in the standardized tests metastasizing through K-12, but also in the calls for assessment now overtaking higher education under pressure from accrediting agencies like the Middle States Association of Colleges and Schools. Texas has even gone as far as to impose standardized measures of productivity on its academic employees. To dismiss these changes as trivial would be short-sighted when they clearly testify to the existence of what Michel Foucault describes as an "episteme"—a fundamental, a priori ordering of knowledge (1973: xxii). Ever since the Frankfort School and Hannah Arendt, critical observers have understood that instrumentalism is at odds with the dialogical relations that are the hallmark of democracy (Arendt 1958: 144 – 58; Horkheimer 1985). But the instrumentalism of our time needs to be understood more specifically as a consequence of two developments: the growing aggressiveness of the Right, especially those who are committed to dismantling of the public sphere altogether, and efforts by liberals to seek out a value-neutral compromise with their determined enemies. For different reasons, both sides have conspired to subordinate education to the logic of instrumentalism: the Right because the erasure of the past clears the road to victory; the liberals because of the mistaken belief that conflict and struggle should be forestalled in the effort to secure a common ground. But conflict and struggle are inescapable, perhaps in the classroom most of all.

REMORALIZING THE DEBATE OVER THE PUBLIC SPHERE

Nowhere in the English-speaking world has the attack on the humanities taken a more open and thoroughgoing form than in David Cameron's Great Britain, where his government in 2010 called for nothing less than the tripling of tuitions—a decision that remained in place even after tens of thousands of students took to the streets. So dramatic was the immediate unrest that observers here in the United States might have overlooked another change, a resolution to eliminate all state funding for the arts, humanities, and social sciences. David Marquand, a former Oxford don and Labour Party luminary, tried to contextualize these events in his 2011 Compass Lecture, a talk attended by Ed Miliband, leader of the Labour Party, and Carolyn Lucas, leader of the Greens:

> One of the great achievements of the 19th and 20th centuries was to carve out a distinct public domain from the private and market domains. Examples include the creation of a career civil service recruited on merit, the so-called gas and water socialism that transformed living conditions in London and other great cities in this country, Lloyd George's national insurance act and Bevan's creation of the National Health Service . . . But, there was a flaw . . . because the guardians and architects of the public domain forgot about the inherent voracity of capitalism that Marx had diagnosed. They assumed that their achievements were safe. That the institutions and norms of the public domain were and would remain inviolate. They failed to see that the market domain is inherently expansionist. And that if it is given half a chance it will invade parts of the public domain. (4 – 5)

The case made by reformers was that public goods, such as utilities, basic schooling, and medical attention, benefited the whole society, but in our time the question of who benefits has been turned against the public sphere with devastating effectiveness. Some people might be chronically ill and require constant support, while others never see a doctor for years, never set foot in a hospital, and die in the beds at age ninety-two. All pay into the common pot, but each draws out of it differently—a fact that observers on the Right decry as manifestly unfair. Much the same argument has been made about British higher education, which benefits only a minority, and mostly the children of the middle class. Why, the logic goes, should Britons from the working class, people who can barely cope with monthly bills, subsidize the children of fellow citizens who are more secure financially and advantaged in other ways as well? The brilliance of this logic becomes evident when one stops to think that every public good will confer its benefits unevenly. Each of us has different needs, just as we have differing abilities.

Marquand observes that in the early days of the public sphere, its champions often defended it with a rhetoric of pragmatism calculated to avoid conflict. Whether one supported socialism, capitalism, or even aristocracy, the public sphere could be defined to include basic, universal needs. But in Great Britain as in the United States, conservatives have shifted the terms of the debate from universal needs to benefits that get distributed unevenly, and this shift has splintered the collective consciousness on which all progressive social change depends. As Marquand suggests, the Conservatives and "New Labour" under Tony Blair found a way around the Left's old appeals to pragmatic common needs. No one disputes the value of good health, and few Conservatives would disagree about the intrinsic merits of music, painting, and literature. But the question of who benefits forces everyone to see themselves as individuals competing for limited resources. Not only has the pragmatism of the Left lost its rhetorical potency, but it actively inhibits Progressives from trying the one tactic that might prove politically effective: a renewed debate about values (Marquand 2011; see also Marquand 2004: 63 – 87). The Left must rediscover, Marquand insists, that its program was always more than merely pragmatic—that it always presupposed a specific set of values we must now regain the courage to enunciate clearly. Progressives must also be willing to unmask the values underlying the actions of the Right. Instead of allowing market paradigms to pass for value neutral, Progressives need to show that "turbo-capitalism" rests on moral presuppositions (2011: 7; 2012). Only by shifting the terrain away from its past pragmatic universalism will the Left have a fighting chance to stake out alternatives. We need what Marquand called in his speech a "realignment of the mind," a shift away from individualism to a collective sensibility based on "equity, professional duty, citizenship and civic virtue" (2011: 4).

Words like *equity* and *duty* seem unobjectionable at first glance, but actually they exist within constellations of value at odds with the motives of corporate capitalism, and Marquand says as much. To speak of "morals" as he does also seems inoffensive until we recognize that politics is what we get when we act on our moral convictions, and that conflict is what arises when those convictions clash. Although Marquand does not put it quite this way, now that the rhetoric of pragmatism has become vitiated, the survival of the Progressive legacy depends on our willingness to accept conflict as the price we have to pay for real alternatives. Here in the United States the communitarian Michael Sandel (2012: 202) has made a similar argument. Unless, he argues, we are willing to push back, markets will "invade" all the other domains of value in our lives: "family . . . friendship, sex, procreation, health, education, nature, art, citizenship, sports, and the way we contend with the prospect of death." Like Marquand, Sandel understands that "the market domain is inherently expansionist" and that questions of value are essential to the survival of democracy itself:

> Such deliberations touch, unavoidably, on competing conceptions of the good life. This is terrain on which we sometimes fear to tread. For fear of disagreement, we hesitate to bring our moral and spiritual convictions into the public square. But shrinking from these questions does not leave them undecided. It simply means that markets will decide them for us. This is the lesson of the last three decades. The era of market triumphalism has coincided with a time when public discourse has been largely empty of moral and spiritual substance. Our only hope of keeping markets in their place is to deliberate openly and publicly about the meaning of the goods and social practices we prize. (202)

By foregrounding the issue of the good life, Sandel evokes a history even older than the one Marquand refers to—the history of classical Greece with its conception of *eudaimonia*. While economists typically represent markets as perennial fixtures of all human communities, their "laws" as immutable as nature's own, Sandel asks his readers to recognize the present moment as a distinct break with the past—a moment of "market triumphalism"—and he explicitly urges a return to a society defined by "open debate."

It is significant, however, that Sandel avoids the word *conflict*, choosing instead the market-friendlier euphemism *competing*. Even while he defends the need to preserve alternatives to the market's logic, he hesitates to challenge the market's view of society—a view based on the centrality of competition as opposed to conflict. Ironically, *conflicting* would be more consonant with Sandel's communitarian aims, since conflict seeks a resolution through change, whereas competition always assumes a *bellum omnium contra omnes*, a war of all against all that ultimately reinforces existing social structures (Marx 1906: 171 – 73, 347; Mills 2000: 343 – 61). But to his credit, Sandel recuperates another, still more loaded word, *politics*, by arguing for the process of deliberation that Aristotle understood as the essence of *politike*. That an argument for politics should even need to be made reflects the contempt with which most Americans hold the very word. And given this sad state of affairs, Sandel's reluctance to place conflict on the table might be seen as a tactical response to a tendency deeply engrained in our culture. When faced with the possibility of political struggle, we can be counted on to turn reflexively to instrumentalist solutions.

THE EVASION OF POLITICS IN OUR PUBLIC DISCOURSE

Quite apart from the merits of Marquand's Compass speech, his remarks would probably leave many Americans uneasy—especially the remarks he made about the relevance of Karl Marx. It seems virtually impossible to imagine a Harvard professor like Sandel praising Marx at a gathering that included, say, President Obama and Bill Clinton or Al Gore. Even though Marx's toxicity would exceed the dread specter of "socialism" by a very wide margin, the real problem with his name's invocation would be that public life in the United States is supposed to "rise above politics." And if we are looking for a locus classicus of this exclusion of politics today, few examples could rival the speech delivered by President Obama (2010) at Cooper Union in New York in 2010, following the financial emergency of 2008:

Now, since I last spoke here two years ago, our country has been through a terrible trial. More than 8 million people have lost their jobs. Countless small businesses have had to shut their doors. Trillions of dollars in savings have been lost—forcing seniors to put off retirement, young people to postpone college, entrepreneurs to give up on the dream of starting a company. And as a nation we were forced to take unprecedented steps to rescue the financial system and the broader economy. . . .

Now, one of the most significant contributors to this recession was a financial crisis as dire as any we've known in generations—at least since the '30s. And that crisis was born of a failure of responsibility—from Wall Street all the way to Washington—that brought down many of the world's largest financial firms and nearly dragged our economy into a second Great Depression.

As I said on this stage two years ago, I believe in the power of the free market. I believe in a strong financial sector that helps people to raise capital and get loans and invest their savings. That's part of what has made America what it is. But a free market was never meant to be a free license to take whatever you can get, however you can get it. That's what happened too often in the years leading up to this crisis. Some—and let me be clear, not all—but some on Wall Street forgot that behind every dollar traded or leveraged there's a family looking to buy a house, or pay for an education, open a business, save for retirement. What happens on Wall Street has real consequences across the country, across our economy.

Perhaps the most remarkable aspect of the speech is its solicitation of Wall Street even though financiers had only recently pushed the world to the edge of collapse—a solicitation more still remarkable precisely because the president concedes that he will probably be rebuffed by the people he is courting. As he acknowledges openly, we have already "seen battalions of financial industry lobbyists descending on Capitol Hill, [and] firms spending millions to influence the outcome of this debate. We've seen misleading arguments and attacks that are designed not to improve the [reform] bill but to weaken or to kill it." Yet in response to this concerted assault, President Obama still invites his listeners to meet him in the middle: "We will not always see eye to eye. We will not always agree. But that doesn't mean that we've got to choose between two extremes. We do not have to choose between markets that are unfettered by even modest protections against crisis, or markets that are stymied by onerous rules that suppress enterprise and innovation." Such rhetoric of reconciliation aimed at an apolitical consensus has become, according to the French theorist of democracy Jacques Rancière (2010: 188), a ubiquitous feature of government in our time, concealing a unity of oligarchic interests behind the pose of debate. By portraying the dispute as a clash between equally inflexible extremes—an extreme Left bent on stifling reforms, an extreme Right supporting total laissez-faire—Obama strategically misrepresents the real nature of the controversy, since the Democrats ventured only modest legislation, whereas their opponents on the Right were opposed to new regulations of any kind. But by distorting the conflict in this way—by creating a false symmetry—Obama was able to represent himself as mature and "statesman-like," above politics, not mired in them.

Obama's consensual rhetoric might be described as quintessentially liberal (Losurdo 2011). When it encounters contradiction, it seeks first to define a middle ground by granting all sides moral equivalence, and then it lays out what Thomas Frank (qtd. in Morley 2011) has called a "technocratic solution," one based on a "pragmatic" calculus rather than on "ideology." Deliberations about larger ends get postponed while means become the dominant focus. In short, instrumentalist considerations endlessly defer a genuine debate over the ethical values that lie at the heart of any real civic life. Value questions are not explicitly ruled out of bounds. Indeed, they have become common talking points. But the liberal response has been to postpone real deliberation by calling for "tolerance," "even-handedness," and "objectivity," all evoked to downplay differences. More than twenty years ago, Iris Marion Young (1989: 252) described what she called "interest group pluralism," in which political disputes are understood as disagreements over policy that must be resolved by appeasing all the players. Young describes this pluralism as a symptom of a "depoliticized society." Like Rancière, she believes that real politics always involves a demand for participation by those who are excluded and lack any normative authority. Because democracy is a process and not a form of government, attempts to forestall conflict inevitably serve the interests of elites. Young describes interest-group pluralism as a "privatization of policy-making . . . consigning it to back-room deals and regulatory agencies." Instead of broadening participation to include the formerly excluded, liberalism in effect attempts to buy off the major players in the game. What Young fails to notice, however, is how closely this pluralism tracks with academia's own tendency to avoid conflicts not sanctioned by the orthodoxy of their fields (Bizzell 1991; Lu 1992; Lynch et al. 1997). Too often the spirit of "toleration" vitiates the heritage of critical thinking the university claims to celebrate—especially now, after the culture wars have intimidated the humanities.

The university's close connections to liberal thinking has a complicated backstory that I cannot unpack here in detail. But academic knowledge has been shaped as much by our response to danger as by our intellectual curiosity. The philosopher John McCumber (1996: 33) recounts, for example, that in "Germany after 1830 . . . reactionary forces purged from academic positions the Young Hegelians—including such able thinkers as Feuerbach, Marx, Max Stirner, and David Strauss—consigning the country's universities to a generation" of neo-Kantians who hid behind their claims to impartiality. The same sort of repression happened here in the United States during the McCarthy era, and it has cast a long shadow, too. English, philosophy, and economics were, according to McCumber, the disciplines most frequently attacked in reports issued by the staff of the House Un-American Activities Committee from 1950 through 1955. Moreover, in philosophy, many of the victims were quite prominent (37–38; also Schrecker 1986). At the same time, distinguished academicians also took an active part in the persecutions, among them the philosophers William Barrett and Sidney Hook and the intellectual historian William O. Lovejoy, author of *The Great Chain of Being*. McCumber claims that in philosophy, the long-term result of the repression was the triumph of the analytic school that still dominates the universities of North America. Even now, he charges, academic "philosophers are directed away from reflecting on the historical conditions of their discipline towards uncovering the logical conditions of the quest of truth; away from [cultural context in] construals of meaning toward a conflation of [meaning] with reference and truth-conditions; away from investigation of the social work and complicities of philosophical approaches, and toward issues concerning the scientific justification of beliefs in general" (45). Of course, what happened in philosophy does not correspond exactly to developments in the field of history, where during the 1960s and 1970s historians like Barbara Tuchman and Staughton Lynd fought for a socially engaged scholarship, or in English somewhat later, when activist intellectuals were thick on the ground (Thelen 1989; Graff 1987). Nevertheless, the more recent, decade-long campaign against "tenured radicals" has had a very real effect, perhaps not silencing dissent, but at least tamping it down. The generation that came to maturity during the 1980s may have no successors in a university more and more defined by commerce, not criticism.

If politics forms and deforms what counts as academic knowledge, the university has also helped to shape the political discourse of our time. It is no accident, after all, that the president should so often sound like the law professor he was formerly, or that he should manifest a studied distance from his supporters' frustrations when his technocratic rhetoric fails—as it did in the year following the Cooper Union speech. Not a single item of Obama's four-point plan made its way to full realization—not limits on the size of the largest banks, nor more transparent financial practices, nor a robust consumer protection agency, nor enhanced shareholder rights. As Thomas Frank (qtd. in Morley 2011) observes, many of the president's supporters were "absolutely furious" about his capitulation to the financiers: because they were the injured parties, they wanted their champion to pursue redress instead of aiming at "neutrality." But Obama and the Democratic leadership simply "didn't get it," for reasons the university might find disquieting. In Frank's words, "The Democrats completely imagine themselves as . . . the party of the professional class. . . . [They] very definitely identify with academia. That's the home of the professions, where they come from" (Morley 2011). Not only is the university today the "home" of the professional-managerial class, but also its knowledge, across the disciplines, has helped advance the "toleration" that marks the president's Cooper Union speech (see Ehrenreich and Ehrenreich 1977; Derber et al. 1990).

Many historians of higher education have noted that the rise of postwar middle class went hand in hand with the explosive growth of American universities. As Christopher Newfield (2003) observes, the middle class was virtually created by the postwar university, which provided ever greater access to the knowledge and skills essential to upward social mobility. And as Newfield also maintains, the middle class made the university in turn a very different place than it had been a hundred years before, when only the wealthy attended. But now the middle class has fragmented in ways that define the postwar period, with its broad access and mobility, as very much a thing of the past. Increasingly, the members of the *upper* middle class—those who occupy the top 10%—have broken away from the rest (Wolff 2010). Some have made their homes in the classical professions of medicine and law, but more typically, they occupy fields that require "knowledge workers" and symbolic analysts—in research and development, finance, the media, higher education—all members of the "creative class" (Florida 2003). Even though they are still classified as a segment of the greater middle, the professional-managerial class (PMC) has its own outlook on the world, and increasingly, the university reflects the interests and needs of the "new class." For the members of the PMC, "management" is the defining skill, management not just of people but of information, resources, and, of course, capital. The ability to find a middle ground, to conciliate opposing sides, to reframe and motivate—these are crucial managerial skills, and they were on display at Cooper Union because they were the ones the president himself acquired on his way first to the *Harvard Law Review*, then to the Senate, and finally to 1 Pennsylvania Avenue.

But "management" is a deeply flawed model for democratic social interactions. In the culture of the PMC, the function of "management" is to empower the members of a "team" or working group, but only within the horizon of goals determined in advance by those at a higher level. Like an organic community, the team members must learn to cooperate, but unlike genuine citizens, they lack the power to decide collectively on which tasks they will undertake: the *how* lies within their purview but not the *what* or the *why*. As a mode of interaction, management is thoroughly instrumentalist even while it pretends to address the needs and aspirations of everyone involved. When management becomes the paradigm that shapes public life, the result is a divided government, though not divided, as we might assume, between the two political parties. Instead, citizens are distracted by a "public" theater-state that appears to be busily engaged with the normal processes of governing but that in fact rigidly confines itself to instrumental concerns—the *how*. At the same time, the real decision making—about the *what* and the *why*—takes place away from public view, not in some mysterious smoke-filled room, but in the complex networks that connect the members of an elite whose interests cut across the traditional boundaries separating the public from the private spheres and the state from finance (Wedel 2009).

Classes at colleges and universities might seem far removed from the president's Cooper Union speech, but in both government and higher education, politics has come increasingly to be seen as dangerous and inappropriate. It was not always so, however—especially at Cooper Union, a school with a long, and progressive, tradition of engagement with civic life. If Obama's presence there was supposed to resonate with that tradition, it also inadvertently underscored how profoundly things have changed for the worse. From the Great Hall in 1860, Abraham Lincoln delivered his own Cooper Union speech, challenging the institution of slavery on legal and moral grounds. In the closely reasoned argument, which salvaged Lincoln's fading career and led to his nomination for the presidency two years afterward, he directly confronted the most explosive issue of his time:

> Wrong as we think slavery is, we can yet afford to let it alone where it is, because that much is due to the necessity arising from its actual presence in the nation; but can we, while our votes will prevent it, allow it to spread into the National Territories, and to overrun us here in these Free States? If our sense of duty forbids this, then let us stand by our duty, fearlessly and effectively. Let us be diverted by none of those sophistical contrivances wherewith we are so industriously plied and belabored—contrivances such as groping for some middle ground between the right and the wrong. . . . Neither let us be slandered from our duty by false accusations against us, nor frightened from it by menaces of destruction to the Government nor of dungeons to ourselves. Let us have faith that right makes might, and in that faith, let us, to the end, dare to do our duty as we understand it. (Holzer 2004: 283–84)

"Groping for some middle ground" was an avenue Lincoln might have pursued, but he rejects it as morally unacceptable. Instead, Lincoln deployed his knowledge of the law in the service of an unapologetically partisan account of the public good; he deployed it, that is, politically, and as Harold Holzer (2004: 231 – 37) argues, the speech launched him on the trajectory that ended with his election. At the same time, Lincoln's speech puts to shame what would come to be the liberal pretense of fairness to "both sides," as though slavery and freedom both deserved equal time and equal respect. If Obama's Cooper Union audience could have been transported to the scene of Lincoln's talk, would they have found it unbalanced, intemperate, scary? Maybe. But at least they would have understood what liberal rhetoric actively conceals: the conflict of incompatible values, and the knowledge that only a fundamental change can bring about a resolution. As Rancière (2010: 185; translation altered) has argued, "Politics is not, as is often said, the opposite of morals. It is the opening of a split within [morality]."

LIBERAL DISCOURSE AND NAKED LIFE

Lincoln's speech represents a kind of Archimedean point outside our current "reality," against which we can take a better measure of ourselves. For another Archimedean point, we might look to ancient Athens, whose citizens would have viewed our lives, confined to the horizon of the *how*, as much closer to the lives of slaves than to those of citizens. In contrast to slaves, free citizens had the power to decide what they would do and why, a power they saw as inseparable from their facility with language. However we imagine it, the polis was created by its language because it was never just a geographic space but also a social process. The "citizen" might be understood as a person capable of speaking to peers who share an implicit linguistic ground made up of common stories, metaphors, paradigms, symbols, turns of phrase, references, vocabulary, grammar, and cadences, all of which identify the participants as members of a collective, a "we." Beyond these commonalities is a shared pursuit of *eudaimonia*, human flourishing or the "good life." As Aristotle famously observes, "If all communities aim at some good, the state or political community, which is the highest of all, and which embraces all the rest, aims at good in a greater degree than any other, and at the highest good" (*Politics*, 1.1.1252a). The capacity to recognize the good and actively pursue it Aristotle sees as inseparable from speech:

> Now, that man is more of a political animal than bees or any other gregarious animals is evident. Nature, as we often say, makes nothing in vain, and man is the only animal whom she has endowed with the gift of speech. And whereas mere voice is but an indication of pleasure or pain, and is therefore found in other animals (for their nature attains to the perception of pleasure and pain and the intimation of them to one another,

and no further), the power of speech is intended to set forth the expedient and inexpedient, and therefore likewise the just and the unjust. And it is a characteristic of man that he alone has any sense of good and evil, of just and unjust, and the like, and the association of living beings who have this sense makes a family and a state. (I.2: 1253a)

Not only does the very existence of the polis depend upon its language, but language injects into the collectivity the question of "good and evil," which Aristotle sees as central to *eudaimonia*, on the macro level of the state as well as the micro level of the family. Yet the choice between "good and evil" is the one that liberal discourse seeks to elide in the name of a pragmatic instrumentalism (recall Obama's "We don't have to choose"). To make "good and evil" disappear, however, is to treat politics as *techne*, a craft that aims at usefulness, whereas Aristotle regards it as a form of *episteme*, a science (*politike episteme*) grounded in the intrinsic character of the human being as a *zoon politikon*, a political animal whose *telos* lies in relations with others (*Politics* 1.2, *Nicomachean Ethics* 1.2 – 6). While Aristotle acknowledged craft as an element of politics, and while he also recognized the need for pragmatic flexibility and spontaneous inventiveness, he could not imagine a politics in which deliberations about means were divorced from the question of ends, the *what* and *why*. If politics aims at the highest good, this divorce would be self-defeating.

By substituting pragmatic workarounds for political contestation, liberals have helped to set in motion a process that threatens to contaminate the whole society to a degree we might underestimate because instrumentalism already represents so powerful and enduring an undercurrent in American culture—influencing many fundamental beliefs about education, knowledge, and literacy. An accounting of that undercurrent would necessarily include some of the preeminent thinkers of America's history—pragmatists like Ralph Waldo Emerson, William James, John Dewey, Richard Rorty, and Stanley Fish—each of whom tried to advance a philosophy of pure action that would avoid certain vexed antinomies, which they only managed to kick down the road. Although both James and Dewey actively pursued a society more open and egalitarian, pragmatism has too easily paved the way for a depoliticized obsession with "results." The regime of standardized testing and the culture of assessment both testify to the failure of the pragmatist tradition or, rather, to the failures produced by its success.

It is hardly an accident that "No Child Left Behind" was promoted as bipartisan, or that the Obama administration took issue with its applications, not its premises. But why should we believe that education, of all things, should strive to be "nonpartisan" when our classrooms have become—as they must be if they matter—the site of some of the most consequential struggles of our time—the struggle, for example, between creationists and the defenders of Darwinian evolution and, more recently, between climate science and deniers?

Aristotle might have pointed to the dangers inherent in our reflexive elision of politics. Instrumentalism, he would argue, confuses the distinction between natural life (*zoe*) and the life we create collectively (*bios*) in a way that greatly diminishes the prospects for human flourishing: "The family is the association established by nature for the supply of men's everyday wants, and the members of it are called by Charondas 'companions of the cupboard,' and by Epimenides the Cretan, 'companions of the manger.' But when . . . several villages are united in a single complete community, large enough to be nearly or quite self-sufficing, the state comes into existence, originating in the bare needs of life, and continuing in existence for the sake of a good life" (*Politics*, I.2.1252b10 – 20). From an Aristotelian standpoint, the great danger of instrumentalism lies in its unwillingness to deal with questions beyond the horizon of the natural, biological life that we share with animals and that we leave behind once our communities have become materially "self-sustaining." In contrast to natural life, human flourishing cannot exist at all without the complex social interactions that produce, through the power of mimesis, our seeing and imitating moral excellence (*arete*) as it is embodied in others. Strictly speaking, natural life is neither good nor bad; standards of value can exist only after we have at our disposal options beyond the scope of mere survival. The possibility of undertaking one action rather than another, or of admiring one person while looking askance at another, places all human relations within the domain of "the political" because the question at hand always requires a moral choice.

The flaw at the heart of instrumentalism, and also at the heart of America's pragmatist legacy, is that the domain of social action is the site of politics par excellence, not the place where we can finally leave politics behind. After the Susan B. Komen Foundation discontinued its funding of Planned Parenthood, Michael Bloomberg (qtd. in Paulson and Taylor 2012) derided the move. "Let's stop playing politics," he said, "and take care of public health." But women's reproductive freedom is inescapably political, and donating to Planned Parenthood—as Bloomberg did from his own pocket—does not set politics aside but, rather, is a political act. Instrumentalism tempts us to believe that because we can sometimes act concertedly even when we might disagree, we have managed to overcome our differences. But people whose reasons are at variance will be unlikely to agree for very long, and then they will face their differences again. Like some forms of vitalist thinking, pragmatism often tries to transcend culture—to transcend ideas, values, history—by supposing that actions can belong entirely to the domain of *zoe*, biological life (Colebrook 2010: esp. 181 – 85). But the face, so to speak, of this vitalism cannot be a human face. It contemplates all outcomes with equanimity because all of them are thought to express the unfolding of the natural life process—whether the event is the invasion of Iraq or Gandhi's campaign against the British. Yet those are the differences that matter most—if we happen to be human. To take this vitalism to heart is to become quite literally an *idiotes*, a stranger to the polis, the fate of which is always collective and so always bound up with questions of ethics.

With some important modifications, the distinction between *zoe* and *bios* has become central to contemporary thinking about the theater-state that now substitutes for real politics. In comments on the discourses of Europe's governing class, Giorgio Agamben decries the same evasive pragmatism heard at Cooper Union in 2010. Since the 1970s, Agamben claims, the European Left has also tried to avoid even the appearance of "politicization" and "partisanship." The "motto that has guided the strategy," he writes, is that "one has to yield on everything, one has to reconcile everything with its opposite: intelligence with television and advertising, the working class with capital, science with [popular] opinion" (2000: 136). Through this process, however—which is not at all dialectical but an evasion of the dialectic—questions about the good life drop away, and we are left in a condition Agamben calls "naked life," which differs from Aristotle's "natural life" because it lies outside the orders of both nature and society. "Classical politics," Agamben writes, "used to distinguish clearly between *zoe* and *bios*, between natural life and political life, between human beings as simply living beings, whose place was in the home, and human beings as political subjects, whose place was in the polis. Well, we no longer have any idea of this" (2000: 137). "Naked life" as Agamben describes it is properly neither zoe nor bios—neither sheer biological existence nor the civic life in the polis—but a condition of pure outsiderness and abject vulnerability. In ancient times, he argues, this "sacred" condition was imposed on banished criminals who became completely liminal, neither human nor animal, and unprotected by the laws that normally prohibited murder (1998: 71 – 90). Far from disappearing in the modern world, these archaic practices have returned with a new urgency in the sovereign's power to create a "state of exception" that places citizens outside the law, like the Jews at Auschwitz or, more recently, the "detainees" at Guantanamo (1998, 2005).

POLITICIZING COMPOSITION

Does the composition class represent yet another "state of exception" from which politics has been excluded? The argument against politics in writing courses goes something like this. Education is a public good, and educators are recipients of the public's trust. As soon as we employ the classroom to advance our private values, we have crossed a crucial line, violating the implicit pact we have made with society. Moreover, writing is a *techne*, a skill, which can be employed by any side in any particular debate. Once we tip our hands and let students see our personal allegiances, they will have reasons to doubt what we say, which should be totally impartial and limited to our proper areas of technical expertise. As professionals we are obliged to avoid distinctions between Left and Right, Republican or Democratic, admirers of *Mother Jones* or admirers of *Atlas Shrugged*, not just in discharging our public roles but even in our private lives, where visible indiscretions can undermine our public probity. And when it comes to our work as professionals, the community that matters is, at any rate, our peers. Our highest obligation is to the profession that has given us the authority we are free to exercise only under these constraints.

But perhaps we should "think again," to use the phrase that Stanley Fish has chosen as the title of his *New York Times* column. It seems incredible at first to claim that Obama's Cooper Union speech, or what we do in English 101, could somehow lead to a scenario like the Nazi genocide. To make such an argument without qualification would be to overlook the many different factors required to produce such a catastrophe—cultural, historical, economic, logistical, and so forth—and, in this spirit, Agamben's critics reject his claims as crude and overblown. Yet thinkers as dissimilar as George Orwell and Theodor Adorno have insisted that how we speak and write will help determine what we will do (Miller 2000). If our words have consequences of some kind, then language can never be neutral or merely a technical instrument, as Agamben (2000: 92) himself understands:

> Exposition is the location of politics. If there is no animal politics, that is perhaps because animals are always already in the open and do not try to take possession of their own exposition; they live simply without caring about it. . . . Human beings, on the other hand, separate images from things and give them a name precisely because they want to recognize themselves, that is, they want to take possession their own very appearance. Human beings thus transform the open into a world, that is, into a battlefield of political struggle without quarter. This struggle, whose object is truth, goes by the name of History.

The account of exposition as a "struggle without quarter" may strike many readers as a formula for intolerance or violence, but even if we might prefer to see struggle as only a metaphor, or as only one of many possibilities, Agamben would insist that nothing less than a life worth living is at stake. To imagine that exposition can somehow bracket out our relations to each other is to deny the very nature of language. But Agamben regards this denial as symptomatic of our time, which he sees as defined increasingly by facilities like Guantanamo, where prisoners and those who imprison them both exist outside the law. Guantanamo is not an aberration, he insists, but the expression of a tendency toward the spread of "naked life" across the globe.

In the university, exposition has been consigned to the lowest level of the curriculum—the humble "freshman English" class. But this demotion might be understood as an example of the liberal logic that has tried to drive politics from every corner of the public sphere. Precisely because exposition is the most fundamental mode of discourse, it is also the most political, as the nation witnessed one January morning in 2012, when the *Today Show*'s Matt Lauer queried Mitt Romney about his criticisms of Obama's call for greater economic opportunities for the "99%":

> **Lauer:** Let me ask you about the choice of words last night when you said we already have a leader who divides us with

the bitter politics of envy. . . . Do you suggest that anyone who questions the policies and practices of Wall Street and financial institutions, anyone who has questions about the distribution of wealth and power in this country is envious . . . ? Is it about jealousy or fairness?

Romney: You know, I think it's about envy. I think it's about class warfare. I think when you have a president encouraging the idea of dividing America based on 99% versus 1% . . . you've opened up a whole new wave of approach in this country which is entirely inconsistent with the concept of one nation under God. And the American people, I believe, in the final analysis will reject it.

Lauer: Are there no fair questions about the distribution of wealth without it being seen as envy, though?

Romney: You know, I think it fine to talk about those things in quiet rooms and in discussions about tax policy and the like, but the President has made this part of his campaign rally. Everywhere he goes we hear him talking about millionaires and billionaires and executives and Wall Street, . . . I think that it's a very envy oriented, attack oriented approach, and I think that it will fail. (Stump 2012)

Note that "policy"—as in Romney's phrase "tax policy"—is a term of art in modern social thought, one that describes the decision making of elites. The authority of those elites, and Romney clearly counts himself as one of them, derives ostensibly from their specialized knowledge and their privileged access to the levers of power. Once a decision has been made, implementation can be delegated within what is known as the "policy cycle" to managers and other professionals who are sometimes disparaged as "bureaucrats" or "technocrats." Romney's responses to Lauer's questioning testify to his comfort with this arrangement, but the audience could also see his growing unease when Lauer dared to inject real politics into what should have been a perfunctory exchange about the horserace of campaigning. Lauer's question is political in just the sense that Aristotle had in mind, concerned as it is with "good and evil" and the "just and unjust," but Romney clearly views it as a breach of decorum, the intrusion of a discourse more properly confined to the precincts of "closed rooms" far from public view.

As I have argued, this distinction between the public and private spheres represents a major departure from the heritage of classical antiquity, when what we call the private sphere was understood to be insufficient for human flourishing precisely because it excluded politics, which was seen as the heart of public life. But in our time "public" and "private" have changed places—the private becoming political, the public becoming value-free—with the effect of stripping away the ethical character of all social interaction, leaving only the instrumentalism typical of liberal thinking. The problem, however, is even worse than that because we are witnessing a wholesale attack on the public sphere by advocates of the so-called free market. Millions of dollars of venture capital are flowing into public education, not only at the college level but even down to the first grade, where the arguments for privatization always start with the alleged ineffectiveness of the old arrangement (see Washburn 2005; Giroux 2007; Newfield 2008; Fang 2011). The charge of ineffectiveness is a claim about means and not ends, a claim we should consider carefully because it completely circumvents politics as Aristotle understood the term—the conflict over what will best serve society as a whole. Instead, the case for a takeover is made on the strength of the private sphere's alleged superiority in delivering "objective" results such as higher scores on standardized tests. Under this regime, which Slavoj Žižek has called the "post-political," the humanities are likely to survive only as a diversion from the disciplines that deal with "real-world" concerns: engineering, chemistry, genetics, economics, business, and management (2000: 198 – 205). As for writing courses, they will become places where no one of intelligence would ever choose to be—neither the teachers nor the students.

CASABLANCA

The best-known American pragmatist is not the philosopher John Dewey; it isn't Stanley Fish or Stanley Cavell. The best-known pragmatist is not, in fact, a philosopher or literary critic. Instead, he was a rather ordinary man who ran a bar or, as he called it, a "saloon," the Café Américain in the port of Casablanca during World War II. Always almost wincing in his white shirt, a cigarette perpetually in hand, "Mr. Rick" has come to signify for generations of Americans the Emersonian mystique of a life above the fray. The fray in this case was Nazi Germany's war of global expansion, its annexation of the

Sudetenland, the humiliation of Poland, the crushing of the British army at Dunkirk, the occupation of slightly more than half of France, to say nothing of the Kristallnacht pogrom, followed by the systematic rounding up of European Jews. But despite all this, Mr. Rick—Richard Blaine—whom we today would call a businessman, still looks ineffably cool, detached. The world around him might be falling apart, but even the flood of refugees willing to do anything to escape does not stir Rick into action. To his Vichy patron and co-conspirator, the venal Captain Renault, Rick says unapologetically: "I stick my neck out for nobody." True, the occasional woman in distress can move him to act in a generous way—we even see him turn down the chance for sex with a desperate young wife. But this is just a personal gesture, not a truly political choice. And given the way Rick has decided to live, without a history, a family, a nation, or even many friends, he has almost managed to put himself beyond politics in just the way that any number of his countrymen still wish they could as well—the archetypal individualist, always looking out for the main chance.

Why some films become iconic probably no one can explain, but the special resonance of *Casablanca* (1942) comes at least in part from our complex regard for Rick's splendid isolation. At the same time that we admire him as *Homo pragmaticus*, we also understand that no human being can sustain so complete a separateness forever and that only someone quite damaged would try. The real story at the heart of the film is how Rick became the man he is, and it centers on the great betrayal that cut his ties with humanity: the woman he loves and hopes to marry disappears just as he prepares for them to flee Paris while the Germans come marching in. His utter dejection so paralyzes him that Sam, the star pianist at his café, has to take him by the arm and help him onto the train. Rick's abandonment, the film wants us to see, is for him a failure of trust so profound that it places all human relations afterward on the footing of exchanges subject to the calculus of costs and benefits—subject to a market logic in which human life has a price while moral value disappears.

The film would not be the work of genius it is if it simply offered us the possibility that Rick might fall in love with someone else. We gradually come to understand that Rick's only way out is to view his experience in a different light, no longer as the story of an individual watching the world from a distance. Instead, he learns to place the events of his life in a larger context, Agamben's "History." This insight comes, not instantly, but step by step through his exchanges with Victor Laszlo, the anti-Nazi partisan who is his rival for Ilsa's love—and who inspires conflict everywhere he goes:

> **Rick:** Don't you sometimes wonder if it's worth all this? I mean what you're fighting for?
>
> **Laszlo:** We might as well question why we breathe. If we stop breathing, we'll die. If we stop fighting our enemies, the world will die.
>
> **Rick:** What of it? Then it'll be out of its misery. [Rick reaches in his jacket for his cigarette case, opens it, and takes out a cigarette.]
>
> **Laszlo:** You know how you sound, Monsieur Blaine? Like a man who's trying to convince himself of something he doesn't believe in his heart. Each of us has a destiny, for good or for evil.

Rick's question—"Don't you sometimes wonder if it's worth all this?"—voices the isolation that has numbed him to his paralyzing sense of loss. It also conveys his anomie and his hunger for the connectedness that holds together friendships and communities, the connectedness that Aristotle knew as *philia*, whose definition falls somewhere between "comradeship" and "love" (*Nicomachean Ethics* 8, 9). Like the movie's viewers in 1942, Laszlo can see that Rick longs desperately for the human contact he belittles, but Laszlo's response throws Rick completely off balance because it asks him to accept his loneliness. Instead of offering Rick the consolation of another shot at romance, Laszlo invites him to recognize that his sense of loss can become the basis for a new form of relation to others. He asks Rick, in other words, to shift his point of view from his life as an individual, now seen irreparably incomplete, to his life as a social being. Pragmatism urges its followers to act as though they had no commitments to any particular future and could simply greet whatever happens with an Olympian indifference. What Rick finds so enticing about Laszlo is his rival's readiness to take part in the shaping of a common future. Indeed, the love affair at the heart of the film is not the one between Rick and Ilsa but the one between Rick and Laszlo, who becomes Rick's ego ideal.

If you have seen the movie, you already know that Laszlo and Ilsa make their escape together, with Rick holding off Captain Renault long enough for them to get away. Not only does Laszlo's sociability rescue Rick from the prison of his solitude, but also Rick's willingness to give Ilsa up, essentially without compensation, transforms the cynical Captain Renault. The story closes with Rick and Renault walking together through the fog, planning out the details of their escape to join with the French resistance.

> **Renault:** It might be a good idea for you to disappear from Casablanca for a while. There's a Free French garrison over at Brazzaville. I could be induced to arrange a passage.
>
> **Rick:** My letter of transit? I could use a trip. But it doesn't make any difference about our bet. You still owe me ten thousand francs.
>
> **Renault:** And that ten thousand francs should pay our expenses.
>
> **Rick:** Our expenses?
>
> **Renault:** Uh huh.
>
> **Rick:** Louis, I think this is the beginning of a beautiful friendship.

We might say that pragmatism secretly desires something like a world of unconditional love, a desire to accord to everyone an equal measure of respect. Or, to put it another way, pragmatism holds out the possibility that all our reasons for fighting one another will evaporate if we just can achieve transparency in our communications. Perhaps this is why our liberal leaders, the president not least of all, keep trying to persuade their mortal enemies to join them on some (imaginary) middle ground. But Rick's unwillingness to discriminate is overwhelmed by the sheer weight of real, and truly terrible, differences. The pragmatist desire to dignify all positions as deserving equal time breaks down in the face of behavior for which "evil" is the only description. Ultimately, no one except an utter cynic can imagine compromising with the Occupation; at some point, even determined isolates have to choose between their friends and, yes, their enemies. And only by choosing their enemies do Rick and Renault discover that the two of them could become fast friends.

In a world imagined by pragmatism—a world where everyone is treated as a friend—real friendship becomes impossible. And what we get instead of friendship is its counterfeit, the universalization of the cash nexus in the form of exchanges that aspire to private advantage, a "good deal." "Value" in such an economy is no longer tied to contexts larger than individual satisfaction, and fungibility takes precedence over all other qualities (Graeber 2011: 336 – 45). This is just what we might expect to see in a city like Casablanca, populated by transients who might not live to see another year and who have few allegiances to the strangers surrounding them. But the long-term effect is to reduce everyone to the status of instruments. Perhaps counterintuitively, the threat of violence and the need to fight back make real value possible again—value in the sense of commitment to a future world worth living in. And this shift is signaled by the change in the status of the money at stake in the bet between Rick and Renault. Before the change, people were just a means; money was the end. But this relation is exactly reversed: the money becomes the instrument of human purposes.

Those of us in composition now find ourselves at a Casablanca of our own. The current understanding of the public sphere as a place apart from all politics has left the whole university, the sciences no less than the humanities, powerless to resist privatization because resistance would have to assume the form of an argument about ends, not means—an argument, in other words, that would appear political and so would run the risk of calling down on us the charge of partisanship. For several generations, we avoided this dilemma by relying on what Fish has called our "place at the table" alongside the other players in the system of professions. But now that the era of professionalism

is coming to an end, our best chance for survival may depend on linking our future more visibly to the fate of the broad majority of our fellow citizens—that is, to more politics, not less. After all, the teaching of literacy is a profoundly political act. And even though English 101 began at Harvard a century ago, the rise of composition has always been inseparable from the fortunes of broad-based public education. How, then, when our field has its origins in the fight against inequality, can we suppress this knowledge when we teach?

Today our society is witnessing events that almost nobody foresaw in the optimistic 1980s: a lost generation of unemployed or underemployed college graduates, trapped in a cycle of debt; a return to a Gilded Age distribution of wealth; the collapse of public commitments to education at all levels; a coordinated assault on labor unions nationwide; the manipulation of the press to discredit global warming; an attack on women's reproductive rights, including access to contraception; the removal of all barriers to money in elections; an explosion of childhood obesity and attendant chronic illnesses; a tenfold rise of anxiety disorders and fivefold rise in rates of depression. In other words, we have ample reason to think that some kind of conflict might be justified. What we lack, however, is not just political will; we lack an intellectual paradigm, something like the theory of "just war," that would allow us to see conflict now as necessary, even noble.

John Dewey (1938: 5) starts *Experience and Education* with this frank admission: "All social movements involve conflicts, which are reflected intellectually in controversies. It would not be a sign of health if such an important social interest as education were not also an arena of struggles, practical and theoretical." But no sooner does Dewey make this observation than he takes the liberal turn. "It is," he writes, "the business of an intelligent theory of education to ascertain the causes for the conflicts that exist and then, instead of taking one side or the other, to indicate a plan of operations proceeding from a level deeper and more inclusive than is represented by the practices and ideas of the contending parties." This confidence in transcending differences has a powerful appeal, but a "more inclusive" unity is precisely what cannot emerge because, as Dewey was willing to admit on other occasions, ideas actually give expression to concrete ways of life, and these ways of life often prove to be impossible to reconcile through any feat of analysis, synthesis, or identification. As the Belgian theorist Chantal Mouffe (2000: 13) insists, the search for a "common ground" sometimes arises from the self-deceiving hope that a truly public space can protect its inhabitants from the exercise of power. But power is actually "constitutive of [all] social relations," and instrumentalism is what we get when we fail to "acknowledge the dimension of antagonism that the pluralism of values entails." Drawing on the work of Rancière, Žižek (2000: 188 – 89; also Žižek 2011: 387 – 402) has made the related point that politics in a democracy is not about resolving differences within some greater unity but about fighting the right battles to preserve democracy itself. Education in a democracy must teach citizens not only that power is inescapable but also that nothing will improve unless they exercise it. The fact that people will disagree about the nature of the good does not exempt them from having to choose. Refusing to choose is not an exercise of power but an acceptance of victimization.

WORKS CITED

Agamben, Giorgio. 1998. *Homo Sacer: Sovereign Power and Bare Life*, trans. Daniel Heller-Roazen. Stanford, CA: Stanford University Press.

—. 2000. *Means without End: Notes on Politics*, trans. Vincenzo Binetti and Cesare Casarino. Minneapolis: University of Minnesota Press.

—. 2005. *State of Exception*, trans. Kevin Attell. Chicago: University of Chicago Press.

Arendt, Hannah. 1958. *The Human Condition*. Chicago: University of Chicago Press

Aristotle. 1984. *The Complete Works of Aristotle*, ed. Jonathan Barnes. Vol. 2. Princeton, NJ: Princeton University Press.

Bizzell, Patricia. 1991. "Power, Authority, and Critical Pedagogy." *Journal of Basic Writing* 10: 54–70.

Casablanca [typescript]. 1942. Screenplay by Julius J. Epstein, Philip G. Epstein, and Howard Koch. TCU Library Special Collections, Digital Archives, www.weeklyscript.com/Casablanca.txt.

Chen, Ellen M. 1989. *The Tao Te Ching: A New Translation with Commentary*. St. Paul, MN: Paragon.

Colebrook, Claire. 2010. *Deleuze and the Meaning of Life*. London: Continuum.

Derber, Charles, William A. Schwartz, and Yale R. Magrass. 1990. *Power in the Highest Degree: Professionals and the Rise of a New Mandarin Order*. New York: Oxford University Press.

Devji, Faisal. 2010. "Morality in the Shadow of Politics." *Modern Intellectual History* 7.2: 373–90.

Dewey, John. 1938. *Experience and Education*. New York: Collier.

Ehrenreich, Barbara, and John Ehrenreich. 1977. "The Professional-Managerial Class," parts 1 and 2. *Radical America* 11 (March-April): 7–31; 11 (May-June): 7–22.

Fang, Lee. 2011. "How Online Learning Companies Bought America's Schools." *Nation*, 16 November, www.thenation.com/article/164651/how-online-learning-companies-bought-americas-schools#.

Fish, Stanley. 2008. *Save the World on Your Own Time*. New York: Oxford University Press.

Florida, Richard. 2003. *The Rise of the Creative Class: And How It's Transforming Work, Leisure, Community, and Everyday Life*. New York: Basic Books.

Foucault, Michel. 1973. *The Order of Things: An Archaeology of the Human Sciences*. New York: Vintage Books.

Giroux, Henry A. 2007. *The University in Chains: Confronting the Military-Industrial-Academic Complex*. Boulder, CO: Paradigm.

Graeber, David. 2011. *Debt: The First Five Thousand Years*. Brooklyn, NY: Melville House.

Graff, Gerald. 1987. *Professing Literature: An Institutional History of English*. Chicago: University of Chicago Press.

—. 1992. *Beyond the Culture Wars: How Teaching the Conflicts Can Revitalize Education*. New York: Norton.

Holzer, Harold. 2004. *Lincoln at Cooper Union: The Speech That Made Abraham Lincoln President*. New York: Simon and Schuster.

Horkheimer, Max. 1985. *Critique of Instrumental Reason*. New York: Continuum.

Losurdo, Domenico. 2011. *Liberalism: A Counter-history*. London: Verso.

Lu, Min-zhan. 1992. "Conflict and Struggle: The Enemies or Preconditions of Basic Writing?" *College English* 54: 887–913.

Lynch, Dennis A., Diana George, and Marilyn Cooper. 1997. "Moments of Argument: Agonistic Inquiry and Confrontational Cooperation." *College Composition and Communication* 48.1: 61–85.

Marquand, David. 2004. *Decline of the Public*. Cambridge, UK: Polity.

—. 2011. "Compass Annual Lecture 2011: A Realignment of the Mind— What Way Forward for Progressive Politics?," 10 February, www2.lse.ac.uk/globalGovernance/publications/articlesAndLectures/compassAnnualLecture.pdf.

—. 2012. "Capitalist Revolutionary/Keynes Hayek." *New Statesman*, www.newstatesman.com/books/2012/03/capitalism-keynes-backhouse.

Marx, Karl. 1906. *Capital: A Critique of Political Economy*, trans. Samuel Moore and Edward Aveling. 3 vols. New York: Modern Library.

McCumber, John. 1996. "Time in the Ditch: American Philosophy and the McCarthy Era." *Diacritics* 26.1: 33–49.

Miller, James. 2000. "Is Bad Writing Necessary?" *Lingua Features* 9.9, linguafranca.mirror.theinfo.org/9912/writing.html.

Mills, C. Wright. 2000. *The Power Elite*. New York: Oxford University Press.

Morley, Jefferson. 2011. "The Tea Party's 'Utopian Market Populism': Thomas Frank on the Dream That Fueled the Right Wing's Improbable Comeback." *Salon*, 28 December, www.salon.com/2011/12/28/the_rise_of_utopian_market_populism/.

Mouffe, Chantal. 2000. "Deliberative Democracy or Agonistic Pluralism." Institute for Advanced Studies Political Science Series, December, www.ihs.ac.at/publications/pol/pw_72.pdf.

Newfield, Christopher. 2003. *Industry and Ivy: Business and the Making of the University, 1880–1908*. Durham, NC: Duke University Press.

—. 2008. *Unmaking the Public University: The Forty Year Assault on the Middle Class*. Cambridge, MA: Harvard University Press.

Obama, Barack. 2010. "Remarks by the President on Wall Street Reform," 22 April, www.whitehouse.gov/the-press-office/remarks-president-wall-street-reform.

Paulson, Michael, and Kate Taylor. 2012. "City Room: Mayor Gives $250,000 to Planned Parenthood," *New York Times*, 2 February, cityroom.blogs.nytimes.com/2012/02/02/bloomberg-to-give-250000–to-planned-parenthood/.

Plato. 1961. *Symposium*, trans. Michael Joyce. In *The Collected Dialogues of Plato*, ed. Edith Hamilton and Huntington Cairns, 526–74. Princeton, NJ: Princeton University Press.

Rancière, Jacques. 2010. *Dissensus: On Politics and the Aesthetic*, trans. Steven Corcoran. London: Continuum.

Sandel, Michael. 2012. *What Money Can't Buy: The Moral Limits of Markets*. New York: Ferrar, Straus, and Giroux.

Schrecker, Ellen. 1986. *No Ivory Tower: McCarthyism and the Universities*. New York: Oxford.

Stump, Scott. 2012. "Romney on Attacks: I Can Handle the Heat and Still Take on Obama" [video], *Today News*, 11 January www.today.com/id/45955862/ns/today-today_news/t/romney-attacks-i-can-handle-heat-take-obama/#.UUoGxFZH7cg.

Thelen, David P. 1989. "A Round Table: What Has Changed and Not Changed in American Historical Practice?" *Journal of American History* 76.2: 393–98.

Washburn, Jennifer. 2005. *University, Inc.: The Corporate Corruption of Higher Education*. New York: Basic Books.

Wedel, Janine R. 2009. *Shadow Elite: How the World's New Power Brokers Undermine Democracy, Government, and the Free Market*. New York: Basic Books.

Wolff, E. N. 2010. "Recent Trends in Household Wealth in the United States: Rising Debt and the Middle-Class Squeeze—an Update to 2007." Working Paper no. 589. Annandale-on-Hudson, NY: Levy Economics Institute of Bard College.

Young, Iris Marion. 1989. "Polity and Group Difference: A Critique of the Ideal of Universal Citizenship." *Ethics* 99: 250–74.

Žižek, Slavoj. 2000. *The Ticklish Subject: The Absent Centre of Political Ontology*. London: Verso.

—. 2011. *Living in the End Times*. New York: Verso.

PRESENT TENSE

Present Tense is on the Web at http://www.presenttensejournal.org/

Present Tense: A Journal of Rhetoric in Society is a peer-reviewed, blind-ref-ereed, online journal dedicated to exploring contemporary social, cultural, political and economic issues through a rhetorical lens. In addition to exam-ining these subjects as found in written, oral and visual texts, we wish to pro-vide a forum for calls to action in academia, education and national policy. Seeking to address current or presently unfolding issues, we publish short articles ranging from 2,000 to 2,500 words, the length of a conference paper.

From GUI to NUI: Microsoft's *Kinect* and the Politics of the (Body as) Interface

In "From GUI to NUI: Microsoft's *Kinect* and the Politics of the (Body as) Interface," David M. Rieder interrogates the role of reflection and critique in immersive natural-user interface (NUI) environments, such as Microsoft Kinect, in which users themselves effectively become the interface. Rieder explains the shift from analyses and critiques of graphical user interfaces (GUIs) to productive projects involving natural user interfaces (NUIs). As we face more and more NUIs in our daily lives, Rieder's exploration—and his Microsoft *Kinect* hacking projects, which are also detailed here—become ad-ditional contributions to the development of new interfaces, thereby chang-ing some of the ways in which we experience the data streams that would otherwise serve convention.

8 From GUI to NUI: Microsoft's *Kinect* and the Politics of the (Body as) Interface

David M. Rieder

Figure 1. Screen capture of passersby registered as potential users by Microsoft's *Kinect* sensor. Image was originally published at the following URL: http://www. pervasive.jku.at/Teaching/lvaInfo.php?key=298

INTRODUCTION: SELFE AND SELFE'S IMPACT ON (GRAPHICAL-USER) INTERFACE STUDIES

In computers and writing (C&W) scholarship, interface studies has been a minor but persistent scholarly topic in numerous publications. Beginning with Patricia Sullivan's article from the late 1980s, in which she argues that scholars associated with technical communication should turn their attention to the subject, "interface" has been explored by scholars in a wide range of fields and sub-fields associated with C&W, including the following: rhetoric theory (Carnegie; Carpenter; Brooke), composition theory and pedagogy (Buck; Haas and Gardner; Mardsjo; Rosinski and Squire; Selfe and Selfe), multimodal composition (Fagerjord; Skulstad and Morrison), and technical and networked communication (Grabill; Spinuzzi).[1] One approach to interface studies that has predominated in the scholarship is related to socio-political issues of equity, identity, and access, and since its publication almost twenty years ago, Cynthia Selfe and Richard Selfe's article, "The Politics of the Interface," has been a touchstone for this critical approach.

Selfe and Selfe's article is an oft-cited reference in articles about the socio-political impact of technological interfaces for good reason. The article is an impassioned call for a "critical and reflective stance" toward the adoption of computers in the classroom (482). It was written at a time when a growing number of administrators and faculty viewed computers as a relatively benign but powerful way to update our classrooms and methods of teaching. Countering that early-adopter fever, Selfe and Selfe challenged us to scrutinize the ways in which software interfaces reintroduce forms of oppression and marginalization that we had been working to extricate from our classrooms. Like a Trojan Horse, the socio-cultural biases against which we'd fought for so long risked being inadvertently reinscribed into the newly established forms of human-computer interaction. After all, technologies are not neutral, and interfaces in particular are expressive of a wide range of socio-cultural and epistemological biases that can impede our pedagogical objectives.

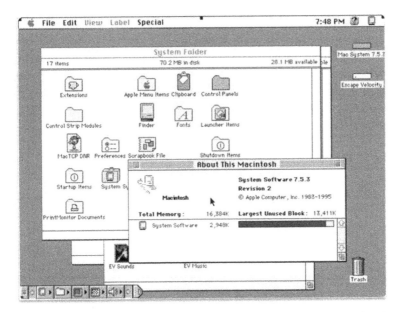

Figure 2. Screen shot of a Macintosh interface around the publication date of Selfe and Selfe's' article

Selfe and Selfe's article is divided in two parts. The first comprises their critiques of interface technologies. It is the longer of the two sections. Three of the arguments they develop are the following. First, computers do not necessarily serve democratic ends: "Computer interfaces . . . are also sites within which the ideological and material legacies of racism, sexism, and colonialism are continuously written and rewritten" (484). Second, the "desktop metaphor" expresses the values of corporate culture, which reinforces the values of white middle- and upper-class users (487). Third, the structure and logic of computer interfaces are aligned with the values of rationality, hierarchy, and *logocentrism* characteristic of Western patriarchal cultures (491). In the shorter second part, they offer three tactics or suggestions for addressing the problems with interfaces that they had just critiqued. First, they encourage a general level of critical awareness about technology issues on the part of both pre-service and in-service teachers (496). Second, they encourage faculty to develop their own interfaces, their own software (497). Finally, they invite students to create mock-ups of their preferred interfaces—interfaces expressive of an alternative (499).

While Selfe and Selfe's article has had a lasting effect on our field because it helped us recognize the socio-politics of the graphical-user interface (GUI), twenty years is a 'long time ago' in the history of popular computing. In that time, the shift from GUI to NUI (natural-user interface) technologies has transformed what a computing environment is. Today, computing environments are increasingly immersive experiences in which it is difficult to distinguish between a user and a system, which means that the ways in which we achieve a critical and reflective stance is changing.

Figure 3. Advertisement for Microsoft's *Kinect*, "You are the Controller!"

Epitomizing the difficulties NUI technologies introduce is one of the tag lines for Microsoft's *Kinect*, "You are the controller!" (see Figure 3 above). If we are the controller/interface, from where do we stand in order to act critically and reflectively? If, in an immersive, NUI environment it's no longer possible to have a standpoint, a point of perspective, how do we critique the technology?

In order to extend the legacy of Selfe and Selfe's contribution to interface studies, I offer two interrelated propositions. The first, related to the exigence of the user-as-interface, is that we redirect our critical attention from the interface on the screen to what Adrienne Rich once called the "geography closest in" (i.e., our bodies)—and specifically to tactical or critical explorations of a body's potential. The power of

NUI technologies is derived from the use of our voice and gestures to engage with a system. At this point, most NUI interfaces with which we interact look like GUIs, but, as NUIs mature, the ways in which we control a computational environment will have less to do with on-screen metaphors, icons, and buttons and more to do with an ethos that we perform. Anticipating this radical shift in computing is an opportunity to redefine the focal point of our critical concerns.

The second proposition is in response to the mainstreaming of computational thinking—in part due to the availability of easy-to-learn programming languages. Since Selfe and Selfe's article was published, programming is no longer something that wizards do exclusively on the other side of the two-cultures split. At this point in the history of popular computing, humanists can engage directly with computational media. Numerous high-level languages have become available that have lowered the learning curve, and several of those languages, such as *Processing*, offer novice programmers powerful ways to design immersive, interactive environments. Related to this point, computers and networks have become fast enough to make programming an expressive art because the historical limits on memory, bandwidth, and processor speed do not constrain programmers to the equivalent of a current-traditional emphasis on conciseness and clarity in writing. Today, alongside computer science, an experimental, ad hoc culture of open (i.e., free and collaborative), experimental work has blossomed.

For these reasons, it's time to focus on the production of novel interfaces that embody our critical values and concerns, rather than limiting ourselves to the analysis and critique of someone else's technologies. In Selfe and Selfe's article, the call to invent new interfaces is overshadowed by a focus on representational critique. As I'll explain shortly, based in part on my experiences working with Microsoft's *Kinect*, socio-cultural critique in immersive NUI environments leads to the conclusion that representational critique must be transformed into an inventional art, a post-representational, tactical pursuit.

NUI on the Rise

Figure 4. Detail from August de los Reyes' presentation, "Predicting the Past"

In a presentation titled "Predicting the Past," August de los Reyes explains that NUIs comprise a suite of human-computer technologies including voice, touch, gesture, and stylus or pen. When you interact with a computer system by speaking to it, tapping or swiping across it, gesturing toward it in the air, or using a stylus to write on a screen, you are using a NUI technology. According to De los Reyes, NUI will be the third paradigm shift in computing. In Figure 4 above, which is a graphic from his PowerPoint presentation, De Los Reyes depicts an evolution in popular computing that begins with the command-line interface, and after the present era of GUI, shifts to NUI. It's also worthwhile emphasizing that the historical movement toward NUI coincides with a movement toward the increasingly intuitive and directly accessed, which means that the implied line separating self and technology is blurred.

It is important to note that some NUI technologies have been around for several decades, but it's the relatively recent explosion of interest in and profitability from products including Apple's *iPhone* and *iPad* and Microsoft's *Kinect* that has led to the uptrend in positive discourse and outright evangelism about them—especially from Microsoft.

In the following three quotes, which are paradigmatic of the optimism and excitement around NUIs, a new age of computing seems apparent. In their book, *Brave NUI World*, Daniel Wigdor and Dennis Wixon write, "Now we stand at the brink of another potential evolution in computing. Natural-user interfaces (NUIs) seem to be in a position similar to the GUI in the early 1980s" (2). Chief Research and Strategy Officer at Microsoft Craig Mundie claims, "The transition to a natural user interface will change everything from the way students write term papers and play computer games to how scientists study global population growth and its impact on our natural resources." Even Bill Gates has responded to the promise of NUI. In an essay titled "The Power of the Natural User Interface," in which he focuses on the *Kinect*, Gates writes, "One of the most important current trends in digital technology is the emergence of natural user interface, or NUI. We've had things like touch screen and voice recognition for a while now. But with *Kinect*, we are seeing the impact when people can interact with technology in the same ways that they interact with each other."

Only time will tell if NUI technologies will be the next computing paradigm, but based on my own experiments with the *Kinect*, I see considerable opportunities for radically new approaches to theory and practice associated with both rhetoric and writing. And if NUI does eclipse GUI, leading to new conventions for human-computer interaction, some of us will turn to Selfe and Selfe's article because of its long-valued contribution to a socio-political approach to interface studies.

EXPLORING THE *KINECT*'S POTENTIAL

My own work with the *Kinect* began in early 2011 with two colleagues in the College of Design at NC State. We developed an interactive art project that enabled users to "write" graffiti on a screen projected on the side of a building. The "Interactive Graffiti Project" was based on the skeletal or joint data streaming from the system. Arguably, the most impressive part of the *Kinect* is that it can identify human figures from everything else in its viewing frame, break each of them down into a set of twenty joints, and track all twenty joints continuously at 30 frames-per-second. This capability had not been so easily available for research before the *Kinect* was released.

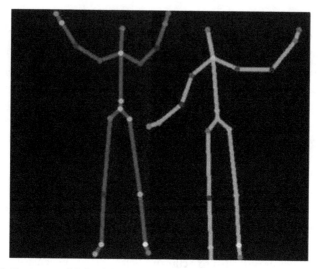

Figure 5. Depiction of skeletal data for two users in front of the *Kinect* sensor

For a programmer, access to the skeletal data means that you have access to twenty three-dimensional data points representative of a user's position and movements around and in front of the sensor, in "real-time." This is the data stream on which most of the commercial games for *Kinect* are based: the ability to make an on-screen avatar kick balls, jump around, or dance is based on your redefinition as a surface comprising twenty points.

Although the *Kinect* defines a jointed body in conventional terms, and many of the on-screen interfaces reinforce that perspective to-date, there's no limit to the ways in which those data points can be redefined computationally. For example, you could redeploy skeletal data from a user as points (or folds) comprising a novel, topological surface. Once we deterritorialize the origin of those points, we can experiment, developing new types of bodily gesture and movement contributing to a new canon of digital delivery. And once a user's movements and position are redefined radically, the environmental feedback from the projected movements has the potential to transform how that user experiences herself, which can lead to new, counter-hegemonic experiences of self. In *Materializing New Media*, Anna Munster emphasizes the potential for developing new experiences of our bodies in our "encounters" with code when she writes,

> Computers offer us multiplications and extensions of our
> bodily actions... These multiplications by no means pro-

vide seamless matches between body and code; the mismatch characteristics of divergent series triggers the extension of our corporeality out toward our informatic counterparts… It is this extensive vector that draws embodiment away from its historical capture within a notion that the body is a bounded interiority. (33)

Munster is not writing explicitly about politics in this excerpt, but her argument extends easily to it. If we equate her description of a bounded interiority with the socio-cultural constraints constitutive of person's sense of self, her point is that mismatches between body and code, which might emerge from a novel redefinition of the skeletal data points, can lead to new experiences of our embodied selves. And if these mismatches are designed tactically, they can change the limits of the bounded interiorities interfacing with the code. Related to the trope of the 'geography closest in,' we might characterize this kind of NUI-based approach to tactical invention as a novel form of geopolitics born of an extensive vector that points beyond the centripetalism of hegemonic relations.

DEPTH IS FLAT

One of the other data streams on which creative work is now based is the depth data. At thirty frames-per-second, the *Kinect* sends a 640×480 frame or image of depth values representative of the depth of every object in the sensor's viewing range. In other words, it streams a 640×480 matrix of depth values representative of an approximately 8×14' space in front of the sensor.

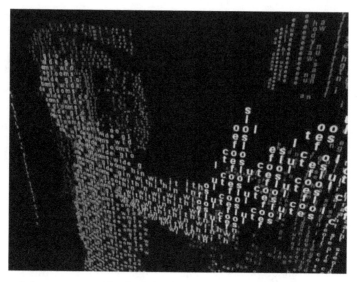

Figure 6. Screen capture of emBody(text) {

In a project titled *emBody(text) {*, Kevin Brock and I used the *Kinect's* depth data stream to develop an embodied, hypertextual environment. Our goal was to create an interactive experience that would be intuitive and compelling for an audience largely unfamiliar with the *Kinect's* technical capabilities. In a way, *emBody(text) {* was our "Hello, World" program. Our digital writing project debuted in a group exhibit titled *ID:ENTITY* at Raleigh's contemporary art museum, CAM Raleigh (see Figure 6 above), and then at the CHAT Festival at Duke University. A few months later, in collaboration with Rachel Bagby, a Twitter-based version of the project titled *emBody(dekaaz) {* was on display at CCCC 2012. For the version at CCCC 2012, the interface was based on the following characteristics:

- We imagined that the space in front of the *Kinect* was divided among ten distinct zones.
- We created ten equivalent zones or layers along the z-axis in the virtual, 3D space of the projected screen.
- We distributed each of the ten most recent tweets to #dekaaz in one of the ten virtual depth planes.
- We made it possible to "mash up" or combine parts of different tweets when participants interacted with two or more zones in front of the *Kinect* sensor.

- We developed a method of identifying which of the ten zones had the most activity at a given moment in order to shift perspective on the 3D space.

The effect of all of this was something like an embodied hypertext. On the second floor of the convention center at CCCC 2012, passive or active participation with *emBody(dekaaz) {* led to mash-ups of the three-stanza poems sent to *#dekaaz*.

As I reflect on my experiences with the *Kinect*'s depth data, it occurs to me that it is a "degree zero" for experimental work because the data is (in Deleuzian terms) an intensive form, pure potential.[2] Whereas you have to "deconstruct" the implied (human) territory or ground of the skeletal data points in order to reach an ontologically flat plane, the depth data is an already-posthumanized space. Ontologically, it's already flat. Working with the depth data puts one in the kind of *uncountry* that Victor Vitanza once characterized as wild and savage (53), and which, due to its savage nature, we might then value as a space in which the *bricoleur* practices a (computational) 'science of the concrete.'[3] The opportunities for developing new forms of interactions are considerable.

Conclusion

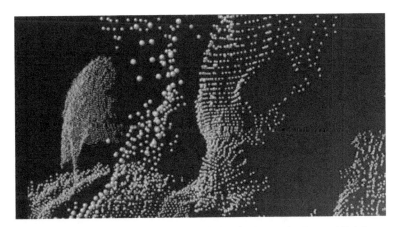

Figure 7. Exploratory "hack" of *Kinect* depth data by Samantha Swartz (click image to follow link)

As Selfe and Selfe explained in their article, politics reside in the interfaces of our techno-mediated worlds, and since the interface of a

NUI environment has shifted, so should the focus of our attention. In Samantha Swartz's "hack" of the *Kinect* (see Figure 7 above), which is based on the depth data, we are presented with a complex, ever-changing series of curving, pointilized surfaces. During the film, we realize that the surfaces are two participants; at one point, we can see them holding hands. But the identifiable hands and arms soon melt away into an intensive swirl of movement. The depiction of those bodies—the projected feedback—is based on the interface that Swartz designed. Swartz's hack is an example of the ways in which the mismatch about which Munster wrote can lead to new relations between bodies and code.

As a field, we have an opportunity to explore new forms of digital writing and rhetoric by critically and creatively engaging with the data streams that represent who we are and what we can be. In immersive NUI computing environments, the politics of the interface are derived from the ways in which we experience the feedback of our selves. In fact, the interface itself is a derivative of a dynamic equation comprising bodies and code; politics associated with interface design is a kind of integral calculus, as we can see in Swartz's experiment. If we contribute to the development of new interfaces, thereby changing some of the ways in which we experience the data streams that would otherwise serve convention, we can accomplish two important things simultaneously. We can extend a critical legacy toward interface studies inaugurated by Selfe and Selfe, and, perhaps most importantly, we can elevate the role and value of invention serving those ends in today's brave new NUI worlds.

NOTES

1. In his article, "On Divides and Interfaces," Jeffrey Grabill hazards that Patricia Sullivan "provides perhaps the first mention of interface design in *Computers and Composition*" (469). I hazard to agree with him.

2. In *Writing Degree Zero*, Roland Barthes characterizes poetic language unrestricted by convention and acculturation as "reduced to a sort of zero degree, pregnant with all past and future specifications" (Barthes 48). My Barthean allusion is meant to characterize the depth data as similarly pregnant with potential. The allusion to Deleuze's concept of intensive qualities parallels the reason for the Barthean one.

3. A "science of the concrete" and *bricolage* are allusions to Claude Levi-Strauss' opening chapter, "The Science of the Concrete," in *Savage Mind*.

WORKS CITED

Bagby, Rachel. "Dekaaz: Word Jazz for the Mind." *Rachel Bagby: Bless Your Voice. Be the Song.* 2012. Web.

Barthes, Roland. *Writing Degree Zero.* Trans. Annette Lavers and Colin Smith. New York: Farrar, Straus & Giroux, 1977. Print.

Brooke, Collin Gifford. *Lingua Fracta: Toward a Rhetoric of New Media.* Cresskill, NJ: Hampton, 2009. Print.

Buck, Amber M. "The Invisible Interface: MS Word in the Writing Center." *Computers and Composition* 25.4 (2008): 396-415. Print.

Carnegie, Teena A. M. "Interface as Exordium: The Rhetoric of Interactivity." *Computers and Composition* 26.3 (2009): 164-173. Print.

Carpenter, Rick. "Boundary Negotiations: Electronic Environments as Interface." *Computers and Composition* 26.3 (2009): 138-148. Print.

De los Reyes, August. "Predicting the Past." *Web Directions South.* Sydney Convention Center. 25 Sept. 2008. Web.

Fagerjord, Anders. "Between Place and Interface: Designing Situated Sound for the iPhone." *Computers and Composition* 28.3 (2011): 255-263. Print.

Gates, Bill. "The Power of the Natural User Interface." *The Gates Notes.* 28 Oct. 2011. Web.

Grabill, Jeffrey T. "On Divides and Interfaces: Access, Class, and Computers." *Computers and Composition* 20.4 (2003): 455-472. Print.

Haas, Mark, and Clinton Gardner. "MOO in Your Face: Researching, Designing, and Programming a User-Friendly Interface." *Computers and Composition* 16.3 (1999): 341-358. Print.

Hayles, N. Katherine. "Deeper into the Machine: Learning to Speak Digital." *Computers and Composition* 19.4 (2002): 371-386. Print.

Levi-Strauss, Claude. *The Savage Mind.* Chicago: U of Chicago P, 1968. Print.

Mardsjo, Karin. "Interfacing Technology." *Computers and Composition* 13.3 (1996): 303-316. Print.

Mundie, Craig. "Computing Naturally." *Microsoft News Center.* 3 Mar. 2010. Web.

Munster, Anna. *Materializing New Media: Embodiment in Information Aesthetics.* Hanover, NH: Dartmouth College P, 2006. Print.

Ramsay, Stephen. "On Building." *Stephen Ramsey Blog.* N.d. Web.

Rieder, David M., and Kevin Brock. "emBody(text) {." *ID:ENTITY. Self: Perception + Reality.* 3rd Emerging Artists Series. CAM Raleigh. 18 Nov. 2011-13 Feb. 2012. Digital Interactive.

Rieder, David M., Kevin Brock, and Rachel Bagby. "emBody(dekaaz) {." Conference on College Composition and Communication. St. Louis Convention Center, St. Louis. 22 Mar. 2012. Digital Interactive.

Rosinski, Paula, and Megan Squire. "Strange Bedfellows: Human-Computer Interaction, Interface Design, and Composition Pedagogy." *Computers and Composition* 26.3 (2009): 149-163. Print.

Selfe, Cynthia, and Richard Selfe. "The Politics of the Interface: Power and Its Exercise in Electronic Contact Zones." *College Composition and Communication* 45.4 (1994): 480-504. Print.

Skjulstad, Synne, and Andrew Morrison. "Movement in the Interface." *Computers and Composition* 22.4 (2005): 413-433. Print.

Spinuzzi, Clay. "Light Green Doesn't Mean Hydrology: Toward a Visual-Rhetorical Framework for Interface Design." *Computers and Composition* 18.1 (2001): 39-53. Print.

Sullivan, Patricia. "Human-Computer Interaction Perspectives on Word-Processing Issues." *Computers and Composition* 6.3 (1989): 11-33. Print.

Vitanza, Victor J. *Negation, Subjectivity, and the History of Rhetoric.* Albany: SUNY P, 1997. Print.

Wigdor, Daniel, and Dennis Wixon. *Brave NUI World: Designing Natural User Interfaces for Touch and Gesture.* New York: Morgan Kaufman, 2011. Print.

REFLECTIONS

Reflections
Public Rhetoric, Civic Writing, and Service Learning
VOLUME 13 • ISSUE 1 • FALL 2013

Latin@s in Public Rhetoric, Civic
Writing, and Service-Learning

Reflections is on the Web at
http://reflectionsjournal.net/

Reflections, a peer reviewed journal, provides a forum for scholarship on civic writing, service-learning and public rhetoric. Originally founded as a venue for teachers, researchers, students and community partners to share research and discuss the theoretical, political and ethical implications of community-based writing and writing instruction, *Reflections* publishes a lively collection of essays, empirical studies, community writing, student work, interviews and reviews in a format that brings together emerging scholars and leaders in the fields of community-based writing and civic engagement.

Chicanas Making Change: Institutional Rhetoric Comisión Feminil Mexicana Nacional

Dr. Kendall Leon addresses change in institutional spaces and examines how Chicanas (Mexicanas or Latinas) use experience to "make" or "construct" things, such as organizations, histories, and practices. Her archival research on Chicana feminist organizations is groundbreaking given the scarcity of this type of public rhetoric analysis, and her personal connections to her archival research with the article demonstrates her responsibilities to her home communities while meeting the expectations set for academics.

9 Chicanas Making Change: Institutional Rhetoric and the Comisión Femenil Mexicana Nacional

Kendall Leon

Abstract: This article draws on an archival case study of the Comisión Femenil Mexicana Nacional (CFMN). Building on my experience as an activist and working in communities and institutions, I argue that it is valuable to examine and translate the histories and practices of organizations like the CFMN to learn the rhetorical abilities we need to operate and make collective change as both part of and outside of publics and institutions. To make this argument, I analyze how Chicanas of the CFMN incited change by writing, theorizing, and making an identity through what might be considered mundane and programmatic writing.

It still always surprises me when I realize that things in my life that I thought happened by pure coincidence in fact, had been building up to this moment and to this place. I am sure many of you can relate to those "aha" moments when your breath is literally suspended as you become aware that the path you have been on was always meant to lead you here. One time this happened was during my dissertation defense when I realized that perhaps I hadn't been lost all along, and that I had resisted giving up any piece of me in order to make this academic thing work. My dissertation braided together all of the pieces of me that on paper looked disconnected and centered on an archival case study of one of the first Chicana[1] feminist organizations, the Comisión Femenil Mexicana Nacional (CFMN). As I had been involved with community and non-profit organizations, I wanted to focus on collectives. As someone who orients to the field through organizational writing, it was also important to me to expand where we turn to for evidence of theorizing and identity making. Through this research I was able to build from the ground up, a theory of a Chicana rhetoric and to extend the making of Chicana to programmatic writing and the building of an organization (Leon, *Building a Chicana Rhetoric*).

Another "aha" moment happened when I was interviewed by a writer from the newsletter for a people's self-help type of housing program, which allowed low income people to purchase and build their own homes in their communities. To participate in the program, potential homeowners had to fall at or below 80% of the area's median income level. For those of you not familiar with these types of programs, the way many of them work is that a group of prospective homeowners who meet the criteria are placed together in a group. The group then collectively builds their tract of homes. The homes are located near and often directly next to each other. I was being interviewed because this program is what allowed my Mom to build a house for my three siblings and I when I was five years old.

Our house was located in a racially diverse and socio economically depressed community, constituted largely by Hmong, Latina/o and African-American families. The neighborhood is located right in the center of the city. But, in a pretty obvious act of ghettoization, the city drew boundary lines around this area to exclude the neighborhood (and the poor and predominately brown skinned people in it) from receiving funds for things like sidewalks and access to other city services. Instead, we were considered "county," despite the fact that we were smack dab in the middle. This neighborhood had its own name that included "town" in it so it really sounded and felt like it was a separate place: It was (and still is) known as "the bad area" to outsiders. I remember when my Mom let me play basketball in the fifth grade and when I participated in the GATE program, I had to bus to other schools because our neighborhood school didn't have either. I was the only Latin@ from the "poor school." Many of the kids who I became friends with in these programs at different schools were not allowed to come over to my house because of where I lived. Yet, to this day, this is the area that I feel at home and supported by the people around me. For many of us, our neighborhood and the people in it became extended family members, which was strengthened by the fact that some of the few owner occupied homes (like ours) were built as part of the people's self-help program.

During that interview for that newsletter, I discussed how in building our houses together, we were building communities. This community building happened in part through the stories or what we might call pláticas, all of our families told together, as the adults struggled to complete the houses, while working one or more jobs, perhaps a single parent like my Mom, with kids scrambling around each other, watched by a rotating slew of older siblings. While I was answering the interview questions, it dawned on me that it was this experience that led me to my interests in working in and later studying collectives. The learning and the relationships that I remember from this place, this place that I turned to for support and protection, were about doing good for your community and peoples; in essence what scholars like Octavio Pimentel have identified as buena gente. According to Pimentel, *buena gente* is a feeling of connectedness and a related "desire to put the needs of 'others' before oneself " (174). The purpose of getting any kind of institutional education was not just about individual status but about how you could leverage what you learned or got access to for the greater good. And while I was still in my neighborhood, I did my best to uphold that part of the deal.

But, when by sheer luck (and really, in my case it was and that's a whole other story!), I ended up in this other place—the university—I found myself constantly trying to reconcile what always felt like disparate parts of who I was and what I was committed to. As Miguel and Franciso Guajardo point out in their writing on this schism, working in the university can further distance us from our home communities and our commitments to the public good. They ask of those who survive and remain in the institution: "what does one keep, what does one give up, what does one sacrifice, and how does one adjust in order to contribute to the public good?" (73). How do we maintain our responsibilities to our home communities while also meeting the expectations for us as academics? Within the university, we are often further limited by what we study and how the bodies we inhabit—and those of the theorists we cite. Just like the city drawing boundaries around the neighborhood I grew up in, we are living the same ghettoization and disjuncture in our field: communities cannot teach us about institutions; the theories of only some people are applicable to all; and if we identify ourselves as Rhetoric and Composition scholars of color, it necessarily means we are given the authority to write about and care about only certain topics or issues.

This is what I experienced in graduate school (what I still experience, several years later as a faculty member), trying to find mentors who get the different parts of me, trying to find out how to navigate this place and figuring out how to make my various commitments and interests mesh together and to make sense to others. This became even more difficult as I shifted my scholarly focus to writing program administration and professional writing. In doing so, I have experienced a disconnect between this interest and my commitment to Chicana rhetoric and Latin@ communities. For instance, as I looked at research on institutional rhetoric and writing program administration, I found little that reflected a commitment to Latin@ communities and rhetorics. When I have shared my research on the CFMN, especially with crowds of people who want me to talk about their poetic writing, their individual leaders, or their more explicitly "activist" performances; or when I have attempted to connect what I learned from their organization to being (materially and intellectually) in an institution and to writing program administration, I am often asked: what does archival research on a Chicana feminist organization have to do with *this*?

And this leads me to another one of those "aha" moments. In talking about this organization with these different audiences, what I have come to realize is that this is the task for us who want to make change—to do the work of rhetorical translation and connectivity. This is precisely the type of ability that I was able to learn from the CFMN through their conscious decision to build an extensive and thorough archival collection so that as past CFMN president Eva Couvillion writes, "we all can refer to it when dark days loom large and we wonder why we are involved anyway" (CFMN's "President's Message"). In a letter to the past national presidents, Beatrice Olvera Stotzer also wrote of the value for future generations in establishing the CFMN archival collection: "This will in effect give historians a legitimate research mechanism which can be added to the data on the Chicana feminist movement. We can only speculate on the immense value of the information that Comisión [sic] will contribute" ("Letter to Past Presidents", 1).

What I want to share with you is an account of the CFMN doing just this type of work to make change, enacting an ability that we learn through stories to connect past and future, as well as community sites and institutions. I want to ground this account in a knowing and know how that is developed out of our material lives. Many scholars have described this grounded, strategic and connective practice. For instance, Chela Sandoval identifies this as "differential consciousness," an ability to "read the current situation of power" and to choose how to respond in a way to push at, or transform the situation. According to Sandoval this is an ability that is "a survival skill well known to oppressed people" and enables coalition building (60). Similarly, Gloria Anzaldúa, describes "conocimiento" as a holistic process of inner and connective work that enables us to build bridges and make change ("now let us shift"). Finally, Delores Delgado Bernal names her "mujerista sensibility" as one that necessitates putting oneself in relation to others and maintaining "a commitment to social change." As part of enacting a "mujerista vision," one has to "cross borders, learn from history, place a priority on collectivity, take care of onself, and be committed to social transformation" (136). Regardless of what it has been called, it has been named. And it has been practiced, as evidenced in the CFMN's building of a Chicana organization and its respective archival collection.

Figure 1: Copy of a CFMN logo

Started with a series of resolutions drafted at the 1970 National Chicano Issues Conference in response to the Chicanas in attendance who felt their issues were being excluded from existent activist movements, the CFMN grew to become a leading collective in the Chicana movement. Figure 1 shows a copy of a CFMN logo that was used for brochures and other publications.

Although the CFMN is most known for their activist work protesting the forced sterilization of women of color,[2] and many of their leaders became well known as individual activists whose writings have been referenced and anthologized, much of their work was in fact programmatic and archival.[3] This work included documenting the building of an organization and the making of a collective identity. As part of my commitment to making connections with histories, I think it is valuable to have a broader sense of how Chicanas have incited change by writing, theorizing, and making an identity. To understand how change occurs, I had to be able to look outside of what might be expected of me as a Chican@ scholar in Rhetoric and Composition—I looked away from the poetic writing and more public performances and instead, researched programmatic writing like the organizational flow chart in Figure 2. This writing was frequently mundane, and often looked like marginalia and small notations on the archival documents.

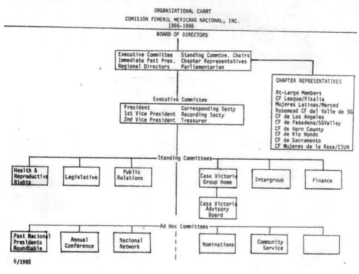

Figure 2: Copy of a Board of Director's Flow Chart

From my experience as an activist and working in communities and institutions, I know that change is often achieved through subtle shifts in behind-the-scenes practices that in order to be recognized require adopting different heuristics. I think this is especially true for Latin@s as we experience being constructed as non-actors in the world of what we might label as "public rhetorics," as if to denote that there is something inherently accessible about such spaces. In other words, for the CFMN, as well as for myself and other Chican@s in higher education, being Chican@ means we are faced with constructions of Latina/Mexican women as not rhetorical in these public and institutional spaces; our challenge is learning how to change this. In response, I argue that it is valuable to examine community-based groups and to listen to histories like the CFMN and Chicana rhetoric broadly, as a way to learn about the rhetorical abilities we need to operate as both part of and outside of publics and institutions.

In my previous writing about this organization, I have discussed two rhetorical practices that the CFMN adopted that reflected and built Chicanidad: La Hermandad (or Chicana sisterhood) and re-envisioning the past to instantiate a historically organizing Chicana (see Leon "La Hermandad"). In this article, I focus on a story told through the archival collection that centers on the CFMN and their affiliate organization, the Chicana Service Action Center (CSAC). This story traces their involvement with accessing and developing employment training for Chicanas, specifically with the California Employment and Training Act (CETA). I examine this story in two ways: first, in the moment as indicative of the ways that Chicanas responded to a historical absence of their experiences in employment training discourse; and second, as indicative of a strategy of action which demonstrates the movement of collective change as working slowly through the nuanced internal work of an organization that was often not visible as public a act.

> "*Spanish origin persons are included in the white population!*"
> —CETA/Manpower and Employee Training Programs

> *. . . just recently, in looking, for example, at publications that the Employment Development of the State of California puts out, over 150 publications for this past year, only three or four had any kind of statistics relating to minorities period. And some of those didn't even have statistics for minority females. I ask you, how can a job training program such as CETA, such as the Job Training Partnership Act be developed around the needs of these women when we don't even know what they are. What are their characteristics?* —Maria Rodriguez, MALDEF attorney and collaborator with the CFMN, Testimony before the Califor-

> nia Legislature Senate Committee on Health and Welfare and Assembly Human Services Committee, "In the matter of: The feminization of poverty"

In the above epigraph, taken from a document in the CFMN files, Maria Rodriguez[4] alludes to a vexing problem that Chicanas faced: a historical erasure of the experiences of minority women that manifested as a lack of statistical employment data. In turn, this altered the ontology of what "minority women" could be and do. To be more specific, as you will see in the following story of the CFMN's involvement with employment training programs, this absence of statistical evidence of the experience of "minority women" resulted in a lack of federal funding for employee training programs for "minority women" because an exigency had yet to be established. The CFMN and their partner organizations existed to redress such absence in the public discourse on employment. These interventions took place though the invention of public issues, in debates about defining the problems at hand, and through strategic behind-the-scenes work that slowly redressed the physical absence of Chicanas in public spaces.

To tell the story about the CFMN's involvement in employment training initiatives, I am going to set up three scenes for you[5]. Scene one provides some context, exigency if you will, for pursuing employment training as a Chicana organization. This scene relays the way that being such an organization meant inventing the issue to begin with. Scene two also provides some context and it relays the "crisis" of this moment for the CFMN. In scene two I focus on a representative sample of texts and actions that are more public: the activist performances that are externally focused and attempt to respond to misconstructions of Chicana identity. Scene three follows a different story that happens at the same time as the first two scenes. While the CFMN forwarded a public strategy to address an issue, at the same time, they enacted a rhetorical knowing and practice that strategically addressed the source of the contention. This is the scene in which I see evidence of differential consciousness in action and to which I turn for a rhetorical education on how to be in institutions.

SCENE ONE: CHICANAS NEED EMPLOYMENT TRAINING—CREATING A PROBLEM AT HAND

During the 1970's, Chicana identity became more widely circulated; its emergence and circulation was a response to the realization that there was a lack of experiential stories told that had *real* consequences. At the same time, the country had a growing need for employment training programs, with a push to train workers in the skilled trades. Prior to the inception of the Comprehensive Employment and Training Act (CETA), the Department of Labor began collecting and distributing statistics on the employment needs of their populace. In their needs assessment report, Department of Labor' s fine print noted "Hispanic populations are included in the white population" (as cited in Flores, "Speech"). As Maria Rodriguez pointed out in her testimony that I used to introduce this case study, the experiences of Hispanic populations, especially Latina women, were not being specified in the data collection and reporting on employment training programs. According to the CFMN, having their lives collapsed within a category of people who were not visibly or linguistically marked in the same way meant that their concerns were not seen as issues. As a result, no one recognized the need. The problem of the availability of jobs or barriers to securing jobs was not seen as a problem for Latinas because their experiences were not accounted for in data collection. Materially, without these statistics to identify a need, the CFMN was unable to obtain federal funding.

Chicanas affiliated with the newly formed CFMN recognized a need to tell stories about accessing employment for their own communities. They knew they had to respond to a historical absence of numerical accounting in order to later redress the issues that they would reveal with their own community-specific data collection. In other words they needed to invent a problem that seemingly did not exist. The CFMN made the invention of this problem part of their organization's mission, which in turn built a trajectory for the organization.

As such, the CFMN decided to conduct their own needs assessment that targeted Latina women. A lengthy questionnaire in the CFMN files dated April 11, 1972 included questions about children (when born and how many); about marital and employment status; formal education received; current childcare arrangement; if the respondent had dropped out of school and the reasons for this; past participation in a job training program and the success of this participation; and interests in receiving training and in what field (Mexican/Chicana women's survey). Now these questions were strategic—they asked about their experiences accessing employment and being employed. They asked about their lives holistically—as women, as mothers, and as wage earners. From their needs assessment, they created two related physical centers that were affiliated with the CFMN: the Chicana Service Action Center (CSAC) and El Centro de Niños, a bilingual and bicultural childcare center. The Chicana Service Action Center, founded in 1972, is an organization located in Los Angeles.

In its earliest iteration, on paper the CSAC was a project of the CFMN. However, in its operation, it was, presumably, the CFMN (until it later split into a separate entity due to disagreements between staff and board members and the realization that the center would best exist on its own). Although it became a separate entity, a relationship persisted due to shared people and historically because the CSAC files are part of the CFMN archival collection[6].

Chicana Service Action Center

Figure 3: Copy of a Chicana Service Action Center flyer

As a result of building these two centers, the CFMN was able to talk to the clients these two centers served. They listened to women relay stories about prevalent assumptions that were effecting members of their communities to obtain employment. One was that the model utilized by available employment training services, which were presumably accessible to all, were really geared toward Anglos and more frequently, Anglo men. For example, when accessing employee training, women in their community were being referred to secretarial and office work—which posed a problem for some monolingual and/ or bilingual women as it relied on particular language use and on unspoken cultural norms about office behavior.

Further, the only apprenticeship training programs that paid apprentices were in the skilled trades—carpentry, plumbing and so forth. As former CSAC director Francisca Flores pointed out in a later letter to an Edna Olivia, a research associate at the University of Texas, the clients they worked with at the CSAC were unable to access the apprenticeship programs that were federally or state funded. Flores wrote, "these programs are restrictive and 'controlled' by the employers hiring the persons (men or women) that are eligible to be trained by the unions in the various industries. It cannot honestly be said that the unions are waiting breathlessly to receive women into the various crafts" (1). In this same letter, she shared some startling statistics on women in the Department of Labor sponsored programs: "Total number of women in California Apprenticeship Program as of January 1980 is 4.1%. Hispanic and Black women, each group, constitute .004%. Total number of minority women in this program are .008+%! (2 of 3).[7]

Accessing these apprenticeships was proving to be impossible for women in general. This was compounded by the fact that Latina women needed paid employment training. However, this was not even consideredan issue because of the stereotypical construction of Latina women. As CFMN representatives pointed out In their publication "Chicanas and the Labor Force," in spite of the construction of Latina women as submissive housewives supported (and controlled) by Machismo husbands, many of the women they saw were single heads of household. In their monitoring in CETA's administration and implementation, the Chicana Rights Project of MALDEF filed an administrative complaint against the city of San Antonio on the basis that the city failed to equally include Mexican American women in their programs (Hernández).[8] The design of CETA intake forms that disallowed women from selecting "head of household" was one way that women were not adequately represented in the program participation data. Just as the Department of Labor data collection enveloped the Hispanic population into the White population, intake forms used in employment training programs concealed a reality that women, and more precisely minority women, faced as they sought employment.[9]

To combat this problem, the CSAC and CFMN shifted an invisible issue in institutional discourse on employment into existence through statistics. These findings were also presented by Yolanda Nava to the California Commission on the Status of Women in "The Chicana and Employment: Needs Analysis and Recommendation for Legislation." In this document, Nava identified a disjuncture between a reductive stereotype and construction of Latina women and the reality that many Latina women were working outside of the home. The CFMN and the CSAC as organizations were being built around the contention that, first, employment statistics did not include information on women and minorities (let alone minority women); second, that training programs did not make available "non traditional" jobs to women in general that would allow for large number of Latina women who were heads of household to support themselves on one wage; and, third, that training programs geared toward women did not factor in language, cultural differences, or expectations in workplace settings.[10] In response, then, the CFMN created a public problem through their data collection and by writing about these research findings in various reports. As a result, they garnered the ability to argue for federal funding.

SCENE TWO: ENTER THE COMPREHENSIVE EMPLOYMENT AND TRAINING ACT (CETA) OR, NOW WE HAVE A DIFFERENT PROBLEM

The CFMN, then, effectively created a public problem: that Latinas were employed outside of the home and needed to access employee training programs. However, the problem at hand shifted. In 1973, the Federal government passed the Comprehensive Employment and Training Act to provide funds for employment training programs as well as job opportunities in the public sector. The implementation of the CETA Act opened up the ability to have a discussion about employment training and created available funding for collecting statistics more broadly. The CFMN acted on this exigency by submitting a request for funding for a special survey of female, Spanish speaking participants in programs authorized under CETA. On the back of a letter in response to their request, a CFMN member left a record of their research and action plan: "1. get L.A. statistics on monolingual women who work in L.A./on welfare/heads of households 2. on some groups who have limited English who need ESL 3. U.S. school young women—poor language skills/to identify/outreach/recruit/refer/and/ or/train—one year/place on job" (Note on back of letter to Pierce Quinlan, re: Reply).

Using this research and action plan, the CSAC secured Department of Labor contract #4047-06. One purpose of the contract was to collect statistics on female, Spanish-speaking participants in CETA funded programs administered by the Manpower project.[11] The CSAC and CFMN shared these statistics in multiple texts such as booklets, presentations making recommendations at legislative hearings, and the well-known and reprinted presentation: "The Needs of the Spanish Speaking Mujer in Woman-Manpower Training Programs." Anna Nieto Gomez delivered a version of this report as a presentation at a Manpower symposium. Gomez began her presentation of this report by stating that the initiative was brought by women attending the Manpower seminar, in response to the fact that the "federal programs are only sensitive to minority groups or to women, it was felt that the needs and issues of Spanish speaking women have not been addressed" (1). If women are addressed, Gomez claimed, it was only along a white/ black breakdown, without considerations for other minority women. Accordingly, Gomez called for further research to study the "socio-economic factors related to the Spanish Speaking women in the labor market" and to develop effective policy that included utilizing community resources (1). Gomez pointed out that many of the training programs developed by Manpower required little English speaking abilities, such as in the skilled trades. As such, Gomez posited that it would make sense to create bilingual and bicultural curriculum to train women in traditional and non-traditional jobs for women, since, given their statistics, there was a "heavy concentration of Spanish speaking women" in "low-paying traditional jobs" that require little or no English speaking language abilities (2).

What Gomez subtly made apparent was the interesting "logic" of the Manpower training programs. If most of the programs did not require English-speaking abilities, then why did they not use bilingual trainers? Also, the jobs that these women were able to access were interestingly paid a lot less than the traditionally male jobs that required similar English speaking abilities. Thusly, Gomez argued, it would behoove the Manpower project—a project dedicated to providing employment training for everyone to improve their lives—"to train and/ or upgrade monolingual women into both traditional and non-traditional jobs for women"(2).

In addition to distributing statistics and recommendations to government agencies, another purpose of the CFMN's Department of Labor contract was to recruit women to participate in a pilot program "through personal contacts, clients who came in [and] referred neighbors" and by using connections with other community organizations and Spanish-oriented media (Department of Labor Contract). As described in her presentation to the Manpower project, the pilot program would create "bilingual/bicultural Spanish speaking, self-development program designed to increase positive attitudes towards women in the labor force and to also expose myths of working women as well as identify the socio-economic importance of women's roles in society" (Gomez 3). This program would approach employment training for Chicanas holistically, meaning that they would include, among other things, a staff of bilingual trainers, access to bicultural child care, vocational training in the trades, communication skills development, and counseling for families and co-workers to facilitate their understanding of the "cultural and economic work patterns of the Spanish Speaking woman" (Gomez 6).

Using the data from their own research and the recommendations they made to the Manpower project, the CSAC ran a pilot program in which they provided culturally appropriate training to meet the needs of Chicanas. The results of their pilot program was that 46% of the women they worked with were placed; 18% were pending placement in jobs or training programs; 9% were referred to agencies; 19% of the cases were closed, and 8% were still pending (MAPC proposal). The CSAC sent the evaluation of their pilot program and the statistics that established the success rates of their program to the local Manpower Area Planning Council along with a request for funding through the CETA ACT to have culturally appropriate trainers given the identified need. In the proposal, the CSAC/CFMN identified to the planning council that current Manpower employment training programs did not meet the needs of Chicana women in terms of employment training: "Skills training and supportive manpower services tailored to the needs of Chicanas are almost non-existent. A lack of skills, age, testing, stereotypes, racial and sex discrimination, all contribute to the plight of the Mexican American woman/ women" (*Manpower Area Planning Council (MAPC) Proposal* iv). The CFMN further contended that the trainers that CETA funded through the Manpower project that the Chicana Service Action Center could access for their clients were all Anglo men. Therefore, they applied for CETA funding from the Los Angeles Manpower Planning Council to work with Manpower to design employment-training program geared toward Chicanas, using trainers who could deliver culturally appropriate training.

The result? The CFMN/CSAC were denied further funding.[12] The reason? Not lack of success, and not inability to establish a need (what used to be the problem). Rather, the Manpower Council denied them funding because the term Chicana was deemed "discriminatory." The Council argued that because the CSAC identified Chicanas as the community they would be serving, and that they were operating as a *Chicana* Service Action Center, that they could not give them funding because they were discriminating against other groups. A flurry of rhetorical activity ensued. Testimonies were given at various government committees, and a general public outcry by the CFMN and CSAC took place: much of this in public hearings and others in the front-page editorials of their newsletters.[13] In one newsletter column titled "A Rose by any other Name..." CSAC director Francisca Flores shared with her reading audience that the Manpower board felt the use of the term Chicana was discriminatory. She wrote that at a later meeting with Manpower's appeals committee, they expounded on their decision stating that their proposal only *"singles out Mexican women to be served...*They said, furthermore, the CSAC proposal was *feminist!"* (1). What is interesting here is that, according to the article, the CSAC and CFMN explained to the commission that 80% of the people in their geographic neighborhood were Mexican American or Chicano, so they were reflecting the background of people who live in the area. In rebuttal, the Manpower Council committee pointed out that Anglos also lived in the surrounding area and were thusly being discriminated against. Therefore, Flores wrote, "With that little stroke of statistical genius the CSAC contention was dismissed"(1).

Whereas before the Anglo population was deemed the universal norm for employment statistics—and it was statistically sound to subsume Hispanic populations in the white population—now the Anglo population was pulled out as being excluded. Small details like the definition of who receives federal funding and based on what criteria often found in the small typeface of government forms and other professional writing documents, help us understand that the implicit issue was about not wanting to give money to the organization *because* of the people they served. While the training programs funded by the government up until that point were in fact exclusionary and catered to English speaking Anglo males as the *CFMN* had proven, they appeared to be inclusive, unmarked, and cohered to the government's guidelines.

In response, the CSAC and CFMN wrote appeals to representatives in Sacramento. These appeals claimed that traditional Manpower training programs were not prepared to effectively train bilingual women (particularly in the skilled trades), that Chicana was not discriminatory, and that the naming was not as relevant as the actual services provided. At some point, it is noted that the CSAC employed the ACLU to work on their behalf. Included in the archives are various letters written by the ACLU to government officials, which argued that the Manpower committee had a "mistaken notion of discrimination." In one letter they wrote that if "if such legally erroneous and uninformed view were prevalent among the members of your council, serious damage could be done to the Los Angeles County participation in the Comprehensive Employment and Training Act" (Ripston, 1 of 2).

Further, the CSAC asked the CFMN members and supporters to attend CETA related meetings whenever possible (Letter to Comision [*sic*] Femenil Members 2 Dec 1974[14]). In another newsletter column titled "A Sequel" Francisca Flores detailed one such meeting with the city of Los Angeles to discuss their denial of funding from the city Manpower Advisory Board. According to Flores, the majority of this meeting was spent discussing "terminology" and not the reasons why they were denied funding. At these meetings, then, the definition—or perhaps more accurately, the signification—of Chicana and of discrimination continued to be a source of contention. In other words, consensus over the meaning of Chicana, or what constituted the actual problem at hand, could not be reached.

SCENE THREE: A DIFFERENT STRATEGY
TO THE PROBLEM AT HAND

Now, it is not clear to me, based on my archival research, if the afore-mentioned lawsuits filed were successful, if public debates resolved the meaning of Chicana or determined whether it was discriminatory, or if these debates settled what constitutes a discriminatory term to begin with. To be honest, I am not interested in following their outcomes. Because what we do know is that something shifted—we see it in the fact that the CFMN have in their records receipt of CETA funding received after having been denied it because of the usage of "Chicana." To see this though, as a researcher, I had to adopt a different method-ological heuristic. I had to turn away from following the actions and exciting rhetorical performances of individuals in order to notice the CFMN's behind-the-scenes connective work that eventually un-did the public problem at hand. This connective work, I argue, displays a type of knowing that Sandoval articulates as the differential: a know-ing of how one is read as a Chicana and an ability to respond in a way to undermine power configurations.

Betwixt the rhetorical activity mentioned that is documented in the public arena, it becomes apparent in the collection that the CFMN employed a different type of strategy: to circumvent the issue of the term Chicana to begin with. This work happened less publicly and more in the nuances of their organizational work. A 1972 press release from the Women's Bureau of Labor about the secretary of labor work-ing to open up jobs to women lists names of representatives (*Brennan Pledges*). The list includes the name of one woman with a perhaps vis-ibly Latina name. The name is underlined—Carmen Maymi—with a phone number written next to it (Note written on *Brennan Pledges*). A few months later, Yolanda Nava of the CSAC and CFMN sent a letter to Carmen Maymi. The letter appears to be a follow up to a conver-sation they have had. In the letter, Nava inquired again whether the CFMN will have input on the "above matter" (presumably the Bureau of Labor working to increase employment opportunities for women). She also asked about the chances for getting a Chicana appointed to one of their boards. At the end of the letter, Nava includes a "CC" to the Secretary of the Department of Labor along with a note (for Maymi to also read) which states that she just wanted to make sure that their office had statistics with the numbers of Mexican and Latina women to demonstrate why they should have representatives on their board (2 Nov. 1973 Letter). This represents a very tactical way, I think, of pointing out the absence of Mexican and Latina women on the board and then alluding that this absence must be an ill informed decision due to a lack of research on their part. Because, surely if they knew the numbers, someone would have been appointed.

We can infer the effectiveness of such a not-so-subtle hint by a later letter from Yolanda Nava to Alan Cranston, forwarding resumes of women to appoint to the Women's Advisory Committee to the Department of Labor and an additional letter sent the following week to a Pamela Faust of the Commission on the Status of Women with the resumes of 17 qualified Chicanas to recommend for appointment (30 Aug 1973 and 1 Sept 1973 Letters). There are several other examples of such work in the archival collection—of newspaper clippings reporting on various government happenings or issues related to employment to reports from US Department of Labor. Many of these documents include some kind of notation of rhetorical activity—names underlined in newspaper articles, stars next to names, someone has written, "call."

After being denied funding from Manpower, an internal memo was sent between the CSAC and CFMN board members. In the memo, the board members raised questions about the members of the Manpower Area Planning Council Board of Directors.[15] In this memo, the board asked about the composite of the Manpower Council, specifically in regards to the selection process and who made the selections. The purpose of this memo was to begin to strategize within their organization. Publicly, they were continuing their outcries in response to being deemed discriminatory; inwardly they were developing a plan that worked at the foundations of the Manpower Council.

Following this internal strategizing, the CFMN sent a letter to Carlotta Mellon of the California State Governor's office. Mellon was apparently in a position to recommend people for appointment to government boards, including the boards that neglected to include statistics of Mexican/Latinos in their accounting and including those that determined funding requirements for employment issues. In response, Mellon sent a memo to the CFMN. In it, Mellon summarized a discussion she had with the Governor's office on behalf of the CFMN. She stated that there was "a commitment to bring many Chicanas into government" and to do this they "wanted to receive resumes so that we could consider Chicanas for appointment." Furthermore, Mellon wrote that she also "had receive[d] loud and clear their [the CFMN's] message of retaining Chicanas in their existing positions and that if any were to be replaced it would be with other Chicanas" (3).

It should be noted that the people the CFMN contacted were not the actual elected officials or the chairs of these committees; rather they were more often than not, the assistants or secretaries to the officials. The assistants were the people responsible for previewing the mail and forwarding necessary mail—including resumes—up the chain of command. It seems that the CFMN and CSAC leaders developed relationships with these people who then would work as allies on their behalf. Through this relationship, they were able to get government officials to agree to not only appoint Chicanas to boards but also to replace any current Chicana members with other Chicanas in order to ensure ongoing Chicana representation.

With this strategy in play, there is evidence of later letters sent from Mellon to then, CFMN president Chris Fuentes, thanking her for recommendations for appointments to a range of government boards. One board mentioned is the California Employment Training Act Council, the very group who funded the Manpower Planning Area Council and who denied funding to the CFMN for being discriminatory. We then see in an editorial for the Chicana Service Action Center 17 Feb. 1975 newsletter, a congratulations to Corinne Sanchez, Administrative Assistant to the CSAC, for being appointed to the board. She would not be the last Chicana from the CSAC or the CFMN to gain access to the CETA council.[16] In other words, Chicanas strategically gained access to the board governing the allotment of CETA funds. Tellingly, CETA funding was later reinstated to the CFMN. A Sept/Oct newsletter column noted, "[on] October 15, 1975, the Chicana Service Action Center, Inc. met with the State Manpower Council to officially sign the state CETA contract which has been awarded them" ("Chicana Center Signs State Contract"). This funding reinstatement happened even without them changing their name from a Chicana Action Center. The members of the CFMN must have known that an agreement over the definition of Chicana could not be reached because of a historical absence of Chicana women on these government boards. Instead of arguing about whether "Chicana" is exclusionary, these Chicanas worked connectively to get appointed to the boards, thereby ascertaining power to actually change the terrain of the discussion. The result is that they effectively made an issue (exclusionary terminology) a non-issue.

Their strategies for accomplishing this happened within their organization and between people and can be realized through paying attention to the rhetorical activity visible in the marginalia on their programmatic documents. During these less public moves, these Chicanas operated with government officials to imbue spaces with Chicana ideology and Chicana presence, so that Chicana became an active part of the policy-making and makers. While they may have lost the public battles of employment training programs, Chicana as a point of contention had less of a rhetorical impact in regards to access to CETA funding. This was achieved from a different approach to activism, through practices that are perhaps equally explicit but operated in less public spaces. The CSAC and the CFMN began to focus on leadership development, and by doing so, placed other Chicanas or like-minded people on the boards and commissions that made decisions that had real impacts on whether or not the CSAC and CFMN could provide the services the knew were vital to their community.

CONCLUSION

Such strategizing evidenced in the CFMN's work to address employment training for Chicanas can be understood as a way of knowing and acting that emerged from being disempowered in institutions. But, the CFMN and CSAC were also aware that they *had* to be able to access government funding for their services. Knowing that they would not be able to reach a shared understanding of the actual problem, the CFMN worked strategically and connectively to redress the situation at hand. This is not to say that the CFMN and CSAC stopped their public protestations against the discrimination claims, or that their testimonies and fiery speeches did not continue to be part of their Chicana activist repertoire. Rather, they developed a rhetoric that was at once responsive and effectual; public and internal; activist and institutional. And they effectively made these seeming contradictions productive as they worked toward an end of garnering federal funding to redress an absence of employment training programs for Chicanas, as well as an absence of Chicanas on federal and state labor boards.

Many of us can relate to seeing absence in institutional spaces. So how do we change this? Part of the challenge for us and for our allies is to do the work of *translations* across time and space: as we can revision history to enable new futures, we also can turn to the work of community organizations to learn about institutions. In this way, we can obviate the reductive binary between institutions and communities that are based on a static subject and space. Had I only sought out the performances of Chicana rhetoric that *seemed* Chicana or activist, I would have overlooked a significant portion of what the CFMN archived and what they considered important to becoming and acting as a Chicana organization. This work included making connections, often within institutions. Likewise, had I only looked at existing scholarship on institutional rhetoric, I would have missed learning from communities whose practices I wish to adopt and reflect in my own work. Each time a Chican@ like myself learns from the CFMN and shares their stories (or of other community organizations), we can create new histories and lineages of change makers. In doing so, we can continue to carve spaces for our commitments into this place of higher education.

NOTES

1. Throughout this article, I utilize "Chicana" when referencing the CFMN's work in building an organization and an identity to better reflect their discourse and the context. I also use "Chicana" in relation to a "Chicana rhetoric" to remain consistent with the terminology I used in the work that I am referencing. Otherwise, I utilize Chican@ to queer its usage.

2. Their participation culminated in the landmark case Madrigal v. Quilligan in 1978 and this case has been written about in and outside of rhetoric studies (see for example, Enoch 2005).

3. It should be noted that the CFMN also included copious copies of writings by other collectives and individuals involved with the Chicana movement broadly, such as activists, academics, as well as policies and legislation that were pertinent to the movement and their communities. I write of these documents as part of the rhetoric of the CFMN as they chose to include them in their archival collection, and to reflect that this is at once a story about an organization as it is about making an oppositional identity and movement.

4. The Mexican American Legal Defense and Educational Fund (MALDEF) worked with the CFMN to file the lawsuit against the forced sterilization of poor women of color during the 1970's in Madrigal v Quilligan.

5. It should be noted that I have constructed this story based on the archival research only. Therefore, as with any story of history, this is constructed by the documents the CFMN included. Adopting the movement

of Chicana rhetoric to work connectively, as part of my methodology, to construct each scene, I did not adhere to a strict linear chronology; instead I drew upon documents that were included in the collection and connected them thematically. This approach also better reflects the CFMN's deliberate arrangement of their archival collection. Instead of a chronological organization, the CFMN elected to arrange the collection to mirror the structure and function of the organization (Guide to Comisión Femenil Mexicana Nacional Archives 1967-1997).

6. Because there is such a significant overlap and sharing of resources (including people) between the CSAC and the CFMN during this time period, it is difficult to distinguish boundaries between the organizations, and therefore, the locus of rhetorical action. In addition, the leaders appeared to intentionally elect to speak on behalf of one of organizations based on an awareness of ethos and audience. Whenever these boundaries are made clear, I will use the appropriate organizational attribution; however, when the boundaries are not made clear I will use CSAC as the identifier when it is clear that the physical employment-training center is being discussed; everything else will be identified as the CFMN.

7. Although almost a decade after the CFMN and the CSAC began working to address employment issues, I think the numbers are telling. Flores also must find the statistics to be shocking, as evidenced by the exclamation mark. We can only surmise how much lower the numbers would have been in the early 1970's.

8. This case resulted in an increase of minorities and women in San Antonio's CETA programs. See also the Chicana Rights Project's summary *CETA: Services to Hispanics and Women* for more information on the impact of CETA on Mexican American women, as well as on their participation in the program.

9. In her later "Testimony at a Department of Industrial Relations Fair Employment Practice Commission" Francisca Flores responded to guidelines the Department intended to implement to remedy sex discrimination. Flores argued that the guidelines did not address the institutional myopia on employment as only about labor. Rather, she states, it "begins at the institutional level" in a failure to educate bicultural children (1).

10. It is important to note that the CFMN/CSAC also explained the difference between an Anglo feminist approach to employment counseling, and that developed by and for Chicanas. In "Employment Counseling and the Chicana," CFMN leader Yolanda Nava outlined this difference. She explained that the CSAC built transitional steps for employment training (i.e. place in small offices where Spanish is spoken), and addressed other issues like family planning. One example was mothers of some of the young women they worked with indicated to the CSAC staff that they were not comfortable talking about family planning but said they were fine with the CSAC em-

ployment counselors discussing it with their daughters as long as they were able to "use discretion." In other words, employment training for Chicanas was much more expansively addressed by the CSAC (*Encuentro Femenil*).

11. The Manpower project was an employment staffing and job training provider that received federal CETA funding in the 1970's.

12. The CFMN were welcomed to access to use the job trainers provided by the Manpower program—these trainers, CFMN charged, were all Anglo men. Further, access to job trainers alone would not comprehensively address all the web of conditions that mediated access to employment for Chicanas.

13. See Flores' "Testimony Before Joint Committee on Legal Equality" and her testimony "Regarding Proposed Guidelines for the California Fair Employment Practices Commission on Sex Discrimination," as well as CSAC published booklet titled "Chicana Status and Concerns," as just a couple of moments where these issues were explicitly or implicitly discussed.

14. Sent internally December 2, 1974.

15. Nov. 1974, "Memorandum re: Refunding of the Chicana Service Action Service a project of the Comisión Femenil Mexicana Nacional."

16. In fact, in May 1975, Francisca Flores was appointed as a chairperson for the newly formed Chicana Coalition's Manpower Committee ("Francisca Flores. . . appointed as chairperson," *CSAC Newsletter* 19 May 1975).

WORKS CITED

Anzaldúa, Gloria E. "now let us shift...the path of conocimiento...inner work, public acts." *this bridge we call home: radical visions for transformation.* Eds. Gloria E. Anzaldúa and Ana Louise Keating. New York: Routledge, 2002. 540-78. Print.

Bernal, Delores Delgado. "La Trenza de Identidades: Weaving Together my Personal, Professional, and Communal Identities." *Doing the Public Good: Two Latino Scholars Engage Civic Participation.* Eds. Kenneth P. Gonzalez and Raymond V. Padilla. Sterling, VA: Stylus Publishing, 2008. 135-148. Print.

Chicana Rights Project of MALDEF (Mexican American Legal Defense and Education Fund). *CETA: Services to Hispanics and Women.* July 1980. Series IX, Box 57, Folder 2. *Comisión Femenil Mexicana Nacional* Archival Collection. CEMA 30. UC Santa Barbara California Ethnic and Multicultural Archives Special Collections, Davidson Library, Santa Barbara, CA. Print.

Chicana Service Action Center. *Chicana Status and Concerns.* 1974. Series V, Box 38, Folder 11. *Comisión Femenil Mexicana Nacional* Archival Collection. CEMA 30. UC Santa Barbara California Ethnic and Multicultural Archives Special Collections, Davidson Library, Santa Barbara, CA. Print.

—."Chicanas in the Labor Force." *Encuentro Femenil.* 1.2 (1974): 1-7. Series IX, Box 56, Folder 7. *Comisión Femenil Mexicana Nacional* Archival Collection. CEMA 30. UC Santa Barbara California Ethnic and Multicultural Archives Special Collections, Davidson Library, Santa Barbara, CA. Print.

—. "Chicana Center Signs State Contract." *Chicana Service Action Center Newsletter 22* (Sept-Oct 1975): 1. Series IX, Box 53, Folder 7. *Comisión Femenil Mexicana Nacional* Archival Collection. CEMA 30. UC Santa Barbara California Ethnic and Multicultural Archives Special Collections, Davidson Library, Santa Barbara, CA. Print.

—. "Corinne Sanchez. . . appointed to California Manpower Services Council." *Chicana Service Action Center Newsletter 22* (17 Feb. 1975): 1. Series IX, Box 53, Folder 6. *Comisión Femenil Mexicana Nacional* Archival Collection. CEMA 30. UC Santa Barbara California Ethnic and Multicultural Archives Special Collections, Davidson Library, Santa Barbara, CA. Print.

—. "Francisca Flores. . . appointed as chairperson." *Chicana Service Action Center Newsletter 22* (19 May 1975): 1. Series IX, Box 53, Folder 6. *Comisión Femenil Mexicana Nacional* Archival Collection. CEMA 30. UC Santa Barbara California Ethnic and Multicultural Archives Special Collections, Davidson Library, Santa Barbara, CA. Print.

—. Letter to Comision [sic] Femenil Members. 2 Dec. 1974. TS. Series V, Box 70, Folder 7. *Comisión Femenil Mexicana Nacional* Archival Collection. CEMA 30. UC Santa Barbara California Ethnic and Multicultural Archives Special Collections, Davidson Library, Santa Barbara, CA. Print.

—. *Manpower Area Planning Council (MAPC) Proposal.* 1973 Sept. 28. TS. Series V, Box 38, Folder 8. *Comisión Femenil Mexicana Nacional* Archival Collection. CEMA 30. UC Santa Barbara California Ethnic and Multicultural Archives Special Collections, Davidson Library, Santa Barbara, CA. Print.

—. Memorandum to Members, "Re: Refunding of the Chicana Service Action Center a project of the Comisión Femenil Mexicana Nacional, Inc." Nov. 1973. TS. Series IX, Box 53, Folder 10. *Comisión Femenil Mexicana Nacional Archival* Collection. CEMA 30. UC Santa Barbara California Ethnic and Multicultural Archives Special Collections, Davidson Library, Santa Barbara, CA. Print.

—. Mexican/Chicana Women's Survey. 11 Apr 1972. TS. Series V, Box 41, Folder 13. *Comisión Femenil Mexicana Nacional* Archival Collection. CEMA 30. UC Santa Barbara California Ethnic and Multicultural Archives Special Collections, Davidson Library, Santa Barbara, CA. Print.

Copy of a Board of Directors Flow Chart. MS. Series I, Box 2, Folder 7. *Comisión Femenil Mexicana Nacional.* Archival Collection. CEMA 30. UC Santa Barbara California Ethnic and Multicultural Archives Special Collections, Davidson Library, Santa Barbara, CA. Print.

Copy of a Chicana Service Action Center Flyer. *Comisión Femenil Mexicana Nacional.* Archival Collection. CEMA 30. UC Santa Barbara California Ethnic and Multicultural Archives Special Collections, Davidson Library, Santa Barbara, CA. Print.

Copy of a CFMN Logo. *Comisión Femenil Mexicana Nacional.* Archival Collection. CEMA 30. UC Santa Barbara California Ethnic and Multicultural Archives Special Collections, Davidson Library, Santa Barbara, CA. Print.

Cortera, Marta. Letter to Francisca Flores. 11 Apr. 1980. TS. Series V, Box 69, Folder 7. *Comisión Femenil Mexicana Nacional.* Archival Collection. CEMA 30. UC Santa Barbara California Ethnic and Multicultural Archives Special Collections, Davidson Library, Santa Barbara, CA. Print.

Couvillon, Eva. "President's Message." Aug. 1982. TS. Series I, Box, 5, Folder 2. *Comisión Femenil Mexicana Nacional* Archival Collection. CEMA 30. UC Santa Barbara California Ethnic and Multicultural Archives Special Collections, Davidson Library, Santa Barbara, CA. 1-3.

Department of Labor. Contract #4047-06. 14 August 1973-15 August 1974. Series V, Box 38, Folder 8. *Comisión Femenil Mexicana Nacional Archival* Collection. CEMA 30. UC Santa Barbara California Ethnic and Multicultural Archives Special Collections, Davidson Library, Santa Barbara, CA. Print.

Flores, Francisca. "Chicana Service Action Center." 18 Mar. 1975. TS. Series IX, Box 53, Folder 6. *Comisión Femenil Mexicana Nacional Archival* Collection. CEMA 30. UC Santa Barbara California Ethnic and Multicultural Archives Special Collections, Davidson Library, Santa Barbara, CA. Print.

—. Letter to Edna Olivia. 20 May 1980. TS. Series V, Box 69, Folder 7. *Comisión Femenil Mexicana Nacional* Archival Collection. CEMA 30. UC Santa Barbara California Ethnic and Multicultural Archives Special Collections, Davidson Library, Santa Barbara, CA. Print.

—. "Regarding Proposed Guidelines for the California Fair Employment Practices Commission on Sex Discrimination." TS. Series V, Box 38, Folder 11. *Comisión Femenil Mexicana Nacional* Archival Collection. CEMA 30. UC Santa Barbara California Ethnic and Multicultural Archives Special Collections, Davidson Library, Santa Barbara, CA. Print.

—. "A Rose by any Other Name. . ." *Chicana Service Action Center Newsletter* 15 (Nov. 1974): 1-3. Series IX, Box 53, Folder 6. *Comisión Femenil Mexicana Nacional* Archival Collection. CEMA 30. UC Santa Barbara California Ethnic and Multicultural Archives Special Collections, Davidson Library, Santa Barbara, CA. Print.

—. "A Sequel." *Chicana Service Action Center Newsletter 16* (Dec. 1974): 1-2. Series IX, Box 53, Folder 6. *Comisión Femenil Mexicana Nacional* Archival Collection. CEMA 30. UC Santa Barbara California Ethnic and Multicultural Archives Special Collections, Davidson Library, Santa Barbara, CA. Print.

—. "Testimony at Department of Industrial Relations Fair Employment Practice Commission." 1974. TS. Series III, Box 31, Folder 3. *Comisión Femenil Mexicana Nacional* Archival Collection. CEMA 30. UC Santa Barbara California Ethnic and Multicultural Archives Special Collections, Davidson Library, Santa Barbara, CA. Print.

—. "Testimony Before Joint Committee on Legal Equality." TS. 12 August 1974. Series V, Box 42, Folder 12. *Comisión Femenil Mexicana Nacional* Archival Collection. CEMA 30. UC Santa Barbara California Ethnic and Multicultural Archives Special Collections, Davidson Library, Santa Barbara, CA. Print.

Gomez, Anna Nieto. "Chicanas and the Labor Force." CSAC reprint from SOMOS, March 1980. Series IX, Box 53, Folder 9. *Comisión Femenil Mexicana Nacional* Archival Collection. CEMA 30. UC Santa Barbara California Ethnic and Multicultural Archives Special Collections, Davidson Library, Santa Barbara, CA. Print.

—. "The Needs of the Spanish Speaking Mujer in Woman-Manpower Training Programs." TS. Series V, Box 42, Folder 3. *Comisión Femenil Mexicana Nacional* Archival Collection. CEMA 30. UC Santa Barbara California Ethnic and Multicultural Archives Special Collections, Davidson Library, Santa Barbara, CA. Print.

Guajardo, Miguel and Francisco Guajardo. "Two Brothers Doing Good." *Doing the Public Good: Two Latino Scholars Engage Civic Participation.* Eds. Kenneth P. Gonzalez and Raymond V. Padilla. Sterling, VA: Stylus Publishing, 2008. 61-81. Print.

Guide to Comisión Femenil Mexicana Nacional Archives 1967-1997 [Bulk dates 1970-1990]. University of California, Santa Barbara Davidson Library. Department of Special Collections, California Ethnic and Multicultural Archives. CEMA 30. Santa Barbara, CA. Print.

Hernández et al v Cockrell et al. SA 76 010. San Antonio, TX. 1979. *Research Guide to the Records of Mexican American Legal Defense and Educational Fund, 1968-1983.* Collection Number M0673. Stanford University. Libraries. Dept. of Special Collections and University Archives. Web. 22 October 2013.

Leon, Kendall. *Building a Chicana Rhetoric for Rhetoric and Composition: Methodology, Performance, and Practice.* Diss. Michigan State University, 2010. Print.

—. "*La Hermandad* and Chicanas Organizing: The Community Rhetoric of the Comisión Femenil Mexicana Nacional Organization." *Community Literacy Journal*. 7.2 (Spring 2013). Print.

Mellon, Carlotta. Letters to Chris Fuentes. TS. Series III, Box 30, Folder 3. *Comisión Femenil Mexicana Nacional* Archival Collection. CEMA 30. UC Santa Barbara California Ethnic and Multicultural Archives Special Collections, Davidson Library, Santa Barbara, CA. Print.

Nava, Yolanda. *The Chicana and Employment: Needs Analysis and Recommendation for Legislation*. 10 Feb. 1973. Series V, Box 38, Folder 6. *Comisión Femenil Mexicana Nacional* Archival Collection. CEMA 30. UC Santa Barbara California Ethnic and Multicultural Archives Special Collections, Davidson Library, Santa Barbara, CA. Print.

—."Employment Counseling and the Chicana." *Encuentro Femenil*. Date Unknown. Series IX, Box 56, Folder 7. *Comisión Femenil Mexicana Nacional* Archival Collection. CEMA 30. UC Santa Barbara California Ethnic and Multicultural Archives Special Collections, Davidson Library, Santa Barbara, CA. Print.

—. Letter to Alan Cranston. 30 Aug. 1973. TS. Series I, Box 11, Folder 11. *Comisión Femenil Mexicana Nacional* Archival Collection. CEMA 30. UC Santa Barbara California Ethnic and Multicultural Archives Special Collections, Davidson Library, Santa Barbara, CA. Print.

—. Letter to Pamela Faust. 1 Sept. 1973. TS. Series I, Box 11, Folder 11. *Comisión Femenil Mexicana Nacional* Archival Collection. CEMA 30. UC Santa Barbara California Ethnic and Multicultural Archives Special Collections, Davidson Library, Santa Barbara, CA. Print.

—. Letter to Carmen Maymi. 2 Nov 1973. TS. Series IX, Box 62, Folder 1. *Comisión Femenil Mexicana Nacional* Archival Collection. CEMA 30. UC Santa Barbara California Ethnic and Multicultural Archives Special Collections, Davidson Library, Santa Barbara, CA. Print.

Note written on Letter from Francisca Flores to Pierce A. Quinlan, re: Reply. N.d. MS. Series V, Box 69, Folder 1. *Comisión Femenil Mexicana Nacional* Archival Collection. CEMA 30. UC Santa Barbara California Ethnic and Multicultural Archives Special Collections, Davidson Library, Santa Barbara, CA. Print.

Note written on *Brennan Pledges 'Partnership with Women' to Open up New Jobs*. N.d. MS. Series III, Box 31, Folder 8. *Comisión Femenil Mexicana Nacional* Archival Collection. CEMA 30. UC Santa Barbara California Ethnic and Multicultural Archives Special Collections, Davidson Library, Santa Barbara, CA. Print.

Pimentel, Octavio. "Disrupting Discourse: Introducing Mexicano Immigrant Stories." *Reflections: A Journal of Writing, Community Literacy, and Service Learning 8.2* (2009): 171-196. Print.

Ripston, Ramona. Letter to Mayor Doris Davis. 19 Nov. 1974. 1-2. Series III, Box 32, Folder 8. *Comisión Femenil Mexicana Nacional* Archival Collection. CEMA 30. UC Santa Barbara California Ethnic and Multicultural Archives Special Collections, Davidson Library, Santa Barbara, CA.

Rodriguez, Maria. *In the Matter of: The Feminization of Poverty.* Testimony before the California Legislature Senate Committee on Health and Welfare and Assembly Human Services Committee. Series III, Box 30, Folder 20. *Comisión Femenil Mexicana Nacional* Archival Collection. CEMA 30. UC Santa Barbara California Ethnic and Multicultural Archives Special Collections, Davidson Library, Santa Barbara, CA. Print.

Sandoval, Chela. *Methodology of the Oppressed.* Minneapolis and London: University of Minnesota Press, 2000. Print.

Stotzer, Beatrice Olvera. "Letter to Past Presidents." N.d. TS. Series I, Box 5, Folder 6. *Comisión Femenil Mexicana Nacional* Archival Collection. CEMA 30. UC Santa Barbara California Ethnic and Multicultural Archives Special Collections, Davidson Library, Santa Barbara, CA. Print.

Women's Bureau. *Brennan Pledges 'Partnership with Women' to Open up New Jobs.* 30 May 1973. N.p. Series IX, Box 62, Folder 1. *Comisión Femenil Mexicana Nacional* Archival Collection. CEMA 30. UC Santa Barbara California Ethnic and Multicultural Archives Special Collections, Davidson Library, Santa Barbara, CA. Print.

THE WRITING LAB NEWSLETTER

Volume 38, Number 3-4   Promoting the exchange of voices and ideas in one-to-one teaching of writing   Nov./Dec. 2013

The Writing Lab Newsletter is on the Web at
https://writinglabnewsletter.org/

The Writing Lab Newsletter (beginning in Sept. 2015, the journal will change its name to *WLN: A Journal of Writing Center Scholarship*), a peer-reviewed publication with five issues per academic year, provides a forum for exchanging ideas and information about writing centers in high schools, colleges, and universities. Articles illustrate how writing centers work in an intersection of theory and practice, underpinned by theory and scholarship. *WLN* aims to inform newcomers to the field as well as extend the thinking of those who are more knowledgeable and experienced. Authors also report on research and describe programmatic models that can be adapted to other contexts.

Going Global, Becoming Translingual: The Development of a Multilingual Writing Center

Noreen Lape places her Multilingual Writing Center (MWC) within the larger academic interest in internationalization, the mission in higher education to prepare students for a globally interconnected world. Her article introduces readers to her writing center that is "for writers and tutors working simultaneously within and/or across multiple languages and writing cultures" (5). Working collaboratively with instructors from her institution's foreign language programs, Lape staffs her writing center with tutors who are first and (at least) second language learners to work with students, some who are non-native speakers of English and all of whom must have studied and written in another language in order to graduate. The outcome, as Lape notes, is that tutors and students become more understanding of what constitutes "good writing" across cultures. The outcomes of cross-cultural writing that are delineated emphasize the value of a translingual writing center as opposed to the more common practice of having a monolingual staff.

10 Going Global, Becoming Translingual: The Development of a Multilingual Writing Center

Noreen G. Lape

In an effort to prepare students for twenty-first century life, many institutions of higher education are seeking to develop "global citizens": students who are "engage[d] in global issues," see the "connection between the global and the local," practice "cultural empathy," and exhibit "intercultural competence" or the ability to communicate effectively across cultures (Green). To educate these global citizens, a growing number of colleges and universities have internationalized their curricula, increased their foreign language offerings, and multiplied their study abroad programs. At the same time, within the discipline of Writing Studies, many scholars have adopted an international perspective and are studying everything from academic genres to intercultural rhetoric to writing programs across cultures. Writing centers have always had a unique awareness of writing in international contexts, thanks to our good work with English language learners (ELL). However, writing centers can adopt an even broader understanding of writing in global contexts—one that not only builds on but extends beyond our work with English language learners. In a truly Multilingual Writing Center (MWC), tutors who are literate in multiple languages and skilled as global citizens can work with writers as they construct their voices—linguistically, rhetorically, and discursively—in order to participate in the global exchange of ideas.

With the internationalizing of academia, a growing number of foreign language writing centers have emerged in recent years. Although a review of the writing center literature yields few studies on the topic, a cursory search of writing center websites reveals the existence of several Spanish and even some French and German writing centers, generally located in foreign language departments. Two notable examples are the University of San Francisco, which provides tutoring in English, French, Japanese, and Spanish; and DePaul University in Chicago, whose Collaborative for Multilingual Writing and Research employs a wide variety of foreign language writing tutors. Recently, the Norman M. Eberly Writing Center at Dickinson College has become a Multilingual Writing Center (MWC) where students writing not only in English but also Arabic, Chinese, Hebrew, Japanese, French, German, Italian, Portuguese, Russian, and Spanish seek the assistance of trained writing tutors who are international students (both visiting and matriculated) and U.S. students who have studied abroad. Established in 1978, the Dickinson College Writing Center mainly has served U.S. students and, increasingly over the years, a growing number of international students learning to write academic English. Like other writing centers, the Dickinson Writing Center would provide sporadic foreign language writing tutoring—on an ad hoc basis—whenever foreign language faculty asked if they could send their writers to English tutors who also happened to be proficient in a foreign language. Then, in Fall 2010, the Writing Center reestablished itself as multilingual, opening its doors to nonnative writers of languages other than English—from U.S. students tackling a second or even third language to international students learning a third language in their second language.

A unique feature of Dickinson's MWC is its collaborative governance structure, which includes members of each foreign language department. Aware of the value of the English writing center, foreign language faculty supported the idea of an MWC staffed by trained and fluent undergraduate peer writing tutors. In fact, the Chair of the Italian Department envisioned that the MWC could build bridges between language departments, bringing together colleagues to discuss language and writing instruction. All saw the value of an MWC with a defined space, consistent staff, permanent budget line, centralized oversight, and mindful pedagogy. As a result, the committee chose to draft a proposal for an MWC. Since then, the committee continues to meet regularly to establish policy, define pedagogy, recommend tutors, and participate in their training. The conversations continually interrogate the interplay between writing center pedagogy, classroom practice, and the development of writing ability.

MULTILINGUAL AND TRANSLINGUAL

In the field of Writing Center Studies, "multilingual" generally refers to nonnative writers of World Englishes; in this essay, the term describes tutors and tutees at a college where all students are first and (at minimum) second-language learners because all must have knowledge of a foreign language through the intermediate level in order to graduate. What's more, two-thirds of those students study abroad at some point during their college careers ("Open"). Thus, in the Dickinson MWC, writers who will or have studied abroad work with tutors who have studied or are studying abroad here at Dickinson.

Multilingual also denotes an open-ended and questioning attitude toward discourse—an understanding that the notion of "good writing" differs across cultures (as does the notion of "good writing center pedagogy.") A multilingual environment, then, is the necessary but not sufficient condition for translingual practice. Bruce Horner, Min-Zhan Lu, Jacqueline Jones Royster, and John Trimbur explain that the translingual approach "address[es] how language norms are actually heterogeneous, fluid, and negotiable" (305). Translingualism opposes the traditional approach to second-language learning, which views difference as a sign of error and teaches "conform[ity] to fixed, uniform standards" (Horner et al. 305). Thus, second-language teachers and students may be multilingual without being translingual if they privilege standard forms of a language. In an MWC, however, where the focus is on process, tutors and writers routinely play with the fluidity of languages as they consider "what the writers are doing with language and why" (Horner et al. 305).

As far back as the early 1990s, Carol Severino imagined a "translingual" writing center, although she did not call it that ("Writing"; "'Doodles'"). While translingualists "recogniz[e] the linguistic heterogeneity of all users of language both within the United States and globally" (Horner et al. 305), Severino imagined a pedagogy that values the "hybridized, 'culturally balanced' styles" of international students ("'Doodles'" 56-57). Her call for a multicultural rhetoric that "allows experimental and culturally mixed patterns" is echoed later by the translingualists ("'Doodles'" 56-57). For Severino, writing centers can cultivate multicultural rhetoric by offering opportunities for "collaborative exploration of cultural and linguistic differences" ("'Doodles'" 57). Severino focuses on English language learners, yet her approach has implications for the MWC model.

Although an MWC calls into question monolingualist assumptions and U.S. concepts of academic writing, tutors must be aware that the personal learning goals of writers may not necessarily include "hybridity" or "linguistic heterogeneity." When writing cross-culturally, some writers find themselves in the contact zone, which Mary Louise Pratt famously defines as "social spaces where cultures meet, clash, and grapple with each other, often in contexts of highly asymmetrical relations of domination and subordination" (4). In a contact zone, writers may resist or subvert culture contact; alternatively, they may find themselves in a liminal position between cultures. Other writers experience cultural immersion when they choose to suspend identity to empathically experience another culture. In cultura-immersion contexts, writers may assimilate or erase the self, even temporarily or partially, and adopt another cultural identity; others may, instead, construct hybrid identities. In an MWC, hybridity is just one potential outcome of writing cross-culturally.

CULTURAL IMMERSION AND WRITING CULTURE SHOCK

Despite some writers' desires to assimilate to the target writing culture and master standard forms of the language, heterogeneity is inescapable. Traditional English-only writing centers tend to have a far more monolingual staff comprised mainly of U.S. native speakers who have variously mastered Standard Written English. In the Dickinson MWC, the tutors represent a variety of writing experiences: native and non-native speakers of multiple languages who have written for professors in the U.S. and other parts of the world. Given this complexity, I wanted to understand how MWC tutors struggled with differing, culturally-specific notions of good writing when they wrote in their study abroad programs. Christiane Donahue notes that "a broadly ignored area of composition work is that of U.S. monolingual students' experiences when they go overseas to study or work and find themselves in universities or workplaces with different rhetorical, discursive, and sociolinguistic expectations, whether that work is being done in English or another language" ("'Internationalization'" 218). Because that kind of composition work undergirds an MWC situated in an institution with a robust global education program, I began to survey each new incoming staff about their overseas writing experiences. Two staff members, Melissa and Grace, were seniors who had just returned from their junior year abroad in Toulouse (Melissa in 2010 and Grace in 2011). Prior to going, they completed the training course for English writing tutors. While studying in Toulouse at the Dickinson Center, they took the required French Methodology and Composition, a course that not only focuses on grammar and vocabulary but also teaches the basic French genres—*commentaire de texte*, dissertation, and exposé oral—that form the basis of university writing (Donahue, "Lycee" 136). Despite the direct instruction in writing, their experiences were very different. Grace found herself in a contact zone suffering writing culture shock as she grappled with feelings of disempowerment within an asymmetrical rhetorical relationship. Melissa, who focused more on genre expectations, seemed to assimilate to the writing culture without much conflict. Their experiences have implications for their translingual work with writers.

Grace and Melissa—whose previous academic writing mainly involved literary and cultural analysis—were taught to value arguing a controvertible thesis, developing an original analysis, and crafting an organic line of argument. Their U.S. professors encouraged them to offer counterarguments and to debate their sources, including the professor. In contrast, as Donahue describes, French academic writing involves the "systematic study of established knowledge about a topic, and the incorporation and synthesis of diverse sources of this knowledge into an authoritative viewpoint" ("Lycee" 156). From Grace's perspective, her professors in France did not value argument/personal voice. She describes her awareness of the rhetorical situation: "Personal voice is not very important. If I want a good grade, I need to write like a professor." She continues, "The professor is God. Do not contradict unless you're feeling real confident." Instead, Grace recalls that "formatting is important," admitting: "I tend to cling to form a bit more in French, where I am less masterful." Grace "clings" to form—for survival, it seems, within a rhetoric that forces her to erase her "personal voice" and form an obedient and submissive relationship to the professor-reader. Her uncomfortable ethos of submission resonates when she refers to her professor as "God"—and a "critical" one at that. She imagines the possibility of developing an argument, but only in the case of extreme confidence.

While Grace experiences a loss of personal voice at the hands of her "god-like" professors, Melissa, conversely, does not express a loss or even much of a conflict as she focuses more on genre expectations than the perceived power dynamics of the rhetorical contact zone. Unlike Grace, who finds French form confining, Melissa quips, "The French adore structure, to the point that it's almost rigid." In addition, she has developed an understanding of French academic genres: "In literature, French professors often ask for a commentaire compose; a very intense, detailed close reading of one particular section of a work, rather than an essay that treats an entire piece. Even larger essays, called dissertations, are different and incorporate multiple works to show one's knowledge of a subject as a whole." Her cross-cultural knowledge extends to conventions, like the problematique, which, she explains, is "different from a thesis statement. Essentially, the *problematique* asks the question that a thesis statement would answer." Both students make astute observations about the differences between the academic writing culture in the U.S. and France. Yet Melissa has a framework that enables her to make sense of the differences. She depersonalizes the rhetorical relationships and refers to "the French" and "French professors." At worst, her criticism is faint: the French are "almost rigid" and "intense." She can clearly explain French genres and criteria of good writing (e.g., they "adore structure"). Rather than writing-culture conflict, she participates in writing-culture immersion.

Grace's and Melissa's conceptions of French academic writing have implications for the mission of an MWC, the role of MWC tutors, and the unique interventions those tutors can offer second-language writers. Tutors who assimilate, like Melissa, can help writers adapt—that is, cross confidently into the new academic culture. She represents the potential of MWC tutors to demystify the educational culture by explaining rhetorical relationships, genre, and discourse conventions. Resistant tutors, like Grace, can be trained to channel their frustrations into translingual questioning, prodding a writer to reimagine her audience and recover her personal voice. Both Melissa's and Grace's insights contribute to the multiple and shifting roles of MWC tutors: to help students understand culturally specific genres and rhetorics, to serve as useful guides who can help prepare students for the transition to another writing culture, to assist in resolving writing culture shock, and to support the creation and examination of hybrid linguistic selves.

BECOMING TRANSLINGUAL

Conversations in the MWC cannot help but interrogate strategies of resistance, assimilation, liminality, and hybridity. The Dickinson MWC cultivates such conversations through the podcast project "Going International: Stories of Second Language Writers" (blogs.dickinson. edu/mwc). In audio narratives students discuss the challenges that accompany learning to research, read, and write in a second language and in a foreign academic culture. The project is based on Severino's "Self-as-Writer II" project in which tutors prompt ELL students to "describe their native writing instruction and experiences" as well as to describe how writing for U.S. teachers differs from writing for teachers in their native countries ("'Doodles'" 49; "Writing" 56). More recently, Ulla Connor has proposed that writing center tutors not only discuss but also "document . . . in a systematic manner" their conversations with writers regarding their home culture and language (73-75).

The "Going International" podcast interviews include not only the visiting and matriculated international students who are writing tutors but also the U.S. foreign language writing tutors who have returned from study abroad. The interview itself, a type of professional development exercise, prompts tutors to reflect upon how their writing experiences in other cultures inform their current approach to writing and tutoring. As Melissa's and Grace's experiences indicate, students bound for study abroad in a non-English program would benefit from working with writing tutors who have "been there" and can serve as "cultural informants" of German or Spanish or Chinese "academic expectations," to quote Judith Powers (41). The actual online podcasts can be used in classrooms and writing center workshops to mediate potential writing culture shock for students bound for study abroad by discussing the rhetorical, discursive, and linguistic choices that face cross-cultural writers.

As the Dickinson MWC evolves, we continue to wrestle with pedagogical issues that problematize traditional writing center practice. First, we struggle to construct pluralistic definitions of "good" academic writing that acknowledge culturally-specific rhetorics and conventions in a world in which English is the *lingua franca*, "the universal language of the intellect" (Canagarajah 41). We also seek to mediate the conflict between the translingual valuing of heterogeneity, multiculturalism, and students' rights to their own language and the individual learning outcomes of writers who choose to adapt—and conform to—the language and discourse conventions of the study abroad university culture. Finally, we grapple with determining the appropriate balance between global revision and sentence-level editing in tutoring sessions. Depending on the writer's level—that is, the extent to which she is learning the language as she is learning to write it, the hierarchical categorizing of global revision issues above sentence-level concerns may not be useful. Instead, we train MWC tutors in "holistic tutoring"—a challenging practice that involves toggling between local and global issues while being keenly aware of their interconnection. Ultimately, the MWC model raises a whole new set of questions about the teaching and learning of writing in international contexts for writing centers and, by extension, foreign language instructors.

An MWC, in essence, is a meeting place for writers and tutors working simultaneously within and/or across multiple languages and writing cultures. True, the conversations take place in a local writing center, but they potentially comprise the world. With the help of tutors, writers can develop a nuanced understanding of the target culture in order to construct meaningful rhetorical relationships, adopt the proper conventions, and make effective linguistic choices so as to communicate proficiently. Thus, the translingual work of any MWC supports the creation of global citizens. What's more, this work potentially serves the discipline as MWCs become thresholds to other writing cultures. As Donahue laments, in the U.S. compositionists "do not often report being in the position of adapting teaching practices from these other countries around the globe" ("'Internationalization'" 220). As more MWCs emerge in the writing center community, perhaps they will serve as portals through which the writing practices of other cultures can enter U.S. universities and inform our own practices.

Works Cited

Canagarajah, A. Suresh. A Geopolitics of Academic Writing. Pittsburgh: U of Pittsburgh P, 2002. Print.

Connor, Ulla. Intercultural Rhetoric in the Writing Classroom. Ann Arbor: U of Michigan P, 2011. Print.

"Dickinson Defined—Global Education." Dickinson College, n.d. Web. 19 Dec. 2011.

Donahue, Christiane. "'Internationalization' and Composition Studies: Reorienting the Discourse." College Composition and Communication 61.2 (2009): 212-243. Print.

----. "The Lycee-to-University Progression in French Students' Development as Writers." Writing and Learning in Cross-National Perspective. Ed. David Foster and David R. Russell. Urbana: NCTE, 2002. 134-191. Print.

Green, Madeline F. "Global Citizenship—What are We Talking About and Why Does it Matter?" NAFSA: Association of International Educators. Jan. 2012. Web. 3 Dec. 2012.

Horner, Bruce, Min-Zhan Lu, Jacqueline Jones Royster, and John Trimbur. "Language Difference in Writing: Toward a Translingual Approach." College English 73.3 (2011): 303-321. Print.

"Open Doors, Open Minds." Dickinson College, 7 Dec. 2011. Web. 7 Dec. 2011.

Powers, Judith K. "Rethinking Writing Center Conferencing Strategies for the ESL Writer." Writing Center Journal 13.2 (1993): 39-47. Print.

Pratt, Mary Louise. Imperial Eyes: Travel Writing and Transculturation. New York: Routledge, 1992. Print.

Severino, Carol. "The 'Doodles' in Context: Clarifying Claims about Contrastive Rhetoric." Writing Center Journal 14.1 (1993): 44-61. Print.

----. "The Writing Center as Site for Cross-Language Research." Writing Center Journal 15.1 (1994): 51-61. Print.

About the Editors

Steve Parks is associate professor of writing and rhetoric at Syracuse University where he teaches entry-level and advanced courses in composition theory and practice. He also leads seminars on community publishing and community organizing. He has published two books: *Gravyland: Writing Beyond the Curriculum in the City of Brotherly Love* (Syracuse University Press 2010) and *Class Politics: The Students' Right to Their Own Language* (Parlor Press 2013). He has also published articles in *Journal of College Composition and Communication, College English, Community Literacy Journal,* and *Reflections.* He established New City Community Press (newcitycommunitypress.com) in Philadelphia as well as Gifford Street Community Press (giffordstreetcommunitypress.com) in Syracuse. Over the past two years, he has been working with democratic activists in the Middle East and North Africa.

Brian Bailie is a PhD candidate in the Composition and Cultural Rhetoric program at Syracuse University. His work focuses on the intersections of protest and media, technology and transnationalism, identity and material rhetoric, and the ways activists exploit, expand, resist, and utilize these intersections to their advantage. Bailie has served as contributor, associate editor, and special issue editor for *Reflections: A Journal of Writing, Service-Learning, and Community Literacy.* His most recent publications have appeared in the *KB Journal* and *Composition Forum.*

James Seitz is Director of the Academic and Professional Writing Program and Associate Professor of English at the University of Virginia, where he teaches graduate and undergraduate courses in writing, literature, and pedagogy. His book, *Motives for Metaphor: Literacy, Curriculum Reform, and the Teaching of English,* considers how English departments might be better served by blurring the boundaries that currently divide the study of composition, literature, and creative writing. Seitz has served as a Carnegie Scholar at the Carnegie Academy for the Scholarship of Teaching and Learning, and he has given dozens of workshops on writing instruction at universities and school districts across the country.

Jessica Pauszek is a PhD candidate in the Composition and Cultural Rhetoric program at Syracuse University. With Ben Kuebrich and Steve Parks, she co-edited a special issue of *Literacy in Composition Studies* on "The New Activism." She is also the assistant editor of *Reflections: A Journal of Public Rhetoric, Civic Writing, and Service-Learning*, and the Managing Editor of New City Community Press. Her current research examines the self-sponsored literacy practices of an international writing and publishing network started in London, England, called *The Federation of Worker Writers and Community Publishers.*

Tamara Bassam Issak is a PhD student in Composition and Cultural Rhetoric at Syracuse University. Her research interests include cultural rhetoric, geographic rhetoric, writing program administration, and composition pedagogy.

Heather Christiansen is a PhD candidate in the Rhetoric, Communication and Information Design program at Clemson University. Her research interests include visual rhetoric, the rhetoric of brand communities, identity, and user experience design. From 2013-2015, she served as the managing editor for *The WAC Journal.*

www.ingramcontent.com/pod-product-compliance
Lightning Source LLC
Chambersburg PA
CBHW031237050326
40690CB00007B/832